LIFE
WITH A VIEW

MEMOIR OF AN AIR TRAFFIC CONTROLLER

ROBIN A. SMITH

iUniverse®

LIFE WITH A VIEW
MEMOIR OF AN AIR TRAFFIC CONTROLLER

Copyright © 2017 Robin A. Smith.

All rights reserved. No part of this book may be used or reproduced by any means, graphic, electronic, or mechanical, including photocopying, recording, taping or by any information storage retrieval system without the written permission of the author except in the case of brief quotations embodied in critical articles and reviews.

iUniverse books may be ordered through booksellers or by contacting:

iUniverse
1663 Liberty Drive
Bloomington, IN 47403
www.iuniverse.com
1-800-Authors (1-800-288-4677)

Because of the dynamic nature of the Internet, any web addresses or links contained in this book may have changed since publication and may no longer be valid. The views expressed in this work are solely those of the author and do not necessarily reflect the views of the publisher, and the publisher hereby disclaims any responsibility for them.

Any people depicted in stock imagery provided by Thinkstock are models, and such images are being used for illustrative purposes only.
Certain stock imagery © Thinkstock.

ISBN: 978-1-5320-2316-3 (sc)
ISBN: 978-1-5320-2318-7 (hc)
ISBN: 978-1-5320-2317-0 (e)

Library of Congress Control Number: 2017909911

Print information available on the last page.

iUniverse rev. date: 08/09/2017

CONTENTS

Chapter 1: They Almost Never Hit 1
Chapter 2: ATC School 25
Chapter 3: Whiting Field..41
Chapter 4: Cubi Point, Philippines 67
Chapter 5: Guam 93
Chapter 6: Oxnard 119
Chapter 7: Tucson 135
Chapter 8: The Academy 153
Chapter 9: The National Air Traffic Controllers Association 163
Chapter 10: The Mimosa Boys 183
Chapter 11: DC 195
Chapter 12: Two Tokens, Ten Dollars 219
Chapter 13: Atlanta... 225
Chapter 14: "Ground, Simon 22 Is with You, Clear of the Active Runway, and Taxiing to the Gate" 229

1
THEY ALMOST NEVER HIT

Tucson, Arizona—August 1992

The obnoxious buzz shook me awake as it had for countless mornings. My clock showed 4:45 a.m., which was good news. Although today was Wednesday, it was *my* Friday, and the clock showed 4:45 a.m. instead of 4:00 a.m., which meant I had a 6:00 a.m. to 2:00 p.m. shift and not the midnight shift. This makes complete sense to controllers but is as confusing to those not familiar with air traffic control as the occupation itself.

My head didn't pound, and my eyeballs didn't fall out when I sat up, so I must've behaved the night before and was not completely opposed to the idea of getting out of bed. Swinging my feet to the floor, I moved as quietly as I could so as not to awaken Roseanne, another future ex-wife. A quick shit, shower, and shave, and I was out the door just in time to admire another sunrise and the beauty of the Santa Catalina Mountains north of Tucson while sipping my coffee: the beginning of another perfect day. However, little did I know I would utter two phrases that day that air traffic controllers never want to say: "radar contact lost" and "at what point did I lose control of this situation?"

It was 5:30 a.m., and I had seen hundreds of sunrises all over the world, from Florida to the Philippines. Each of them was memorable in its way, but sunrise over the mountains of the Santa Cruz Valley held a special place. Tucson, Arizona, is a jewel in the desert, assuming, of course, you find 110 degrees during the peak of summer attractive. Fortunately, there are few people with their heads screwed on straight and IQs greater than the temperature of ice water who do. Arizonans like it that way. They're independent and tolerant almost to a fault, and they rarely let a sometimes-fickle Mother Nature alter plans to enjoy life.

Comfortably nestled in a picturesque bowl and surrounded by 9,500-foot mountains, Tucson sits on the edge of the Sonoran Desert, just north of the Sea of Cortez. During the summer monsoon season, the sea provides moisture, which is one of the three essential elements of the monsoon equation. *El sol* is the second element, and the third is the breeze generated by the tilt of the earth in concert with the summer solstice. Most people associate monsoons with constant downpours in Southeast Asia, but the monsoon is a trend associated with wind currents that play a part in generating those downpours.

In Tucson, even during the monsoon season, mornings typically begin with a cloudless, cobalt sky, allowing an unencumbered sun to paint the Santa Catalina Mountains a soft reddish-orange. When a day begins with this combination of scenery and color, it forces you to stop and enjoy nature.

Days such as this give us a sense of well-being that settles into our souls. The feeling wraps around us and administers a feeling of security and serenity like a nap on Grandma's front porch after a Thanksgiving dinner. We're emboldened to go forth, bite off a piece of life that we can chew for a while, and reap an experience on which we can reflect when nothing else goes right. Life on this day is a rarity. Throw caution to the wind, dig deep, and resurrect that cavalier, devil-may-care attitude time-capsuled years before. Have another margarita, put the top down, worry about no cops today—say, "I am in complete control of my destiny and one with the universe."

As I drove to work that morning, the memories of perfect days ending less than perfectly were as hidden as the back side of the Santa Catalina Mountains. Only the beauty that surrounded me consumed my thoughts.

I drove into the radar room parking lot and, as always, hopped the cement divider. It was a routine accomplishment for my beat-up four-wheel-drive truck, and I did it for two reasons. First, it allowed a quick getaway. Hopping the cement divider, I faced the exit without backing in. Second, it ticked off Big Al. I never figured out why, but Al was a law-and-order sort of guy, which is a tendency that flies in the face of being an air traffic controller. He spotted me more than once performing this ritual and each time shook his finger, raised his voice, and questioned my right to exist in a civilized society. It wouldn't have been any fun if I didn't believe he was truly upset with the manner in which I flaunted the rules of the parking lot and scoffed at his authority. Besides, I was the parking lot police. Ask anyone.

I had been awarded the "parking lot police" title for running air force personnel out of our parking lot. The Tucson radar approach control building was Federal Aviation Administration (FAA) property but was located on Davis-Monthan Air Force Base. We had a small parking lot restricted to FAA air traffic controllers. However, when the air force played war games, a large building across the street became a major center of activity, and participants quickly filled our lot. Our facility manager refused to stand up for us, so I did, which brought the ire of the base commander down on our manager's narrow shoulders. I was the embodiment of the 80/20 rule: 80 percent of your time will be taken up by 20 percent of your employees. I always wanted to be in the upper percentile.

Big Al was older than most of us and one of a few who hadn't walked out during the air traffic control strike in 1981. Although he and I had opposite opinions about the way the world should be run, I had a great deal of respect for him. Al was a Vietnam veteran who had worked as a navy Seabee and, while in-country, had been routinely shot at while sitting atop his bulldozer. I think his firm sense of fair play and decency came from the chaos and absence of both in war.

At one point he proclaimed, for reasons unknown to us, his heritage as a Native American. We called him "Big Al" because he was. He was also one of the whitest guys I've ever known and had a great deal more scalp showing than hair. Irish, maybe, but Native American—that's a toss-up.

However, being politically correct, we felt it our duty to christen him with an appropriate Native American title, and Al, being big and white, started as "Big Ass" and then became "Big Crack," before we finally compromised with "Big Cloud." The thought of someone as Anglo as Big Al having such a cool title caught on, and very soon, names such as "Dances with Sheep" and "Stands with Hard Ding-Ding" were floating around the radar room. Naturally, Big Al took offense to this attitude, and we all became good gene-deficient hoodlums.

Al rode a Honda motorcycle to and from work to save gas money. It was at least one or two sizes smaller than it should have been, and I was sure that if he had done the math, Al would have found that, with his girth, it would have been cheaper to buy a Honda car. One night, on an evening shift, it was getting close to quitting time, and Al noticed the latest weather observation showing the temperature in the low thirties.

He remarked, "Gonna be frost on the pumpkin!"

I replied, "Nah, you'll be wearing a helmet."

He laughed. On occasion, Al had a good sense of humor.

Big Al didn't meet me in the parking lot that morning, and I immediately felt cheated. Maybe the day wasn't so perfect.

Everything controllers do is inherently contrary to law and order. We tell pilots where to go and what to do with no ability to inflict consequences. Amazingly, the pilots comply. Unlike real law enforcement or Mr. Murphy (Murphy's law: if something can go wrong, it will), controllers cannot levy a fine or pass and execute a sentence at will.

With one exception; delay vectors. Noncompliant pilots occasionally find themselves on the receiving end of delay vectors. Many, but not all vectors (turns) are followed with a reason for the vector. "Turn right heading zero-four-zero, vector for the visual approach, runway one-one left" was sometimes adjusted to read "for controller amusement."

Or the controller might order, "Turn left ten degrees for noise abatement."

Aircraft, "Approach, we're thirty miles south of the airport over the desert. What noise abatement?"

"Two airplanes hitting makes a lot of noise. Traffic, twelve o'clock, five miles opposite direction at your altitude."

Delay vectors are sometimes issued just to give the pilot time in the penalty box for not paying attention.

In general, though, pilots comply with instructions without question, believing that the voice in their ear is omnipotent. They would realize how asinine the concept is if they could see what happens in the control room. Ignore the voice behind the microphone.

Controllers have a tendency to behave in a less than professional manner, and I now attribute the adolescent happenings in towers and radar rooms to a release of anxiety. People ask me if air traffic control (ATC) is a stressful job. In the early years, it was. But as knowledge combines with experience, controllers eventually find their comfort level, and the stress diminishes. You come to know yourself and begin to recognize personal limitations. Depending on daily circumstances, performance may fluctuate slightly, but a dozen or so years and after a controller has been certified to work traffic at a few different airports, it remains pretty constant.

After years of entertaining the question, I came up with a suitable analogy. Imagine a sixteen-year-old working his or her first lunch rush at a fast-food joint. Chaos. However, a year later, the teen knows the routine, and it's just busy, unless a cash register goes out or a fryer quits. Then he or she adjusts and compensates. It's the same with ATC.

Good-weather days with all the equipment operating as advertised are busy, but nothing a controller hasn't seen hundreds of times—not easy, just busy. When a thunderstorm moves in and takes away part of the normal pattern, or the wind blows from the wrong direction, making a runway unusable, a controller still must work the same amount of traffic but with fewer resources. That's when the job becomes stressful and a controller's limitations may come into play.

We could see it coming; there were all the earmarks of a typical monsoon day. Beautiful in the morning, puffy clouds forming around 10:00 a.m., and severe thunderstorms developing in the afternoon. Temperatures over the desert floor rise easily over 100 degrees Fahrenheit, driving the elevator that lifts moisture into the sky. With the ambient air temperature around 110 degrees, the elevator would be running at full power. Size and intensity of afternoon storms depend on the amount of moisture riding the elevator into the upper atmosphere, where it cools and condenses, forming clouds and eventually succumbing to the laws of nature to fall as rain. As with the fast-food noon rush, we anticipated the adverse effects of the monsoon and were prepared to adjust accordingly.

I grabbed my headset, performing a quick, cursory check of the earpiece and mike boom, and then walked into the radar room. Checking my earpiece, or "bippy," had become automatic after the day I dipped a coworker's bippy in a tub of Vaseline. When he stuck it in his ear, the expression was priceless. I didn't want to suffer paybacks, but I knew payback would come in due time and in some appropriate form. That's just part of the game. But, I would not let a gooey bippy serve as retribution.

How do you eat an elephant? One bite at a time. Likewise, the airspace is divided into bite-sized pieces. Each piece is known as a sector, and each sector has a radar scope assigned to it. Controllers train and qualify on each sector until fully certified throughout the facility. Years before, during my days in training, I had certified on three sectors at Tucson and was training on the most difficult sector, the arrival sector. The arrival sector sequenced aircraft into the Tucson airport, and I was having some trouble figuring out how some pieces of the puzzle fit together. Imagine airplanes coming into your sector from all directions, each at a different speed and different altitude and each aircraft having specific capabilities. It reminded me of a crazy salad of military fighters, commercial air carriers, and package-laden cargo flights.

I was a little early for one of these training sessions and decided to watch a certified controller, Ty Welsh, for a while and hopefully pick up some pointers. As with most trainees, I took every opportunity to learn from seasoned controllers, but Ty was probably not the best choice. He had a few letters of reprimand and was not ashamed of them. I was not a shining star by any stretch of the imagination but was determined to complete the training program successfully, so I plugged in, hoping to learn something from Ty.

Tucson had sixty F-16s from the Tucson Air National Guard that flew twice a day. This morning, the F-16s were just beginning to come home as I plugged my headset into the jack and began watching Ty. There were about forty-five F-16s scheduled to return in the next thirty minutes, usually two to four aircraft per flight, and a quick look at the other sectors showed air carriers being sequenced for the Tucson airport. Ty knew it was going to get busy. Among other aircraft, Ty had a single F-16 flown by pilot with the call sign, Hondo, and an America West Boeing 737. All other aircraft were far enough away not to be a concern, but these two were a DAT, or "dead-assed tie." Considering their respective locations from the airport, one aircraft had to slow down, allowing the other to go first. I had seen this scenario many times and screwed it up routinely, so I was very interested to see how Ty would handle it while remaining within the confines of ATC law.

The Tucson Air National Guard trained F-16 pilots, who generally left early in the morning and again shortly after lunch, with an occasional training mission after dark. Exercises were frequently dependent on each other and grouped together, making launches and recoveries look like coveys of quail coming and going from a watering hole.

The pilots were a gang of fun, consisting of seasoned aviators who were making the transition from piloting another aircraft (such as a cargo aircraft) to piloting the F-16. They took their duties seriously, maintaining an air of professionalism, yet rarely missed an opportunity to have some fun. Controllers accommodated whenever possible and turned a blind eye to deviations from the norm, especially when they resulted in comic relief.

My first ATC instructor in the navy (and good friend since 1977), David Dodd, gave me advice to live by during my first training session working live tower traffic. It was the summer of 1977 at a small naval air station in the Florida Panhandle, and I was working ground control for the first time.

Dave asked, "Do you know the rules?"

"Yes," I answered.

"Good," he responded. "Now, if you're going to break a rule, just know which rule you're breaking, and be prepared to deal with the consequences."

Fair enough.

Ty knew the rules, broke them on a regular basis, and had the letters of reprimand in his personnel folder to prove it. He looked at me, knowing I saw the DAT and wanting to see my reaction for himself. Since Hondo was at an odd angle and farther away from the airport, I figured he would slow Hondo and put him behind the Boeing. It was the logical choice from my perspective.

Still looking me in the eyes, with his focus turned away from the radar presentation, Ty keyed the mike, told Hondo about the Boeing, and informed him that if he could "keep his speed up," Hondo could turn direct to the Tucson airport and would be number one in the sequence.

Hondo knew that the only other option was to slow his aircraft down and take a long way home, following the commercial jet. Fighters hate to go slow; their airplanes handle like tugboats in a typhoon. So naturally, Hondo replied, "Hondo will keep the speed up, is number one, going direct to Tucson."

For this to work, Hondo would have to bump his airspeed up to 400 knots or more, breaking some speed restrictions and increasing the chances of someone ending up on the carpet to answer for violations of federal air regulation. Ty, being a sly old dog, had thrown down the gauntlet and dared Hondo to fish or cut bait. Ty also knew that the wording of the speed assignment would allow him to successfully argue his way out of any responsibility for Hondo's action. "Keep your speed up" is arbitrary and open-ended. Ty never told Hondo to increase his speed to over 400 knots.

However, Hondo was no fool and knew that the consequences of his actions could jeopardize any hope of flying for the airlines and the fat paycheck that came along with the job. The next question put the ball squarely back in Ty's court.

"Tucson Approach, Hondo ... define 'keep your speed up.'" In other words, *I'll see your game of chicken and raise you a letter of reprimand.*

I smiled. Plugging in with Ty was becoming a lesson in how to have fun and what not to do. Maybe this time Ty had been trumped, and for a brief second, I wondered if he would fold his hand, eat crow, and buy a round at the next FAA/Air National Guard golf tournament.

Nope. Ty was the union president, so they weren't going to fire him. Career aspirations of becoming a supervisor had gone away with his third letter of reprimand. Once, at a post funeral gathering for a fellow controller who had passed away long before his time, Ty posed a question to all the women as they arrived. "Any tan lines? Can I see them?" At a funeral! That's Ty.

Ty was a good controller and enjoyed playing the part of Ty much more than playing the political game required of management. True to form, Ty keyed the mike while sporting a crooked, roguish grin and replied, "Firewall that baby."

"Roger!" Hondo replied, and I swear I could *hear* the smile on his face. It was on the tapes for all to know, and with dreams of an air-carrier salary intact, Hondo put the F-16 into afterburner, lit the can, and delightfully executed air traffic control instructions. I pictured in my mind coyotes and rattlesnakes scrambling for cover as Hondo dropped to the desert floor and threw coals on the fire.

Hondo's target speed jumped from 300 to 400 knots in just two sweeps. The single-engine fighter covered thirty miles so quickly that Ty had to switch Hondo to the Tucson tower frequency on the next transmission. It was a brief but well-fought duel of wits between seasoned sportsmen. Ty had blinked and been left holding the bag, but this time, unlike others, it did not contain a shit sandwich.

Back then, ATC tapes were recycled every fifteen days, and we both knew that if the incident went unreported, we would be laughing about this one in two weeks. I filed the lesson away under the heading of "fun stuff to do when nobody is looking."

Shifts in air traffic control facilities revolve around traffic density, and sectors are opened and closed accordingly. During the midnight shift, all sectors are combined into just one, with one controller on watch upstairs in the tower and one in the radar room from 11:00 p.m. to 7:00 a.m. This was Tucson, not LAX, and throughout most of the night, one controller had the airplanes outnumbered.

The first controller of the day shift relieves the midwatch controller at 5:45, works an eight-hour shift, goes home, and comes back in that night at 11:00 p.m. and works until 7:00 a.m.—hence the 4:15 a.m. wake-up instead of 4:45 a.m. This week, I had two day shifts, and no midshift. We worked midwatches every other week, so this was my off week. Therefore, I was the second to show up for the day shift. As with countless other mornings, plugging in my headset, I opened the arrival sector, and with that, the routine of another perfect day had begun.

Too early for an arrival rush, I watched as the other sectors sent Hondos, Ninjas, Pizzas, and other F-16s on their merry way, knowing I'd be talking to them soon enough. They would return, tired from pulling Gs and low on gas, with students happy to have completed another syllabus on the schedule and to be one step closer to graduation.

The F-16s are identical in form but as unique as fingerprints when a warm body climbs into the cockpit. Pilots choose their call signs, and therein lies the real distinction. Call signs tell controllers what we can do and what we can't do, except for people like Ty, who was nondiscriminatory, pushing his luck just to see where it would run out. But, the pilots are unique and their call signs are an extension of themselves. Names such as Moron, Nafod, Ballz, and Hokahae ooze with character.

I remember my first encounter with Moron during my one-year tour in Tucson tower. When I got to Tucson in March 1989, the tower and radar room were combined. That is, all controllers worked both the tower and radar room. Shortly after I got there, for many reasons, the FAA decided to separate the controller workforce into tower controllers and radar controllers. So, I spent one year working in the tower before transferring to the radar room.

While I was working ground control in the tower one morning, a single F-16 exited the runway using the call sign "Moron" and requesting permission to taxi to the Air National Guard ramp.

I approved the request, and, thinking my headset was going bad, asked for a confirmation of the call sign. He reiterated, "Moron." I then inquired as to how such a highly descriptive title had been arrived at and the reasoning behind his voluntarily using it. Moron stated that his previous call sign had been used by pilots at other bases, and he was tired of it. A call sign is personal property, and just because you have a cool call sign doesn't mean another pilot can use it. So, when this pilot transferred to the Tucson Air National Guard, he picked a call sign nobody else would use. Mission accomplished, Moron.

Moron was fun to work with, and his call sign created opportunities to add to the "fun stuff to do when nobody is looking" file. One afternoon, Moron departed as part of a flight of four aircraft, two instructors, and two students. Moron returned early from the mission southeast of the Tucson airport as a single ship (solo), using the call sign "Moron 1." I asked him what had happened to the rest of his flight, Morons 2, 3, and 4. Apparently, Moron found his student to be an idiot and felt it better for all concerned to leave him in the hands of the other, more tolerant instructor. I asked if the other three aircraft in the flight would return using "Moron 2" as a call sign.

"Heck no!" he said. "They are taking the other instructor's call sign."

Once again, mission accomplished, and for the moment, Moron's call sign was safe. Moron had a reputation and, like a former spouse, was not terribly easy to live with.

Moron stated that he needed a practice instrument approach at the Davis-Monthan Air Force Base and then wanted to go home and to the Tucson airport for some touch-and-go work. About the same time, I accepted control of "Willie23," a jet trainer from Williams Air Force Base, located a hundred miles north of Tucson, on the south side of Phoenix. The Willies came down quite frequently for practice approaches and flew T-38s, two-seaters, flown by a student and an instructor. I issued a heading and altitude to Moron for the practice approach, but the student in Willie23 read back the instructions.

Keying the mike, I stated, "Willie23, that was for the Moron. I need you to fly heading two-seven-zero and climb and maintain eight thousand, vector for the instrument approach, runway one-one left at Tucson."

The Willie23 instructor acknowledged his instructions, and I reissued Moron his heading and altitude.

Having trained under experts in antagonism such as Ty and David, I recognized the opportunity that had been dropped in my lap and felt I had sailed my little boat into a school of hungry fish. Moron was definitely in a cranky mood; admonishing and then abandoning his student had proved it. How about the Willie? Was he a major-league player?

Keying the mike once again, I chummed the water. "Moron, you're going to have to change your call sign again."

"Why?" he responded.

"The Willies are answering for you."

Like a black marlin on a fat squid, the instructor in Willie23 took the bait. "My student may not be the brightest bulb in the ready room, but he ain't a moron!"

Whoa! Pay dirt!

Moron, not one to let this assault on his character go unchallenged, replied ever so calmly, "And the instructor?"

I was now content to watch my handiwork chart its own course, but the frequency had gone cold. Dead air. My fish had taken the bait and danced on his tail above the waterline, but this time I hadn't been quick enough and had failed to set the hook.

It is important to understand that the air force trains pilots and either sends them on to squadrons or retains them at the training base to instruct new pilots until a suitable assignment opens up. The Willie23 instructor had been retained at the training base and was being very mindful of his Ps and Qs until offered a better gig. He knew that getting smart on a recorded frequency with an F-16 instructor pilot over a stupid remark by a jackass controller was not going to land him an assignment flying F-15s, so Willie23 accepted his car-antennae spanking with a tight lip and clenched jaw. Moron may have been Moron, but he was our Moron, and we loved him. I filed the incident away and vowed to set the hook next time.

The call sign Nafod (pronounced "Nae-fod") was an acronym for "No Apparent Fear of Death." Hokahae (pronounced "Hoke-uh-hay") was supposedly a Native American word meaning "It is a good day to die." I'd have to ask Big Cloud for an interpretation of that one.

"Ballz," on the other hand, was an abbreviation for Balzerac, an instructor pilot's last name. Balzerac is obviously too long for a call sign and too difficult to say when you are busy, so he shortened it. We all knew that sooner or later, a call sign like "Ballz" was going to get someone lathered up, so his fellow aviators, not wanting to fight an Equal Employment Opportunity battle, leaned on him to change it.

As I understand it, Balzerac was half in the bag at a going-away party for a Canadian F-18 squadron that had been conducting joint training exercises during the winter months in Tucson. With his wits in a diminished state, the opportunity emerged to convince Balzerac of the futility of his stance on the issue. However, Ballz was not as much in the bag as previously thought and mounted a hefty defense. His aggressors were on the verge of conceding when Ballz made a fateful mistake.

When asked why he was so special as to require the entire team to go to the mat and protect his call sign, he replied, "I'm the king!"

It stuck, and upon Balzerac's return to work Monday morning, his call sign had been officially, if not unceremoniously, replaced with "Elvis." A life-size cardboard cutout of the original owner of the name now keeps watch in Balzerac's cubicle while he protects the skies and defends the freedoms of all. It became a game with us, and Balzerac took it in stride. When returning from the operating area and checking in with ATC, he would proclaim, "Tucson Approach, the Flying Elvises, Tucson chapter, are with you on the Pima recovery."

The day progressed as usual, and I slowly worked my way through it, always mindful today was my Friday. Controllers typically work two hours on a sector, followed by a twenty-minute break. Each trip between the break room and the control room reemphasized the fact that it was monsoon season. The radar scope resembled a teenager with acne, becoming increasingly cluttered with building thunderstorms. My day was set to end at three in the afternoon, and at two o'clock, I was assigned a final shift on the departure sector.

All radar scopes are aligned with the top representing north, which makes the area directly to the controller's right east, with south at the bottom and west on the left. Tucson and Davis-Monthan Air Force Base are in the center of the scope, with Davis-Monthan above, or north, of the Tucson airport. Looking at the radar for the first time after a twenty-minute break, I was astonished at how quickly the storms had matured. Previously isolated thunderstorm cells had congealed and moved north from the border of Mexico, positioning themselves on the west side of both airports. We had just completed a runway change and were on a northwest configuration, forcing departing airplanes to take off heading northwest, or directly into the arriving thunderstorm.

Although independent of each other, Tucson and Davis-Monthan are only four and a half miles apart, divided by Interstate 10. The storm had become enormous and occupied airspace from just southwest of Tucson to a point due north of Davis-Monthan, effectively surrounding the departure corridor for both airports. Waiting for the storm to continue its track northward was the only way to avoid its effects.

Southern Arizonans look forward to the monsoon season like schoolchildren to Christmas. It brings relief from the scorching heat and provides moisture essential to quelling mountain fires and quenching the thirst of paloverde, mesquite, and saguaros. As with the snows up north, a little can be a lot, and a lot is usually too much. The desert floor is as hard as concrete and absorbs water just as effectively, resulting in floods when summer rains are measured in inches per hour. Knowing the possible effects of this thunderstorm made me a little queasy.

Contrary to popular opinion, ATC cannot deny an aircraft a takeoff clearance just because the weather looks bad. There is a bold line between ATC authority and the pilot's responsibility for the safe operation of their aircraft. These rules are dictated in the air traffic procedures manual, the code of federal air regulations, and controllers are thoroughly schooled, tested, and retested in them throughout their careers. With a weather cell this large, I knew no pilot in their right mind would fly through it, but that did not mean pilots wouldn't take off into it.

This appears to be a contradictory statement, but there was a good chance some pilot would take off into the black hole and ask for an immediate turn off the runway, thereby avoiding the severest portion of the weather. However, pilots on the ground did not have my perspective on the situation and could not tell that there was nowhere to go. This cell was rapidly wrapping itself around both airports so completely that even the quail and coyotes were taking cover—probably together, if all else failed.

The Tucson terminal radar approach control (TRACON) is located in an old tin-roofed building on the Davis-Monthan Air Force Base. Thick insulation muffled the thumping of raindrops announcing the storm's arrival, but with the clock indicating my imminent departure, I was fairly confident that I was going to be a passive observer and not a combatant in this particular battle with Mother Nature. I had seen my fair share of crappy days, vectoring airplanes around bad weather while hoping a pilot didn't declare the path I had selected impassable, so the silence, in this case, was golden.

My contentment was shattered by a voice from Tucson tower: "Northwest 551, Boeing 727, taking the runway for departure."

"Are they looking out the front window?" I asked.

The tower controller assured me the pilot saw the storm. Needing confirmation that my radar was in proper working order, I asked, "Does it look as bad out the tower window as it does on radar?"

The tower replied simply, "Yep," and I briefly wondered if I had heard the voice of Mr. Murphy.

I knew the Northwest pilot was betting on the come and would ask for a turn immediately after takeoff. Since they were taking off heading northwest and destined for Minneapolis, which was northeast, the preferred course would take them in a right turn, directly over the Davis-Monthan Air Force Base.

As long as no aircraft took off from Davis-Monthan airport, I could issue an immediate turn, and the Northwest jet would merely skirt the storm. This assumed, of course, that the air force pilots at Davis-Monthan had enough sense to look out their windows and opt for another Coke in the ready room and a game of Crud while waiting for the black hole to pass over.

A controller is only as good as his or her bag of tricks. A bag is issued the first time a control instruction is transmitted, and the bag is filled over the years. Like a bell curve, it fills rapidly at first and then more gradually as certifications are acquired at different airports, until the accumulation tapers off, as familiarity becomes experience. A full bag of tricks meant always, always having a backup plan, a way out of every situation. Bad weather, however, was a hole in the bag, decreasing options and increasing the pucker factor.

Satisfied that I had a way out, I was just beginning to let my thoughts drift to post work activities when the other shoe dropped. The tower controller at Davis-Monthan tower popped into my headset and announced, "Simon 22 is departing."

My first impression was that the air force was not as bright as I had originally given them credit. Then I read the flight strip belonging to Simon 22, which showed that Simon 22 consisted of four navy A-7s. The A-7 was a workhorse of both the navy and the marine corps. The air force had a few too. The A-7 was designed as an attack aircraft capable of delivering a few times its weight in bombs, but not designed to go fast or climb very well, and was therefore known as a "lead sled."

Being an old navy guy myself, I chalked up Simon 22's decision to fly in such hostile surroundings as a combination of mission necessity and a wish to show the air force how to fly an airplane. The flight strip showed they were headed west toward Gila Bend, en route to Miramar Naval Air Station, San Diego, which was undoubtedly home. "Get-home-itis" is a disease common among aviators and, in this case, constituted mission necessity. The disease typically inhibits synapses between the neural nodes that are essential for deductive reasoning, and the side effects are frequently the subject of National Transportation Safety Board (NTSB) reports.

I quickly reevaluated my original plan and concluded that even with the departure of Simon 22, I could turn the Northwest B-727 over the top of Davis-Monthan. This was possible for one reason: Davis-Monthan tower routinely announced an aircraft's departure as the flight was turning onto the runway. Military flights taxi onto the runway, lock the brakes, run through a checklist, and then start their departure roll. Tucson tower, on the other hand, performed the rundown function when an aircraft was starting its takeoff roll. Commercial aircraft typically "turn the corner with authority" and throttle up toward full speed immediately. For a flight of four, as in Simon 22's case, the taxi onto the runway and run-up process would easily take three to four minutes, and by that time, Northwest 551 would be climbing through Reddington Pass, twenty miles northeast of Tucson, and passing through ten thousand feet. At least that's what would have happened on a perfect day.

As expected, Northwest 551 checked in a minute later. "Tucson departure, Northwest 551 is with you, climbing out of three thousand seven hundred for seventeen thousand."

Before I could key the mike and reply to the Northwest, another voice announced its presence—not an unfamiliar one, but one completely unexpected. "Tucson Departure, Simon 22, a flight of four A-7s, off Davis-Monthan, climbing through three thousand six hundred for seventeen thousand."

Both targets appeared a sweep of the radar later, and the automation system recognized their transponder codes and labeled them as "NWA551" and "Simon22." I issued "radar contact" to each aircraft and subconsciously acknowledged that my bag of tricks had just become a great deal lighter. As all five-aircraft climbed into the thunderstorm, I watched the storm change size and shape like an amoeba in a high school science movie. Each passing sweep of the radar emphasized the inevitable, and time slowed. I had been here before, and I was not comfortable. I could see the future but could do nothing to stop it.

As expected, Northwest 551 asked first. "Tucson departure, Northwest 551 is requesting an immediate right turn for weather."

My worst-case scenario had just become very real because I had violated the cardinal rule of air traffic control. Even with all my years of training and experience, I didn't have a way out. My only option was to restrict Simon 22 to six thousand feet (the minimum altitude to clear the Tucson Mountains directly ahead) and send Northwest 551 over the top of the A-7s *after* Northwest 551 had climbed through seven thousand feet, thereby ensuring the minimum one thousand feet of vertical separation required by ATC.

Good idea, but there was one problem. By the time Northwest 551 had the necessary altitude for the turn, forward momentum would put all five aircraft in the worst part of the thunderstorm. The futility of my plan was obvious. Boeing 727s ("three holers" because they had three engines) were fast but didn't climb very well. None of the aircraft could climb fast enough to meet the turn restrictions I had given without entering the worst part of the storm.

In the next few seconds, Northwest 551 would rapidly encounter severe turbulence, forcing crew members to wrestle with controls. The loss of control would be compounded by hail, which would sound like rocks hitting the cockpit windshield at 250 knots, sending the crew a mental picture of titanium engine blades doing their best to cope. Microbursts, extreme downdrafts of air present in mature thunderstorms, would compound the difficulties.

I replied, "Northwest 551, unable immediate right turn, traffic directly off your right side, four miles, four A-7s leaving Davis-Monthan. They will be stopped at six thousand; leaving seven thousand, turn right heading zero-four-five."

The next response from Northwest 551 sent a chill down my spine. "Northwest 551 is declaring an emergency and starting an immediate right turn, northeast bound."

The voice was as calm and definitive as Moron's had been. Once a pilot declares an emergency, the book and all its rules go out the window. The pilot in command is free to do whatever is necessary to ensure the safety of the aircraft, crew, and passengers.

I felt like a parent who had just finished a fifteen-minute dissertation on the ill effects of sticking a finger into a light socket to his two-year-old. I had been explicit and direct and had painted a clear picture to the Northwest flight crew of the hazards on their right side. However, just like the two-year-old who insisted on testing the dynamics of free-flowing electrons, NWA 551 heard and understood my game plan, but it just didn't fit with theirs. The NWA 551 crew was completely familiar with elements constituting a thunderstorm, and from a strictly statistical view, the chance of hitting one of the A-7s was lower than the chance of losing a wing or an engine in the black cloud so, a right turn it was.

Immediately, the air traffic control automation system calculated a drastic reduction in separation between the aircraft, initiating a flashing "CA" for "conflict alert" adjacent to both targets. An associated aural warning caught the shift supervisor's attention, forcing him to look up from yesterday's Anaheim Angels box score to evaluate the situation.

After eight years as a navy controller and even more time as an FAA controller, I could see the next logical event in this sequence. Military flights operate in extremely close proximity, relying on visually acquiring their wingmen. If weather such as this prevents one pilot from seeing another, a condition known as "Lost Wingman" is declared, and all aircraft immediately execute a predetermined turn. This turn, generally ten degrees each per aircraft, gives them immediate and steadily increasing separation.

As if on cue, the next transmission I received was "Tucson Departure, Simon 22 is Lost Wingman."

I now had five aircraft in the middle of a severe thunderstorm who were unable to see each other and unwilling to accept my instructions as they approached downtown Tucson and flew directly over the University of Arizona.

It took a second or two for the realization to sink in, but once it did, and the radar confirmed the intentions of NWA 551, my responsibilities were reduced to traffic calls and damage control. I raised my hand, not like a schoolchild who is proud of knowing the answer, but one who was about to pee his pants and desperately seeking permission to go, once again, drawing the attention of the shift supervisor.

I knew the thunderstorm had reached its peak when the radar scope clutter turned to complete blackness. This storm was so dense that my radar could no longer see into it, much less see through it. The only aspect of control I had left was the ability to issue traffic advisories, and that bit of control was eliminated as the targets disappeared into the blackness.

Keying the mike, I made traffic calls to the five aircraft, knowing my efforts were meaningless. As with previous incidents, this one would continue with the express intention of occupying its place in time. I had become an observer with no opinion in the decisions. Mr. Murphy had walked through the door of our little approach control with rain on his shoulders and thunder in his heart.

I explained my situation to the supervisor between traffic advisories, which were based not in reality but in belief regarding aircraft locations. Since my radar had been rendered useless, my calls were shots in the dark, as I guesstimated the location of the aircraft. The only other option was to do nothing, and, being an air traffic controller, that was not an option. "Make a decision, even if it's the wrong decision!" was a mantra I had heard beginning day one of my career. Seconds passed with no information from my radar or voices from the cockpits, and in this case, no news was not good news. I truly believed Mr. Murphy had held court, had decided on guilt, and was executing the sentence. This was the calm before the aluminum showers.

Following the radar sweep through the storm for the fifth time, I caught a glimpse of a primary target heading northeast. The automation system recognized a transponder, confirming my belief, and NWA551 finally answered a call for a radio check. The next sweep showed two of the four A-7s heading northwest, in accordance with prescribed procedures, each separated by ten degrees and now a few miles apart. I identified the third A-7 two sweeps later and searched desperately for the fourth, issuing a radio check and instructions for a radar identification. A voice crackled and gave me a glimmer of hope when the Simon 22 flight leader informed me he had made radio contact with all Simon 22 aircraft. Two sweeps later, the fourth Simon 22 member was radar-identified, and I issued headings to join them as a flight again.

As quickly as it had begun, it was over, and all aircraft were separated. I issued headings commensurate with the aircraft's original flight plans and sent them on their way. The view from their windows surely showed black spots on the horizon, but with all the maneuvering space ahead, those storms would be negotiated easily. I'm confident the pilots performed a quick skivvy check and kissed their lucky charms. There is an old saying in aviation: "There are old pilots and bold pilots, but no old, bold pilots." These pilots had taken off boldly, and if they used this as a learning experience, they stood a good chance of becoming old pilots.

I sat back with the supervisor still looking over my shoulder and took a deep breath. The weather was now north of both airports, leaving behind shaken aircrews, a confused controller, and a city full of people who would not read in the morning paper about an incident in southern Arizona that had claimed a bunch of lives. No call to the Los Angeles FAA regional office or the NTSB would go out that day.

The supervisor contemplated the situation for a minute and asked if I had lost separation between any of the aircraft involved. What had happened had happened, and there was nothing he could do about it, but if separation had been lost, an investigation was in order, and he was obligated to launch it. I told him that I had lost radar contact with all of them once they entered the worst part of the storm, so I really didn't know if separation had been lost. They couldn't hang me without proof of loss of separation, and from where I was sitting, there was no proof.

His next question hit me the same way the announcement from NWA 551 initiating its right turn had. "Did you initiate 'radar contact lost' procedures when you lost contact with the aircraft?"

"Shit! I didn't have time!" I shouted.

I was astounded. After what had just happened and the possibilities that hadn't occurred, he was interested in my compliance with standard procedure. But his job was to ensure we stuck to the book.

My response shocked him back to reality, and he looked at me for a second before asking if today was my Friday. I told him that it was and that I was out the door in thirty minutes. He quickly found someone to relieve me from the position, and I left the radar room for the last time that week.

Driving home, I replayed the entire scenario over and over, desperately seeking solace in the fact that I had done nothing wrong. Experience clearly projected a picture of potential disaster, but I had become comfortable and, to some degree, complacent with normal operations. Bad weather and conflicting courses of aircraft were comparable to running a fast-food shift with two fryers, a cash register failing, and three cooks sicking out—except at fast-food joints, customers who aren't served just go hungry.

As a controller, I could have put both airports on hold for just a few minutes and averted the entire situation. However, I knew management would have drilled me on the reason behind the decision, citing unnecessary delay of the aircraft. How do you use gut instinct as a reason? How do you prove your beliefs when an event is a nonevent? What was I to say? "I can't see the future, but I have seen the past"?

Controllers live in a world in which "close" is pretty damned good. Aircraft arrive on time because of a string of pearls—a line of airplanes, minimum separation between each, stretching thirty, forty, even fifty miles from the airport. It's a beautiful sight and something of which a controller should be proud. Airplanes depart on time because of squeeze plays, which require "cocking" the runway by putting an aircraft on it immediately after a landing aircraft crosses the landing threshold. Cocking the runway allows a controller to clear the departing aircraft for takeoff as soon as an arriving aircraft turns off the runway but prior to the next landing aircraft. It's tight. Sometimes a squeeze play doesn't work, resulting in a go-around that costs the airline a lot of money in fuel and ticks off the approach controller, who has to build another hole in his or her already cramped sequence.

Squeeze plays and a string of pearls don't just happen; they're planned and executed with flawless precision. Engineers may view mistakes as learning experiences, but controllers read about their mistakes in the morning paper, testify about them in court, and worse, live with them forever.

"Scraping paint" is a term controllers use instead of "midair collision." Ironically, this is less harsh than uttering the obvious, which is contrary to the typical controller's demeanor. We're direct, no-bullshit kind of people. Ask a controller a question, and you'll get an answer, but don't expect any sugarcoating. There is only one exception: scraping paint. A reference to "scraping paint" is our way of acknowledging that one of us may have made a mistake. There are approximately 325 million people in the United States. There are approximately 13,000 FAA air traffic controllers. That's a small percentage of the population. Even a music major can do those numbers in their head. We're a tight-knit community with extremely high standards for admission. As in most every other profession, admitting that a member of our ranks made a mistake or, worse, failed to do the job, is painfully difficult.

———•◆•———

As I drove home and gazed at the Santa Catalina Mountains, now partially obscured by the remnants of the nemesis storm, images of past perfect days that had ended not-so-perfectly emerged. Was there shame in a pilot believing in a hunch, taxiing back to the ramp, and opting for a soda and a burger? Or a controller relying on gut instinct to play it safe?

After a few beers and a leftover painkiller from an old rugby injury, I finally accepted the facts of the day. I had gone toe-to-toe with Mr. Murphy and decided the fight was a draw. A tragedy that could have happened had not, so victory was not Mr. Murphy's. But I had not outwitted him, so victory was not mine either—an air traffic control push, I guess.

The military sometimes uses a form of self-separation referred to as "MARSA": "military assumes responsibility for separation of aircraft." It is used to relieve the controller of separation responsibility in certain situations, allowing military aircraft to operate in very close proximity. Dave Dodd coined a term that applied in this case and, sadly, too many others: GARSA, or "God assumes responsibility for separation of aircraft."

As I lay in bed that night, staring at the ceiling, I realized once again that I was a controller, but not really in control. Comfortably self-medicated, I fell asleep pondering the same old questions: "At what point did I lose control of this situation? Was I ever *in* control?"

But on that perfect summer southern Arizona day, nobody had scraped paint, so in the world of air traffic control, it *was* a perfect day. Welcome to the world of an air traffic controller. Welcome to my world.

2
ATC SCHOOL

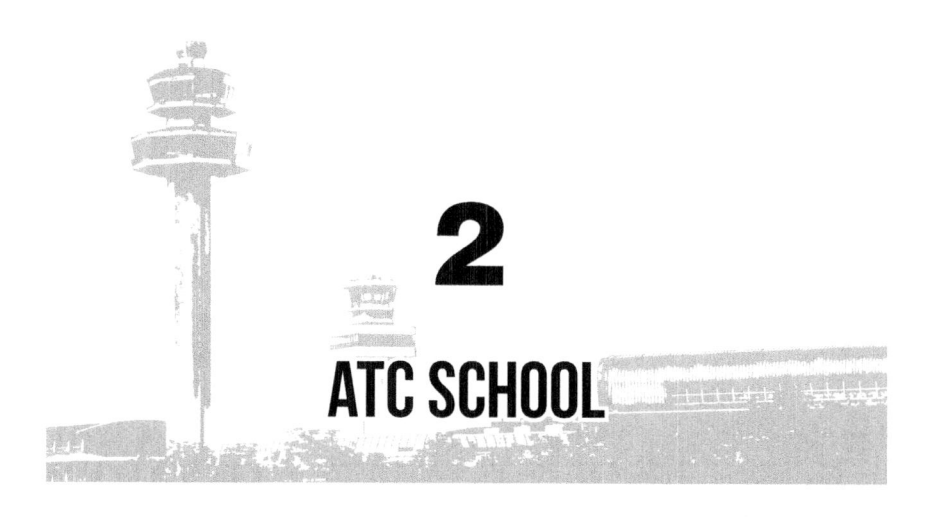

Conroe, Texas, 1976

It was a cold January evening in Conroe, Texas, just north of Houston, when I was seventeen. I sat on the front porch with my dad, chewing the fat and discussing my future. He was a short, stout man, much the same as his father. He had been raised on hard labor, doing anything that needed to be done in the oil fields, resulting in an intimate understanding of building roads, hoisting rigs into place, and running them in all conditions. Authority to make decisions such as these and to lead or discipline roughnecks came with the job. He was at the top of a rig in west Texas during a sleet storm late one night, shortly after graduating high school, when his glove stuck to a metal shaft and stayed there. Continuing his work with one glove, he made an unconscious decision that it was time for a career change, and he enrolled at Texas A&M shortly thereafter. Upper-level education lasted barely a year, and he soon found himself at the mercy of the navy. He soon was off to boot camp and air traffic control school.

My story began in 1958, when I was born in Lake Charles while Dad was working his first job with the FAA in New Orleans. By the time our cold, cold conversation occurred, he had been an air traffic controller for nearly thirty years and ran not only his life but also mine and my older sisters' with the authority and discipline he exercised in the oil fields. Like most fathers, he was focused on my best interests, and I couldn't blame him for that, but four years of high school were coming to a close, and the time to plan my next move had arrived, so we sat and planned. Charlie Daniels once sang, "A rich man goes to college, and a poor man goes to work." We weren't rich, and even if we were, I was not ready for college, so our planning session was short.

High school is a coming of age for young men. I guess it was a coming of age for me, but not in the conventional sense. I never fit any mold. Friends and schoolmates grew up, got married, had kids, acquired mortgages, and all the rest. Mom and Dad divorced during my freshman year, making my high school days a gumbo of joy and agony—sometimes too much cayenne and other times not enough okra. When the two people you love most in the world can't spend ten minutes with each other without resorting to name calling, leaving the nest is easy.

My dad learned air traffic control in the navy, so following in his footsteps seemed logical. I took the Armed Services Vocational Aptitude Battery and scored high enough for everything but nuke school, which was fine with me. Being seventeen, I needed my parents' signature on an enlistment waiver, so Dad and I discussed my career aspirations on the porch that night. My future, according to Dad, had always been a four-year accredited learning institution, and I was very concerned he might not be willing to sign the authorization. So I tiptoed around the subject until just the right moment.

When the time was right, I made it appear to be his decision, and he agreed to sign my enlistment authorization, on the condition that I would go into the navy and became a controller. Whatever you say, Dad. My dad was a controlling authority, but in this case, he realized that I was not mentally prepared for college and that my going would've been a waste of my time and, just as importantly, his money.

My sister insists, even to this day, that I was running away from life. Conroe, Texas, is located fifty miles north of Houston and in 1976 had a population of about 12,500. I didn't dislike Conroe; it was a quaint, homey small Texas town, and the people were down-to-earth. But I did not like Houston, and Conroe had nothing to offer. So I left.

I took the signed paperwork to the navy recruiter and found myself skipping school one day the following week to take my physical in downtown Houston—a one-hour ride I'll never forget. For the first thirty minutes, the recruiter coached me on what to say and what not to say. "Remember—you've never smoked pot. You've never had sex with another guy. You've never done this, never done that." The emphasis was on pot. Marijuana testing didn't exist back then, so just saying no worked.

My physical went routinely. I answered all the questions correctly, but the recruiter's routine made sense that afternoon during the ride back to Conroe. More than a few dumb-asses in my group had knuckled under to the pressure of the doctor and fessed up to smoking pot—just once. I managed to get through the summer, installing air-conditioning ductwork in new homes and counting the days until I hopped an airplane and headed for Orlando, Florida, and boot camp.

Boot camp was uneventful except it was a few weeks longer than usual. Going in at the end of October 1976, I was part of a "Christmas company." I got to Orlando too late to finish boot camp before Christmas, and like the rest of the federal government, most of the base shut down for the holidays. There was a two-week suspension of our training, so the navy gave us the option of going home for the holidays or staying in boot camp. My dad, always the pragmatist, convinced me that coming home was not the best idea. After all, I had seventeen Christmases under my belt, people would laugh at my haircut, and I would be spending my "new-car money" saved during boot camp on airfare. Besides, nothing had changed back home in two months. So I hung out with the other disenfranchised and passed the time working at the pool as a lifeguard. It was my first Christmas alone but wouldn't be my last.

I went into boot camp bilingual, speaking English as a second language and Texas redneck fluently. After three months of total immersion, I left boot camp trilingual, with a whole new vocabulary. Walls were bulkheads, floors were decks, and left and right were port and starboard. A gun was now a weapon, and my ding-ding was now a gun. Toilets were known as a head. How did a room—or in navy talk, a compartment—housing a toilet become known as a head?

For the first time in my young life, I was introduced to Yankees. The Texas definition of a Yankee is anyone born and raised north of Dallas. They had their own language, which confused things greatly.

"Y'all" was "youse guys," "yep" was "oh shooah," and "her" was "huh," and they had a tendency to add the letter *r* to words like "wash." There were, however, some words common to us all, making communication possible. "Shit" and "fuck" had the same meaning on both sides of the Mason-Dixon Line.

My most eye-opening event in boot camp happened in the dispensary, where I was introduced to the government health care system after breaking my foot, a stress fracture, from running on pavement. Running on pavement in hard-soled boots: what genius came up with that idea? A navy corpsman decided that either I was malingering or I had fallen arches. Unable to prove malingering, he issued me a set of A1 navy arch supports and told me to come back in two days. I returned in more pain than before, and he decided that they hadn't had enough time to take effect. Another two days later, as he was examining me and I was screaming, a real no-kidding navy doctor walked in and decided to take some x-rays. Even to me, the break was clearly visible, so they put a cast on my foot and issued me a set of A1 navy crutches. Government health care? No, thanks. Had some. Trying to quit.

In four months, I had been introduced to new and different people, customs, and languages. I had a cool navy haircut, a cool navy uniform, and a fresh outlook on life. Boot camp had not been nearly as tough as some had made it out to be, but I was happy to be finished all the same. Having learned how to live in the world of the navy, I was now prepared to go to Memphis, Tennessee, and learn air traffic control.

I was very young the first time I had seen Memphis, when my mother, my older sister, and I went to visit Mom's sisters, Sis and Jimmy. I never blinked an eye at names such as Bubba, Junior, or Runt or at having an aunt named "Jimmy" until I joined the navy and my shipmates raised north of the Mason-Dixon Line made me question my heritage. Although I can't remember any relatives who played the banjo, *Deliverance* suddenly made sense.

The second time I saw Memphis, in January 1977, I was eighteen, and it was covered with an inch of ice. I was certain it was colder outside than our Texas freezer had ever been. My entire world was now navy blue and, quite possibly, soon to be haze-gray (the color of navy ships) and underway.

Air traffic control school would prove to be a turning point in my life. It didn't matter how cool you were before raising your right hand and swearing to the Almighty to protect the constitution; you were now in the navy, and during the 1960s and '70s, the military was definitely uncool. Although we wore blue jeans and tennis shoes off base, 90 percent of the rest of the male population had Ted Nugent hair, so we might as well have been wearing our uniforms in public.

ATC school was four months long and divided into four blocks: control tower operator (CTO), airport, tower, and radar. CTO was the worst two weeks of my life. The block was designed to prepare us to take the CTO permit exam, which is the primary requirement for talking to airplanes. It signifies that the permit holder has enough knowledge to *train* for certification in an air traffic control facility. The two-week syllabus was a combination of classroom instruction, programmed instruction, and intensive study, followed by a comprehensive hundred-question test. Failing the exam meant washing out of school and going directly to the fleet. In the fleet, without a job specialty, you became some boatswain ("bo-sun") mate's plaything. Navy ships are in constant need of maintenance—chipping, painting, cleaning of heads, and buffing and waxing of passageways (halls). Washouts became professional buffers' mates for the rest of their enlistment.

After two weeks of studying for the CTO exam, the time came to take our test. I had no earthly idea what air traffic control was all about and was scared to death of failing. Fear is a great motivator, and unlike my high school days, I had been studying until 2:00 a.m. regularly, including weekends. We were scheduled to take the exam on a Friday morning, and the afternoon before, I requested counsel with our instructor. He was a handsome, young-looking chief petty officer who had been dinging an attractive blond wave (female sailor) in our class. Although this was a forbidden and punishable offense, he flaunted it. Likewise, she pushed the envelope, hoping an intimate relationship with an instructor would secure her orders to Bermuda. One afternoon, with our entire class looking on in amazement, he picked her up outside the school in his convertible—ballsy, but stupid. I would later learn that this behavior was typical of air traffic controllers: find a rule and break it. Poking a sleeping bear was just clean fun.

The afternoon before our test, when he and I were in his office, I explained my complete failure to grasp the concept of air traffic control and my fear of the inevitable. The instructor assured me that he had seen this many times before and that I had nothing to worry about. He chalked it up to pretest jitters and told me to go back to the barracks and get a good night's sleep. I didn't sleep, but I dragged my butt into the classroom the next day, prepared as best as I could be and hoping for the best.

The test was composed of one hundred questions, requiring 70 percent to pass. I completed it and handed it in. As I stood in front of his desk and watched, he slapped the instructor answer sheet containing the correct answers on top of my answer sheet and began grading. Holes in the instructor's answer sheet indicated correct answers. Each hole without my pencil mark below it indicated an incorrect answer. With a red grease pencil, he began marking blank holes, and there were a lot. Under my breath, I counted red marks, hoping that I would not reach the fateful number of 31. Each red mark sucked a little more air from the room. The grease pencil slowly painted the picture of a ship at sea with a grungy, sweaty, smelly boatswain's mate grinning broadly in anticipation of my arrival. Fifteen, twenty, twenty-three—a game of hangman for real. Twenty-four, twenty-five. I counted while he ever so slowly approached the one hundredth question.

As my calculated lack of understanding passed twenty-six and twenty-seven, he stopped, pulled the answer sheet away, and looked up with a mustached smiled. "There ... see! I told you there was nothing to worry about!"

I had scored a seventy-one. If this was any indication of my future, I was in serious trouble, and air traffic control was going to be a stressful occupation. But block one was in the books, and that was something to celebrate. So we did.

That night, in less than an hour and a half, I drank four hurricanes at the enlisted club. Falling down once for each drink on the way home, I ripped the knees out of a brand-new pair of jeans and woke up the next afternoon with a hangover I still remember. It was my first aspirin-resistant celebration, but not my last.

With the exception of the CTO exam, if a student had trouble and

ATC SCHOOL

didn't pass a class, a review board could be requested. The board would assess a student's situation, looking at test scores and participation, and then recommend either washing out or recycling through the previous class.

One of the most colorful characters I've ever met is Kyle Goon, who joined our class as a recycle as we were starting block two. He showed up one afternoon with one hand wrapped so completely in gauze that it looked like a white bowling ball. The gauze was at least five inches thick, and his fingers stuck straight out like quills on a porcupine's butt. Apparently, he had been involved in some sort of moronic game that wound up stretching and tearing ligaments in his hand. I pictured a navy corpsman using him to instruct a class in Gauze Wrapping 101—illustrating the proper technique, turning to his class of corpsman wannabes, and saying, "There. Got it? Now you try. Then you and you and you. Tomorrow, we'll talk about fallen arches."

In the present, the instructor shouted, "Goon! What the hell are you doing back in my class?"

I said, "Hey, go easy on the guy. There's no reason to call him names!"

The new arrival looked at me matter-of-factly and calmly stated, "Goon is my name."

Kyle Goon was six foot four with red hair and a kinda-sorta beard that reminded me of a Texas lawn in August: patches of green St. Augustine grass interspersed with brown, grub-eaten turf and a clump of unmown, two-foot-tall weeds indicating the location of the septic system. He had a cleft palate, skewing his mustache to one side and resulting in what appeared to be a permanent snicker, which fit his personality.

A setback was generally the first step down a slippery slope, indicating a washout in the making. With a name like Goon, we all assumed it was merely a matter of time. As it turned out, Goon was very intelligent, and his setback had been directly related to his injury. Apparently, the A1 navy doctor had prescribed a lot of painkillers for his injury, and Kyle had taken them all in fewer days than he should have. One of those days was a final exam—hence, the poor test score and the setback into our class.

Block two was everything we needed to know about airports, runways, lighting, aeronautical charts, publications, approach procedures, and weather. There was a solid week of weather—eight hours a day, for a total of forty hours of weather. At the end of a week of learning cloud identification, the characteristics of frontal passage, and the difference between a wind gust and a squall, I just wanted the test in front of me or an ice pick to stick in my ear, and I didn't care which. Fortunately, there were no ice picks in school, and we all passed the test. On to block three!

Block three, the tower block, was four weeks long, with a midterm at two weeks and a final test given at the end. The tower course was taught with a large table painted to resemble an airport in the center of the room and a tower cab mock-up in one corner. The students who weren't in the tower cab being controllers acted as pilots, walking around with walkie-talkies on their hips and plastic airplanes at the end of a stick as they pretended to be patrol, fighters, tankers, and cargo aircraft. The final test graded students on their phraseology, knowledge of rules and procedures, and handling of situations such as emergencies, using the students with plastic airplanes to create the scenarios.

As the morning wrapped up on the last day of block three, half of our class had taken and passed the final test: me, Goon, and a few others. Two of the instructors saw this as a reason to celebrate at the Petty Officer Club for lunch. So we did. Besides, how much trouble could we get into with the instructors? Seven sailors plus nine pitchers of beer equals two problems. One, despite all our navy training, we didn't have enough time to drink that much beer and be back in the classroom on time, so we were late. Two, the rest of the class still had to take their tests and didn't need drunk pilots. We returned to face the music. The instructors were dealt with by the lead instructor, but we were the personal property of the sergeant.

Most people don't realize it, but the marine corps and the navy go hand in hand. The navy keeps sea lanes open and safe for merchant ships and commerce. The marines perform a lot of functions today, but they were originally formed to keep ports open for those merchant ships. The navy gave them a ride to the port and provided firepower support. So we had marines in our class. They were great, and it is important to note that aviation marines are not considered part of the corps by "real," no-shit marines. Aviation marines are not seen as having an elevated status in the corps, but they are viewed as a separate element. The navy is similar. Real "black-shoe" sailors refer to aviation sailors as "Airedales." Black-shoe sailors wear black shoes. Airedales are authorized to wear brown shoes—sets us apart.

In school, class leaders are not elected or even selected. This was the military, so the senior person, in our case a marine sergeant, was our class leader. He was a good guy—evenhanded, honest, and fair, with a good sense of humor. School was school, the field was the field, and things were a bit relaxed in school because it was a tough program with a graduation rate of only 60 percent.

But after we returned to class nearly an hour late, totally in the bag, the sergeant's pleasant demeanor and accommodating manner were nowhere to be found. Before air traffic control school, he had been some sort of ground-pounder or infantry or cannon shooter. I'm not exactly sure. But he was a no-kidding marine who had seemingly left the better part of his military bearing on his last bivouac—until we so blatantly abused the relaxed good order and discipline we had taken for granted.

In the military, punishment is administered in appropriate amounts in appropriate places and times. Apparently, the sergeant decided the dressing-down we were about to receive would be more effectively and appropriately administered in private. Punishing us in front of the rest of our class, awaiting their final exam, would have been distracting and unfair, so off we went. In accordance with his no-kidding marine training, he escorted us into another room, flaunting his standard thirty-six-inch marine stride, hands tightly cupped and swinging rhythmically, turning corners with a ninety-degree pivot. When the grunt lifestyle that was embedded in his soul emerged and assumed control, I knew we were screwed. The entire event, as I remember it, was brief and to the point.

The sergeant was a head shorter than me, and at five-eleven, I was otherwise the shortest of the bunch, but somehow, he looked us all directly in the eye, even Goon. Without laying a hand on any of us, which we fully expected, he instilled the fear of God in all of us. The sergeant's words were carefully chosen, further illustrating his experience, and he documented each and every one of our violations of the Uniform Code of Military Justice. However, nothing he said hit us the way his final words did. "I'm extremely disappointed!" With that, he turned and marched back to the lab, and we very quietly followed.

Walking back into the class, our heads hanging like two-year-olds who had just crapped their pants, we apologized to the class for our behavior and got on with business, doing our level best not to screw up for the other students. Everyone passed the final exam, continuing to the radar training portion of the school and our final four weeks.

I had a healthy respect for the marine sergeant before that day, but after witnessing justice administered the way it should be, I realized he had been around long enough to acquire not only intelligence and experience but also, and more importantly, wisdom. The sergeant made us feel like jackasses with minimal words or actions. A smacking would have been easier to take.

In the navy, "captain's mast" is a term for nonjudicial punishment (punishment other than courts-martial). It comes from the old days of wooden ships and iron men when the captain would gather the crew at the main mast and mete out penalties for infractions such as sleeping on watch and drinking too much. Even though the sergeant wasn't an officer, I felt it was my first and only captain's mast, but it wouldn't be Goon's. I liked Kyle Goon, but if you could get caught doing something, Goon got caught.

I went back to the barracks that day not feeling like I had dodged a bullet, but like I had learned a valuable lesson. Years later, I would be in charge of an air traffic control crew and would find myself reflecting on that event when I was put in the same situation. Imitation is the sincerest form of flattery.

Everything is relative, and the rest of ATC school went relatively smoothly—except for incidents with Lance Corporal Robinson and our graduation party. Robinson was a tall, black Magic Johnson look-alike from New York City. A handsome guy with a deep voice, a great sense of humor, and an enormous politician's grin that made you want smile too. Robinson ran around with a fellow marine named Estes, who was equally tall but otherwise quite his opposite. Estes was conservative and quiet with a quick dry wit, and he claimed to have been a motorcycle gang member before deciding on a tour in the corps. The last week of school, he showed us a picture taken before boot camp, and with one look, we all agreed he was the real deal. The picture showed a guy with hair down near his waist, a beard to match, and the physique of a redwood tree. All of us together didn't stand a chance against Estes.

It was Robinson's first experience in the South, and I don't think he fully grasped the implications of being black in Memphis, Tennessee. It might have been 1977, but it was not New York City. Designated drinking fountains and restrooms were gone, but those were just physical manifestations of a culture that remained firmly intact.

A new class started every week in ATC school, and with it came a batch of fresh faces. We were about halfway through school when an attractive, outgoing brunette from New York City began her education. She was loud and had a Brooklyn accent that couldn't be denied. Having so much in common with her and seeing that she had no one to help her with the ins and outs of air traffic control school, Robinson delegated himself the navy/marine corps ambassador and offered his services. Soon, it became obvious to all that a close relationship was growing.

Over the next few weeks, I watched their association continue, and although I was young and somewhat inexperienced, the logical conclusion was obvious. I had a few drinks with a fellow student, Don Scott or "Scotty," one night and broached the subject. He suggested that they were both students and weren't breaking any laws—*written* laws. Scotty was born and raised in Florida, but in the redneck part of Florida, so he understood my point.

Don't get me wrong—what Robby and Ms. NYC did was between them. I liked Robby, but I could see storm clouds on the horizon in the form of Shelby County's finest. Interracial relationships up north might have been accepted, but in the heart of Dixie, they were a bit more than frowned upon.

Sure enough, one Monday morning the always early, studious, clean-shaven, and smartly pressed Lance Corporal Robinson was nowhere to be found. Estes hadn't seen him since Sunday and knew only that Robby had planned on going to a get-together at Shelby County Park with Ms. NYC. Hours passed, and the scuttlebutt filling the halls indicated that they had been discovered in the back of a Ford doing what two people do, not fully comprehending the consequences of the fact that Robinson was black, Ms. NYC wasn't, and they weren't in New York City anymore.

Without military discipline for being late or in custody of the local constabulary, Robinson returned to school the following day. We welcomed our classmate warmly. No mention of the incident was made, and we all now understood the importance of being a team. Our numbers had been diminished by nearly half since CTO, and graduating would require each person to support the other. It was my first experience with the power of teamwork, which was the foundation required of a controller.

The second event, and a fitting end to a tumultuous sixteen weeks, was our class party. Throughout my career to come, I would encounter controllers who had heard about our class party. Very few of them knew the members of our class, but the events were legendary.

To this day I don't know who was responsible for organizing our class party. Two of the instructors had a townhouse far from the base, and it was decided we would be safe there. Besides, technically, after graduation we weren't students anymore, so how much trouble could we get in with the instructors? I've always been a slow learner.

We decided to invite anyone and everyone who wanted to come. After all, it was our graduation party and the more, the merrier. The party started Saturday morning around ten, and by the time early afternoon arrived, we had a lot of people—*a lot* of people.

When Estes showed up with Robinson and Ms. NYC, I should have recognized the implications. Things were getting loud and crowded. A couple of instructors who had been stationed in the Philippines made a trash can full of Mojo, which proved to be the beginning of the end. Mojo is loaded with liquor, and fruit juice is added to cover up the bitter taste. I lost track of Scotty and Goon after one of the instructors declared it was time for a road trip in his new Bronco. He was in no shape to drive, but between the Mojo and other stuff (we'll leave it at that), I could see my controller career ending before it started, so a road trip it was.

The only "seat" left wasn't a seat at all, but room between the backseat and the tailgate. I was joined by another controller, and with the two of us facing each other, the space got very cramped. We were gone for several hours and returned to cheers for having made it back alive and with sore butts from four-wheeling. It was almost dark, I had to pee, and the time to end the celebration was fast arriving. As I walked into the townhouse, I recognized my CTO instructor, and he congratulated me. Was there anyone from the school who had not been invited? Or who had not shown up?

Climbing the stairs to the one bathroom, I noticed a line, became mentally prepared for a long wait, and put my bladder on standby. However, upon assuming my place at the end of the line, I realized the line was not for the middle door housing the toilet, but for the two doors on either side—the bedroom doors. Confused, I asked about the availability of the head and was ushered up the stairs, where I took care of business and descended past the line and back into the confusion. Without asking for confirmation, I assumed some illegal drug was the order of the day and concluded I did not need to press my luck any longer. I gave Scotty the option of staying and finding a ride or leaving now with me. He took one look around and joined me in heading back to the barracks. Goon, as expected, stayed.

The following Monday morning was a big day at school. We were scheduled to attend graduation ceremonies and receive our next duty station assignments. Senior Chief Nona Makinson, a woman I would see again later in my career, stood in front of us and delivered a doubled-edged message. First, she said, "Congratulations on graduating. However, graduating from this school does not make you air traffic controllers. It merely gives you the ability to walk into a tower or radar room and *train* to be an air traffic controller."

Well, there's a backhanded compliment, I thought.

Makinson frowned. "Your graduating class is a lot smaller now than when it started. And statistically, approximately one-third of you will wash out in the field."

Are you considering a postnavy career as a motivational speaker, Nona? I wondered. *Your style needs work.*

Assignments followed. Goon and I were assigned to Whiting Field in Milton, Florida, a training command about a half hour from

Pensacola. Then Makinson got to Scotty. "Airman Don Scott, you're going to Diego Garcia, and I need to talk to you after we finish here."

Scotty replied, "Just one question—where is it?"

The senior chief responded, "It's in the middle of the Indian Ocean, a few thousand miles from anywhere."

So here we were: Goon, a setback who was lucky to have graduated, and I, looking to go anywhere overseas, both had been assigned choice duty in Florida, and Scotty, who wanted anything in Florida, was being sent to the middle of the Indian Ocean. Is the navy fair? Nope. Ironically, I *almost* traded orders with Scotty. Yep. I enlisted to go to the nether regions, and I wanted to go. But life on the beaches of Pensacola overrode all that.

After Makinson finished, the commanding officer in charge of the air traffic control school walked in and announced that some of us needed to report to his office immediately. Hmm, this put some bad vibes in the air, especially since Goon and I were on the list. As we sat outside the commander's office in our white dress uniforms, fresh from graduation ceremonies, I replayed in my mind all the events of the party, but nothing came to mind. Goon agreed that he could think of nothing earth-shattering that had happened. The commander walked out and called for Goon. Ten or fifteen minutes passed like ten or fifteen years. Finally, Goon emerged sullen-faced, not revealing anything, and kept walking down the hall.

I walked in and was introduced to my first Naval Investigative Service agent. He asked me the questions I expected: "Were you at the party?" "How long?" "Did you see any drugs?"

My recruiter training kicked in, and I answered each question very simply: "Yes." "A while." "No."

Then he asked me about the events upstairs, and I answered truthfully. "I do not know what you are referring to." And I didn't.

I must have been persuasive because as quickly as the interrogation had begun, it ended. "Anything you want to tell me, Airman Smith?"

"Nope," I replied.

"You're dismissed," he said with finality.

Later, we found out that someone had invited two of the local ladies of the evening to our party. They mingled with a house full of drunk sailors and, deciding a profit was to be had, set up shop in the bedrooms—hence, the lines. Maybe the Mojo makers, fresh from the Philippines, had brought with them more than a taste for Mojo and had taken a cut of the action. That would explain the Naval Investigative Service interest. To my knowledge, the issue was looked into and dropped due to lack of evidence. The naval investigators asked, but nobody told.

Thirteen years later, I ran into a fellow FAA controller, and through the course of casual conversation, it was established that we both had been at the academy around the same time. He recalled the incident and admitted to attending our graduation party as well as a subsequent question-and-answer session with Naval Investigative Service. He asked when I had graduated, and his eyes lit up and mouth opened when he realized it was my class that had caused the trouble. I smiled but could not dismiss a nagging feeling that I knew him from somewhere. As I inquired about any participation he might have had in the road trip, I realized I was looking at the guy who had sat across from me in the back of the Bronco. It is truly a small world.

Tuesday was checkout day. Wednesday morning, we said our goodbyes, loaded up our cars, and set out for our first duty stations.

On to the beaches!

Postscript

Scotty had to stay another month waiting for a port of call (navy talk for transportation arrangements) and a passport. Scotty had successfully completed ATC school without being called on the carpet once. However, he was now facing one month of waiting, but in the navy, idle hands are not the devil's workshop because they are filled with the handles of a floor buffer. Determined to avoid time-consuming activities such as working in the chow hall or sweeping, swabbing, and buffing barracks passageways, he used an old teenager trick. Unlike Goon and me, Scotty was a quick learner, and he told the barracks chief he was in advanced school; he was going to night classes and sleeping during the day, so he asked not to be disturbed. With Nona Makinson's roster showing him detailed to the barracks as an aviation buffer's mate and the barracks roster showing him in night school, Scotty was free to roam the base at will until his port of call came through. He became a regular in the pool hall, hustling new arrivals for beer money.

He completed his one-year tour on "the rock" and then received orders to the Philippines. I hooked up with Scotty in the Philippines two years later and shared a house with him until he transferred back to the States. He was hired by the FAA after the strike and retired in 2012.

The blond wave who dated our CTO instructor during school, hoping to curry favor and receive orders to Bermuda, did get orders to an island: Guam.

Estes completed his military obligation, was hired by the FAA after the strike, and recently retired from Tampa tower.

I was told Robby became a marine corps officer and retired as such. Bravo Zulu, Mr. Robinson!

Kyle Goon and I spent two years in the Florida Panhandle, where he got caught some more but always managed to land on his feet. He was hired by the FAA and spent a short career at the Albuquerque tower and TRACON. After he was diagnosed with an enlarged heart, the flight surgeon revoked his medical clearance, and he was medically retired after just a few years.

3
WHITING FIELD

Following ATC school, I planned to spend two weeks at home visiting my folks and friends while catching up on history-altering events that had occurred in Conroe, Texas, during the past four months. The latter task took exactly one hour of the first day, and I found myself bored to tears, trying to find something to do while all my high school buddies were at work. I was forced to reevaluate the best use of my vacation, and the contemplation clearly illustrated what a waste of time it was to stay in Texas. I had orders to Whiting Field in Milton, Florida. Tough decision: summer on the beaches of Florida or boredom in Conroe, Texas? My dad agreed, and we plotted my departure.

Looking at the map, it was obvious that I would take I-10 eastbound until I hit Pensacola. Simple, right? I had just come from four months of ATC school, where I had learned, among other things, the intricacies of navigation. However, some of the critical elements must not have sunk in—first and foremost among them, basic navigation skills.

Houston is divided into four quarters, with I-10 and I-45 converging in the center of town. I hopped into my brand-new 1977 Celica GT, headed south on I-45 until I hit I-10, and hung a right—westbound, toward California. Three hours later, I finally realized that San Antonio was getting closer and closer, which was, if I remembered correctly, not on my route to Pensacola. Frustrated, I pulled over, bought a soda, and dug out the map my dad had so lovingly photocopied and highlighted for me. After realizing that San Antonio was in fact not even depicted on his map, I loudly summed up the situation in one word: "Shit!"

Everyone in the Circle K parking lot looked at me, and I was sure they understood what I had just figured out: I was a dumb ass. Three hours driving in the wrong direction. So I gassed up, pointed my little hot rod east, and backtracked down I-10.

By the time I reached Houston, it was nearly noon, and I had a decision to make. Should I go north on I-45 back home, get a good night's sleep, and start over in the morning or drive straight through and get into Pensacola around 6:00 a.m.? I could not face my dad and admit that I had done something as stupid as driving three hours in the wrong direction. So I kept going, east this time, on I-10. Around 2:00 a.m., just outside of Pascagoula, Mississippi, I succumbed to sleep deprivation and pulled over at a rest stop for a few hours of shut-eye.

Reaching Pensacola the next morning, I followed the few signs posted giving directions to Milton, Florida, and Naval Air Station (NAS) Whiting Field, which was to be my home for the next two years. After asking for directions twice, once in Gulf Breeze and again in Jay, north of NAS Whiting Field, I once again backtracked and found my destination. I really sucked at navigation.

NAS Whiting Field is named after a naval aviator who was considered a real pioneer in his time. The tall pine trees obscuring anything and everything made the place seem like an exact duplicate of Conroe, Texas. It was not that I didn't like Texas; I hadn't been anywhere else and could not possibly know how good, or bad, a place it was. But I had orders to Florida, which to me meant three things: beaches, babes, and beer, not a naval air station five hundred miles east of Texas that looked and smelled just like Texas. I concluded that this was definitely *not* Florida and that I was a much worse navigator than I had imagined.

I drove through the main gate and saw navy training aircraft on static display, a T-28 on one side and a big Huey H-1 and a Bell Jet Ranger on the other, painted white, orange, and black. With the base commander's office in the background looking like the White House, I knew I had arrived where the action was.

I checked in at the White House and was told to go to the enlisted barracks for a room assignment. The next morning at 7:00 a.m., I would report to the personnel office to complete the check-in process. It was just past 11:00 a.m. by the time I finished my business at the barracks front office, found my room on the third floor, and came face-to-face with none other than Kyle Goon, who was my new roommate.

There are a few things in my life I distinctly remember, and my first look out the barracks window at NAS Whiting Field, seeing T-28s flying overhead and hearing the rumble of their engines, is just one. I recall thinking that I was going to be there for two whole years! To a nineteen-year-old, two years seemed like a lifetime.

Goon gave me a quick tour of the base, the airports, and the towers (there were two airports: one for the fixed-wing aircraft and the other for helicopters), and then we headed to the enlisted club for first-day formalities. Several pitchers of beer later, we concluded my first day with a trip into Milton, Florida, landing at the local Pizza Hut. A few more pitchers of beer and a huge pizza later (Goon could eat! I once watched him consume a single, a double, and a triple cheeseburger all in one sitting at a fast-food restaurant), we headed back to our barracks room.

I had just dozed off when the tower evening shift showed up: Merlyn Eldred Albert (I've always called him Eldred), Mark Bachand ("Baashand"), and Steve Hall. Merle was from Fond Du Lac, Wisconsin; Mark was from Boston, Massachusetts, with the accent to prove it; and Steve was from Syracuse, New York. All three had grown up playing hockey and now chose to continue the tradition in Florida despite no puck, no sticks, and no ice. They referred to their bastardized version as "hall hockey." It consisted of brooms for sticks, a hall for ice, and a round, one-inch-thick piece of four-year-old yellow Colby cheese for a puck. It was past midnight, and they were lit. Screaming and hollering, they played this stupid game just outside my and Goon's room. I asked Goon what was going on but got only snores in response.

I threw the door open and turned to my right to find Eldred and Steve standing there with brooms in hand. I shouted in my best Texas accent, "What the haaa-ell are y'all doin'?" (Only southerners can expand single-syllable words into two, three, or four syllables.)

They froze, looking not at me but through me, and I heard a voice behind me say, "Y'all! Who the haaa-ell are y'all?"

I turned and came face-to-face with Mark's chest. Looking up at all six feet four inches and 230 pounds of Bachand, I realized the time had come to ditch the Texas accent. I stood my ground by turning to face Eldred, who was six-one but nearly as skinny as me, and Steve, who was closer to my five-eleven and even skinnier. Confronting either of them was preferable to taking on a Wookie from Boston.

"I'm trying to get some sleep here and can't because of the noise," I said in more of a pleading manner.

"Ah!" Eldred said in a convincing, professor-like, cheese-head accent. "You must be da new guy. We'll try ta keep it down for ya."

"Thanks," I said, half-believing him.

I turned, walked into my room, shut the door, and crawled into bed, expecting to fall asleep immediately. I was only half-disappointed when the raucous activity resumed immediately. Using my pillow, I covered my head and concluded that this was just the way it was going to be and that would okay.

For those of you who have never served in the military, enlisted members salute officers as a sign of respect. It's protocol. Junior officers salute senior officers too. Because Whiting Field was a primary training base for pilots, it had an officer-to-enlisted ratio of approximately six to one. That is six officers to every enlisted person, a ratio just shy of the typical air force base. Navy ensigns and marine corps second lieutenants (looeys) were everywhere. An enlisted person couldn't walk a block without saluting thirty times. It was ridiculous. However, we did have fun with it. We would pretend to salute an ensign and then scratch the back of our head instead, just to see if someone would critique us for insubordination. No one ever did.

I did have a marine second looey chew my butt on the flight line for not saluting. In the navy, sailors don't salute uncovered (a "cover" is navy talk for "hat"), and covers are not worn inside a building or on the flight line. On the flight line, covers tended to get blown off and sucked into jet engines, causing a great deal of damage and costing the navy a lot of money. Marines, on the other hand, salute anytime and anywhere. Marines are really into the whole "military" thing.

On my way to the South Tower one morning, I walked past a marine first looey on the flight line and didn't salute because I was uncovered.

He spun around and shouted, "Hey, sailor!"

I was on a navy base with sailors everywhere, and I was a controller, so naturally, I thought he was addressing a sailor, not me, and I ignored him. This pissed him off, so he chased me down and grabbed my arm, spilling my coffee. Screaming over the jet engines, he proceeded to dress me down for failing to render the appropriate indication of respect. I let him rant for a while until we were joined by his navy instructor, a lieutenant commander who simply watched as his student made a complete ass of himself before explaining the navy protocol. Because we were standing on the flight line with helicopters turning all around us and jet engines screaming, I could no more hear the instructor–student conversation than I had been able to hear the first looey's words as he screamed at me. But I could tell by the look on his jarhead face that he heard his instructor loud and clear. The commander finished, and the first looey turned to me. He shouted more unintelligible babble, shaking his head up and down and then sideways, and shrugged his shoulders, finalizing the apology with a slap on my back, a sheepish smile, and a thumbs-up for good measure. He was content to have righted a wrong.

Tower Basics—Part 1

In the typical tower, there are three basic positions: tower (also referred to as "local," although the really old controllers sometimes call it a "A stand"), ground control, and flight data/clearance delivery. The tower or local controller position owns the runway and is responsible for clearing airplanes for takeoff and landing and for sequencing aircraft in the touch-and-go pattern. It is typically the most difficult position in tower and the last position on which a controller trains.

The ground control position owns all the taxiways and ramp areas. Ground control issues taxi clearance to and from the runway and controls all the emergency vehicles such as crash trucks, ambulances, and security trucks. Whenever a vehicle wants to cross the runway, the ground controller asks the local controller for permission and either issues a crossing clearance or instructs the vehicle to hold short of the runway.

Tower Basics—Part 2

The flight data or clearance delivery position is more administrative than anything else, coordinating runway changes, issuing clearances to aircraft, and handling miscellaneous other information.

Training in a tower environment typically starts with the flight data/clearance delivery position. This allows a controller to interact with adjacent agencies responsible for other aspects of the ATC operation while observing the total operation between local and ground control. The flight data controller coordinates cancellations of flight plans or changes in flight plans with the receiving approach control and with other towers whose airspace may be affected by the change. These duties are fundamental to nearly all flight data/clearance delivery positions, but the job can very well encompass a wide range of other responsibilities as dictated by the facility.

This is a very important point to make regarding the entire ATC system: everything varies from airport to airport. In effect, each facility is completely different and accommodated independently. This difference requires air traffic controllers to certify at each facility. In other words, it doesn't matter if a controller was fully certified at Chicago, LAX, Atlanta, or New York approach controls and towers. If a controller transfers to Birmingham, Alabama, he or she still must successfully complete the training syllabus before being designated a fully certified controller at Birmingham.

There are also generic descriptions of all aspects of ATC. For instance, the definition of the tower's airspace is five statute miles around the geographical center of an airport, up to but not including three thousand feet above ground level. Some tower airspace rises above this definition, some rises to less than that, and some airspace is extended beyond the five-mile range to include approach corridors. So the next time some reporter on the evening news says, "The tower was talking to the aircraft at thirty-one thousand feet," you know that the reporter did not do his or her homework.

Whiting Field was an air traffic controller's dream and the perfect place to learn the profession. It has two identical yet completely separate airports: North Field and South Field. North Field was set up for fixed-wing aircraft, and South Field was set up for rotor aircraft (helicopters). North Field had seventy-five or so T-28 "Trojans." They were big radial-engine, two-seat trainers. The radial engine allowed oil to congregate in the lower cylinders, which burned profusely when the engine started. The resulting black cloud completely engulfed the Trojan, making it disappear until the turning propeller generated enough wind to clear the smoke. The T-28s were big and loud, and I loved them—real no-kidding aviation. The T-28s could cruise at two hundred knots or slow to seventy knots on final approach. They routinely crashed off base and a day or two later would roll through the front gate on a flatbed truck with no wings and pine branches or cornstalks wedged in the engine cowling, indicating their final resting place. Depending on the extent of damage, it was not uncommon to see a crashed Trojan airborne a few weeks later. The pilots loved them, believing that any landing you can walk away from was a good one, and a pilot could land a T-28 in a lower Alabama pine forest and still walk away.

North Field was a hornet's nest. All of the T-28s flew two to three times a day, from six thirty in the morning to eleven at night. A typical morning started with twenty-five or more aircraft at the approach end of the runway, waiting for takeoff. I can still remember working my way down the line, asking call signs and numbers.

i.e., "Number fifteen holding short, say your call sign."

"Fairdale 202 is number fifteen", all the way to twenty-five or more. We loaded the runway four or five airplanes at a time, and they departed in five to ten second intervals.

Since this was a training command, North Field was also a place for aviators to practice touch-and-goes. Aircraft went out at the same time with the same amount of fuel, so they all came back at the same time, with just enough fuel to do a few touch-and-goes, creating an enormous pattern full of airplanes. It wasn't unusual to have ten to fifteen aircraft in the pattern at any one time.

During the 1970s, we had no radar in the tower to help us keep track of who was who and where they were, so we wrote down aircraft call signs as they entered the pattern and scratched them off the list as they landed. Although there were some controllers who preferred to work alone, when things were that congested and busy, another controller would assist by manning the binoculars and advising the tower controller when to send, or "break," an aircraft to the downwind.

So let me explain about patterns and runways. There are two ends to each runway. The approach end is the end that an aircraft crosses when landing, which is also the end where aircraft taxi to for takeoff. The other end is called the departure end—the opposite of the approach end. An ATC pattern is a racetrack consisting of four legs: upwind, crosswind, downwind, and final. Imagine flying to an airport at an altitude of five hundred feet, planning on performing a touch and go, and looking directly down at the approach end of a runway. After the aircraft crosses the approach end, touches down and takes off again, it is now on the upwind leg. At the departure end of the runway, turn left to the crosswind leg. Fly approximately a half mile and turn left again to the downwind leg toward the approach end of the runway. After passing the approach end, turn left again to the base leg. Take one more left turn to the final approach leg and descend to the runway for landing.

A word about the final approach leg. The next time you're on an air carrier, listen for the the "ding, ding" five to ten minutes after takeoff and thirty minutes, or so, before landing. This is a signal from the cockpit crew to the flight attendants that the aircraft is either climbing through 10,000 feet, or descending through 10,0000 feet. This is important. In the cockpit, conversation below 10,000 feet is kept to an absolute minimum as the arrival checklists are pulled out and the flight crews attention is wholly focused on the aircraft arrival sequence. Seriuos business. Ironically, either pilot could be flying the plane. Four stripes on a pilots' shoulderboard indiate the Captain. Three indicate the First Officer; referred by TV people as "Co-pilot." But, to the professionals, it's First Officer or, FO. They are both fully certified to fly the airplane and swap the "Pilot-In-Command" (PIC) duties. FO's have to get flight hours to move up in the ranks, so, they split the time. Whoverer is flying, the other does the talking to ATC and other administrative duteis.

Climbing out of 10,000 means the flight attendants can start their beverage routine among other duties. Descending through 10,000, they start putting things away. Here's the irritating part from a Controller's view. The "descending" notification is always followed by a flight attendant saying, among other things, "We've been cleared to land." No, you haven't. The final approach leg can be as far as a few hundred miles, (as with the profile descent int LAX) or as short as two miles. But, ATC will not issue a landing clearance when a airplane is descending out of 10,000 feet. Too many things can, and do, happen between 10,000 feet and touchdown, and a landing clearance is only issued when the controller is satisfied all safety issues have been resolved. Safety is *always* first and foremost, and many unsafe situations can arise between 10,000 feet and the runway threshold. Generally speaking, landing clearance is issued five to ten miles from the runway.

Back to the pattern and touch and goes. The downwind leg to final approach, in the military, is reduced to two 180-degree turns and is referred to as an overhead pattern or as the "break." It simplifies the process of landing while allowing a lot of airplanes to operate in a very small area.

Upon entering the pattern, an aircraft is assigned another aircraft to follow. However, flying an airplane is complex, especially for student pilots. So with fifteen aircraft in the pattern, it was not easy for pilots to fly their aircraft and maintain sight of the traffic they were following. At Whiting, the controller assistant with binoculars, called the "spotter," monitored the pattern to ensure that no aircraft turned downwind until there was adequate spacing.

Imagine driving a car in a parking lot that has no boundaries with ten other cars, all of the cars following a racetrack pattern, making only left turns, all maintaining a speed of ten miles per hour. There are cars parked in the center of the racetrack pattern, and that is your goal: to park your car. Organization is the key to safety, so cars come in from one specific corner of the parking lot, the upwind leg, and drive in a circle until a space to park is ready.

Your car enters the parking lot pattern on the upwind leg and is instructed to follow a car directly ahead of you. This way, the parking lot controller can adjust the size of the pattern in relation to the number of cars to park. More cars equals a bigger racetrack pattern; fewer cars equals a smaller racetrack pattern. And you can't stop. You and all the other cars must maintain a constant speed of ten miles per hour. No more, no less.

No problem, right? You can see all the other cars in the parking lot racetrack pattern—some in front of you, some making the left turn to the other side of the racetrack pattern, and some on the other side of the racetrack, moving in the opposite direction. Now imagine a layer of light fog in the parking lot, making it difficult, but not impossible, to maintain visual contact with the car you're following. You look down at the airspeed indicator to make sure you're not going too fast, and when you look up again, the car you're following is missing. What do you do? Do you ask the parking lot controller where your traffic to follow is, or assume the car you were following turned left following its traffic? In the pattern, more often than not, students didn't want to admit losing visual contact with the traffic they were following by asking the tower controller, so they just assumed the aircraft had already turned left to the crosswind leg, and they did the same. Sometimes they got lucky, and it worked. However, more often than not, they turned too early and turned in front of the aircraft they had been told to follow.

Now imagine that you lose sight of the car you're following, you don't ask the tower for help, and you turn anyway. You wind up pointed directly at another car on the other side of the parking lot pattern, the downwind leg. You are about to T-bone another car. The responsibility of the spotter was to ensure that all aircraft followed their interval, maintaining an orderly operation and preventing a midair collision while the tower controller cleared aircraft for takeoff, landing, and touch-and-goes. Simple, right?

Pilots are officers. Enlisted sailors do not tell officers what to do, except in the case of controllers. We were the only occupation—that I'm aware of anyway—in which an enlisted person could tell an officer where to go and what to do when they got there. When the pattern had ten aircraft in it, with novice pilots constantly creating conflicts, and there were twenty aircraft waiting for takeoff, the job got very stressful. The controller had to get *very* aggressive and control the frequency. We got very good at telling pilots (officers) exactly what to do and when to do it. Consequently, we had a tendency to become rather full of ourselves. Justified or not, when you walk out of the tower after having your backside handed to you and no one scraped paint, your self-esteem is pretty high, and being humble becomes somewhat challenging.

The training was brutal. Your instructor continually reminded you (usually shouting) to take control, or something bad was going to happen. I wish I had a dime for every time my instructor said, "Give me the mike! You're going to kill someone!" It was very intimidating and separated the wheat from the chaff. Makinson was right: not everyone who graduated ATC school made it through the training program to certification. The failure rate? I don't know what it was at the time of my training, but I do know that later in my career with the FAA, at some facilities, it was 30 percent or more. At one time, Atlanta TRACON had a failure rate of 50%. The FAA Inspector General was called in for an investigation. I never read the final report, but, the general consensus was; the failure rate was justified. The job isn't for everyone and pulling someone off the street, sticking them in one of the world's busiest TRACONs expecting success, just isn't realistic.

Failing training must have been a tough event in a person's life. During my career, I would certify at all but one facility. At a duty station in the future, my military obligation (enlistment) was coming to an end, and I would have certified and then left the navy. Management made the decision to terminate my training, which was a practical decision. But I was already certified on a few positions and trained controllers on those, so I was productive and not a washout.

Controllers must put their emotions in a box and rely on deductive reasoning. When the walls are caving in and you're running out of options, it's extremely difficult to remain calm and focus on priorities, but controllers do. It's self-gratifying in a way. Certification meant working on your own, without an instructor, in a very stressful environment and every day.

After certifying in the tower, our confidence (arrogance) grew. We became more flippant and had a tendency to use unapproved phraseology to tell pilots they were turning inside their traffic and instruct them to turn back to the upwind. Practicing this technique required the utmost discretion to avoid being called on the carpet in the operation commander's office. Used correctly, our technique emphasized to student pilots the necessity of paying very close attention to air traffic control instructions. The fact that an enlisted controller like one of us was belittling an officer was generally ignored by the instructors.

However, each of us crossed the line on occasion and found ourselves facing the music. I was no exception. On one occasion, a T-28 had not once or twice but three times lost sight of his traffic and attempted to turn downwind early, which meant he could have flown directly into downwind traffic and caused a midair collision. All three times, my spotter caught the guilty party, but since I was running the show, it was the third strike. I had a pattern full of Iranian student solos performing touch-and-goes and no time to monkey with a US solo who kept screwing up.

So I keyed the mike and said, "Philander 202, North Whiting Tower. Climb and maintain eight hundred, then turn left heading three-six-zero, and contact Pensacola Approach for re-sequence. If you can't get it right the first time, you'll just have to try it again."

"Tower, Philander 202. Do you know who I am?" he replied.

"No, Ensign, I don't," I said, "but if you ask your instructor, I'll bet he can tell you."

Shit, I thought, *I don't know who you are, what college you graduated from, or who your daddy is, and I don't care. I'm up to my ears in airplanes, and you're not helping matters.*

He took the instructions without any more complaining and turned north. An hour or so later, the bitch box (a metal box we used to communicate with the other tower, base operations, and the office) came alive with the operation officer's voice. The instructions were simple: have the controller who worked Philander 202 report to his office after the shift and bring along his supervisor.

My supervisor, David Dodd, chewed my ass off while half-laughing all the way to the ops officer's office. However, as I went into Commander Pifer's office, I noticed a navy commander in his khakis sitting in the entryway. Navy commanders do not sit and wait to see other navy commanders unless a higher-ranking officer such as the base captain is in the office or the ops officer is about to have a come-to-Jesus meeting with some poor, dumb-ass enlisted controller—in this case, me.

Commander Pifer was waiting for me. My supervisor, the air traffic control officer, the air traffic control leading chief, and I were instructed to sit down and shut up. Commander Pifer was a no-nonsense kind of guy. He was a man of very few words, and when he spoke, people listened. He played the tape of my escapade, and I was somewhat impressed with my voice and handling of the situation until I heard Philander 202. As it turned out, Philander 202 was not an ensign at all, but a squadron commander—a full navy commander. I rapidly deduced that the commander sitting in Pifer's entryway was most likely Philander 202. I was screwed.

Pifer asked for my side of the story, and I told him.

He played the tape of the event again to confirm the facts and said, "Stick to approved ATC phraseology, and do not *ever* speak to a commissioned officer in this manner again. *Got it*, Petty Officer Smith?"

"You betcha, Commander!"

"Now get outta my office!"

"Yes, sir!"

We all left, after which I took a little ass whipping from the air traffic officer, Lieutenant Firmbach, who thought the whole incident was funny. Before dismissing me, Lieutenant Firmbach asked, "Where did you learn to be so abrasive?"

"My instructor, David," I responded.

He laughed and said he didn't want to see me again.

As I walked past the commander's office, I heard Pifer's voice loud and clear, chewing Philander 202's ass for being such a shitty pilot and threatening to send him to the air force to fly C-130s to and from Diego Garcia. Right then, I realized that there was justice in the navy.

Training in my first tower consisted of massive amounts of belittling, constant questions about whether I had two parents, and an unrelenting emphasis on my ability to control my bowel movements because I obviously couldn't control airplanes. Now and then, there was an almost indistinguishable attaboy, usually in the form of "Well, you didn't screw that up too badly, so I guess the session was okay."

David was my primary instructor and used his command of the English language to emphasize areas needing improvement. It all served a purpose, one that I would not recognize until I was fully certified, but a purpose all the same.

Airspace towers and radar units are split into pieces with appropriate names. The tower, for example, has a few pieces: runways, taxiways, and ramp areas. The tower controller is responsible for clearing airplanes for takeoff and landing.

Terminal radar approach control (TRACON) is a bit of a misnomer. The TRACON airspace is generally defined as the airspace around an airport up to ten thousand feet and out to twenty-five statute miles, not including the tower's airspace. Just as the tower is divided into pieces, so is the TRACON. The TRACON is divided into sectors such as approach and departure, as well as west, east, low, high, and overflight. Sometimes sectors are named after another airport or airports that are serviced by that sector such as Ryan or Avra Valley.

Each sector has its little piece of the TRACON pie. As the traffic increases, sectors are split off and opened and the pie is split up. This spreads out the amount of traffic each controller works, making heavy traffic loads manageable. Conversely, when traffic loads decrease, sectors are combined, allowing controllers breaks, lunch, dinner, and so on.

Back at Whiting Tower, I certified on flight data/clearance delivery at North Tower and started training on ground control. My first day on ground control, my instructor Dave asked, "Do you know the rules?"

"Yep," I replied.

"Good. Now if you're gonna break a rule, just know what rule you're breaking and be prepared to deal with the consequences."

"Um, okay," I said. Of course, I had no idea what he was talking about, but I found out quickly.

There was something incredibly exciting about getting up in the morning at 3:30 a.m., going to work in a control tower, and watching airplanes departing into the sunrise. I was young, full of piss and vinegar, bulletproof, and boilerplated. There were not enough airplanes or emergencies to dim my enthusiasm—until I saw my first crash, "first" being the operative word.

I walked into the tower for an evening shift at 2:00 p.m. on a late summer day. It was my first day as a certified ground controller. Dave, the supervisor, told me to work ground control and to expect a runway change due to a thunderstorm passing north of the airport. Almost immediately, he began the runway change coordination, informing me that the third T-28 on final approach would be the last arrival for runway 22. Then we would switch to runway 4, completely in the opposite direction.

The laws of aerodynamics dictate that airplanes *must* land going into the wind—ergo, runways. Otherwise, all airports would be identical, and life would be a lot easier.

As the thunderstorm passed, the prevailing wind changed direction, and Dave initiated the runway change. Two of the last three T-28s struggled to land on runway 22 with a moderate tailwind, landing long, which is aviation talk for "too far down the runway to leave an acceptable amount of room for error." But they landed safely and kept their aircraft on the runway, turning off at the last taxiway.

The last T-28 for runway 22 was not so fortunate. With a fifteen- to twenty-knot tailwind, he first touched down three thousand feet down a six-thousand-foot-long runway and promptly bounced back up in the air about thirty feet, finally touching down hard—very, very hard—on the right main mount (tire) and nose gear. The main mount broke, sending the T-28 careening off the right side of the runway, where the right wing hit the ground, breaking off and splashing fuel on the engine cowling. Immediately, the aircraft erupted in flames, and I just watched.

I simply could not believe what I was seeing. It's all fun and games until someone gets poked in the eye. For me, ATC had been fun and games. I heard noises behind me but could not take my eyes off the fireball in front of me. Then I felt a clipboard smack my head. Dave had been screaming for me to transmit "Signal Delta" to the crash captain (code words that allowed the crash crew to cross the runway and access the disabled aircraft). I had been frozen. Finally, keying the mike, I followed established procedures without another hitch.

I had practiced emergency scenarios and the procedures associated with them a million times, but nothing prepared me for my first crash. One thing I do remember from all the crashes I have seen is the feeling of slowing of time. It's as though the event is happening in slow motion. Many of my controller buddies have experienced the same slowing of time. It is a very eerie feeling.

Since the beginning of aviation, airplanes have crashed. I saw a cable TV special illustrating the ten best fighter aircraft. The Sopwith Camel was among them. The Sopwith Camel was responsible for nearly as many deaths associated with pilots learning to fly the damned thing as combat deaths. Fortunately for aviation in general and me in particular, the ratio of crashes had diminished by the time I got to ATC school. However, there were times during my tour at Whiting that I would have argued the point, and this was one of them. I had been at Whiting a month and a half when I worked my first crash.

The party that night was at least as big as my full tower certification party four months later. A controller's first crash at Whiting was something to be remembered. But first, we spent the rest of the afternoon and part of the evening transcribing the tapes, literally word for word. We would play the tape for five seconds, stop, write, and play it again to make sure we had everything right. If not, play it, stop, write, play it again. We let the tape play for five to ten seconds at a time at the very most. I was in controller hell.

After we finished the transcription that night, we headed off to the enlisted club for what we called a "debrief." In air traffic controller language, a debrief is a gathering of controllers at a local watering hole to discuss the day's events and better ways to handle situations. At least that was what the married guys told their wives. We drank, played pool, played pinball, and drank some more. I don't think the wives were foolish enough to actually believe that we discussed better ways of doing business. Then again, they had married controllers in the first place, so an argument could be made.

Whenever my favorite ex-wife, Roseanne, complained about anything I had done, I just reminded her that she was the one who had said yes, and I hadn't waited until after we were married to become a jerk. I then smoothed things over by reminding her that she was my favorite ex-wife. It's the little things in life that count.

My first crash ceremonies were straightforward. I bought round after round and went home as I would many times in the future: navy drunk. The whole situation was surreal. Two pilots had nearly died. Both had been carted away on stretchers, flight suits and helmets blackened from the fire. A stark aviation reality had played itself out, and I was no longer a nineteen-year-old kid from Conroe, Texas. That night I reflected on the event, trying to understand exactly what had occurred, and wrestled with it psychologically. I was uncomfortable with my lack of emotional response. I thought I should've been more of a wreck.

The manner in which we celebrated a near disaster was strange, but I would find later in my career that it was just one of many escape valves used to prevent a complete controller meltdown—like moats around our castles filled with piranhas and alligators to keep all the ugliness and atrocities out of our lives. This was my first crash, and both pilots had survived, but that night I was confident that the time would come when pilots would perish, and I would have to deal with the consequences of a breached moat.

But I was still a young guy and tried to look at the bright side. I had become a member of a society, controllers who would never let me down and who had an unwritten rule to never leave a man behind. I would become a member of the brotherhood, and I liked that idea. I was part of a team, not a baseball team striving for a score that would mean nothing the next day, but a team playing the game of reality, which never had a final inning and had a score that accumulated endlessly—and the score did mean something the next day. It was the brotherhood that kept me going.

Merlyn Eldred Albert, mentioned earlier as a hall hockey player, became my good friend at Whiting and still is. As explained to me by his grandma, he was named after a tuba payer in a polka band. I don't know if that is true or not, but I did spend the Christmas of 1978 in Fond Du Lac, Wisconsin, which was all I needed to validate the explanation.

I grew up on the bayous of southern Louisiana and in down-home, no-bullshit Texas. I've never been smart enough to pretend to be someone I wasn't, which made it very easy for me to be me. Fond Du Lac, Wisconsin, is about two thousand miles north of where I grew up, with a distinctly different accent and bratwurst instead of beef brisket.

At Eldred's grandmother's place for Christmas dinner, she pointed to a bowl of peanuts and told me, "Sonny, eat the peanuts before the grandkids get here because then they'll all be on the floor." I did eat them because a grandma was telling me to and because I was in Fond Du Lac (the coldest place on earth) and I needed the carbs to weather the environment. To spend Christmas in Fond Du Lac, Eldred and I had left Pensacola with temperatures in the midseventies and landed in Chicago, where it was snowing and the temperature was in the low thirties. Changing planes in Chicago, we ran across the ramp to an old DC-3, pounded on the door until the flight attendant opened it, and finally flew to Oshkosh, Wisconsin, where Eldred's parents picked us up. Wisconsin was a lot colder than my freezer in Texas ever got. The wind was blowing so hard that Merle's dad had a hard time keeping the 1966 Dodge Dart on the road. I spent two weeks in Wisconsin, and the daily high temperature broke zero three times. A small creek running next to Eldred's house was running the day we arrived, but before we left, it was frozen solid enough for snowmobilers to use as a highway.

After returning to Florida, Merle and I moved out of the barracks and into a bachelor pad—a single-wide mobile home. An old farmer owned it, and when we rented it, he made a point of telling us not to soil his beds by sleeping with a woman who was "in season." In season? Dogs and cats go into and out of season. I've slept with a woman or two who wasn't a model, but none who could be considered in season. Our goal as young men was to get laid as often as possible, so I just figured he was referring to Eldred.

Merle was tall, athletic, and handsome with blond hair that readily bleached as evenly as his skin tanned in the Florida summer sun. He had a great sense of humor, was always ready to try something new, and took the outcome of those endeavors in stride. During our time as roomies, we lived in two places: the mobile home and a two-bedroom apartment. Each place had one large bedroom and a much smaller second bedroom. Each time, I convinced Eldred we should flip a coin to determine who got the large bedroom. I won the first coin toss at the mobile home, and Merle tried desperately to argue that he should be afforded the large bedroom in the apartment by default.

I never mixed it up with Merle, partly because he would have easily whipped my ass, but mostly because he was nonconfrontational by nature. Years later, when it came time to get married, he proposed to his wife, Dawn, over the phone.

Astonished at that time, I asked, "Why?"

Merle replied, "I don't deal with rejection very well, and if she said no, I figured I could just hang up." Eldred in a nutshell.

We debated the larger bedroom in the apartment until he agreed to another flip. I won again. Eldred took his losses as he did everything else in life, with a shoulder shrug, a smile, and a chuckle.

Typically, in the navy, the wheels watch guy is positioned at the approach end of the runway, making sure each and every landing aircraft has its wheels down. The wheels watch has a pair of paddles for daytime operations and a flare gun for nighttime operations. Normally, this position is staffed by a junior enlisted sailor, but since Whiting had so many ensigns and second looeys, they got the job.

To get the wheels watch to and from the runway, we also had a duty driver in a truck with a radio who asked ground control for permission to cross the runway. NAS Whiting Field had three duty drivers, two male and one female. One August morning during heavy air traffic operations, one of our male duty drivers took the wheels watch, a male ensign, across the runway to the wheels watch station.

This typical August day in Florida was very hot and humid, and this ensign knew there were no female pilots in any of the cockpits, so he decided to mitigate the heat by shedding his flight suit. After all, he was at the end of the runway, surrounded by forests, a mile from the tower, and no one could see him in his skivvies and flight boots but other pilots.

Wheels watch shifts were a few hours long, and during this guy's stint the duty driver's shift ended, and guess who assumed the afternoon shift? Yep, our only female driver. We in the tower couldn't see the ensign at the end of the runway, so we didn't know he had autonomously altered the uniform of the day until the female duty driver called for permission to cross the runway. David was working the tower position. I was working ground control, and he gave me clearance to cross the duty driver "with no delay" (hurry) because of a landing aircraft on "short final," a quarter mile from the end of the runway. In other words, it was a squeeze play. Standard runways are two hundred feet wide, and the duty driver had just started to cross the runway when she saw the wheels watch guy in nothing but his skivvies and flight boots. Abruptly slamming on the brakes, she performed a right 180-degree turn in the middle of the runway.

David screamed. I screamed. The T-28 on final was flaring to land directly on top of the duty driver truck. The pilot must have realized something didn't feel right because he added power at the last second, which was the only reason our duty driver truck did not become a duty driver/T-28 truck. The whole situation scared the living shit out of all of us, including the duty driver and her ensign passenger.

Our supervisor, Ernie, otherwise known as "fuckin' Ernie," broke the silence. "Robin, hold the duty truck short of the runway."

"No shit, Ernie," I replied. This was why we called him fuckin' Ernie.

After finishing the shift (and cleaning our drawers), we retired to a debrief at the club, laughing our asses off about the whole situation. We awarded Ernie the prize for dumb-ass statement of the day, and he bought pitchers of beer until we said to stop—which took a while. It was the near miss of all near misses, but with all the disasters we had seen at Whiting, nobody had scraped paint, so the operation was a success.

The wheels watch position was responsible for one other very memorable experience. It was an evening shift around 9:00 p.m., and I had a pattern full of T-28s performing touch-and-goes. The T-28s had small white lights on the landing gear so that the wheels watch could verify a "wheels down" configuration at night. One T-28 turned for its final approach and showed only two lights, so the wheels watch got on his radio and told the tower, me, that the aircraft was showing only two lights and I asked the instructor pilot if he had "three in the green" from the cockpit.

In the cockpit, when the wheels are lowered, there is a green light for each wheel that is down and locked. The pilot acknowledged that "three in the green" were indicated, but he wanted to make sure, so I asked another aircraft in the pattern if he would fly next to the problem child and visually check his gear. The whole process went off without a hitch, confirming our belief that the landing gear was down and locked. We figured the white light was merely burned out and decided to press on with business as usual. And it *was* business as usual, until the changing of the guard at the wheels watch station. Apparently, during the change-of-command ceremonies, the outgoing wheels watch neglected to tell his relief about the burned-out landing gear light.

The two-eyed T-28 turned final again. I cleared him for touch-and-go, and our new wheels watch recognized an absence of lighting. He could have keyed the mike and told me, but choosing the second option in his arsenal of options, he waited until his quarry was within the very limited range of the flare gun before faithfully executing his assigned duty and pulling the trigger on the flare.

As I understood it, wheels watches were instructed to fire the gun ahead and well over the aircraft, ensuring the pilot would see the flare and take the appropriate action. This guy must have slept through that part of the class because he hit the T-28 smack in the middle of the canopy. The flare exploded like a Roman Candle when it struck the canopy, illuminating the silhouettes of the instructor pilot and his student against a scarlet background.

Dave, Merle, and I stood speechless in the tower. The T-28 pilot added power, aborted the touch-and-go, and struggled to fly upwind, wings rocking up and down.

Some smart-ass pilot in the pattern keyed his mike and, in the finest fuckin' Ernie tradition, stated the obvious. "Tower, I think the wheels watch hit that last T-28 with a flare!"

The target T-28 pilot responded, "Yeah, and I can't see a damned thing!"

Not to be outdone and let an opportunity slip away, another unidentified pilot weighed in. "Must be some marine second looey practicing his marksmanship."

Once again, everyone lived, and the wheels watch submitted his report along with ours, noting that the flare gun kit was short one flare.

Crashes continued to happen on a far-too-regular basis. Next to my first, one of the worst occurred when I was working local control, with Dave spotting for me. Whiting Field was split in half by Langley Road running from the front gate to the back gate, and a particular runway configuration, runway 31, had the aircraft flying over that road before landing. One aircraft turned final and was really low on the far side of the road. David noticed it about the same time I did and suggested I say something to the pilot.

"What am I supposed to say?" I said. "He's flying the airplane."

"Tell him he appears to be very low from the tower!" David insisted.

I repeated Dave's suggestion verbatim, and the pilot acknowledged it by simply saying, "Roger!"

When there was no change in his altitude, Dave made me repeat my previous transmission. This time, the pilot responded, "Tower, I'll fly the aircraft."

And he did. Right into the ground. A few seconds after my warning, the aircraft impacted the ground on the far side of Langley Road. With heavy five o'clock traffic heading out the back gate, the aircraft went airborne once again, over the road and the traffic, impacting the ground for the final time on the tower side of the road. Simultaneously, the right wing and the aircraft nose slammed into the grass, and the aircraft cartwheeled a few times before coming to rest on its canopy, wheels sticking straight up. Unlike my first crash, this time I knew exactly what to do: sit and watch.

David was a facility watch supervisor, and the crash occurred short of the runway, so I left the particulars to him and simply asked, "Is the runway still operational?" In other words, would the crash/rescue effort be affected if I continued air traffic operations?

Calmly, he said, "Yes, you're good. Keep working."

After nearly two years of heavy air traffic operations and too many crashes to count, I knew that aircraft in the pattern were my concern. They'd be low on gas and forced to divert to another airport if they couldn't land at Whiting. Most importantly, there was nothing I could do for these two pilots who, despite my best efforts, had landed short of the runway. Both pilots lived. So much for Darwinism.

My time at Whiting Field came and went so quickly that I am fortunate to have a handful of pictures from that time to supplement all the memories. When my time there was done, I was two years older and not necessarily wiser but definitely more experienced than the average twenty-one-year-old. Merle and his hall-hockey buddies, Bachand and Steve, were now haze-gray and underway. They had received orders to carriers and were continuing the honorable service of their country from the high seas. Goon had called for orders a few hours before I did and had received an assignment to the USS *Constellation*, an aircraft carrier homeported in Los Angeles. All male controllers leaving Whiting for the previous five years had been assigned carrier duty, and I accepted my destiny hoping, at the very least, to get a carrier on the West Coast, preferably the Connie with Goon. Goon and I had become good friends, and with five thousand swinging dicks on the Connie, I would have at least one friend.

That afternoon, the leading chief of Whiting Field air traffic control, Tony Waugh, called the detailer (typically a senior or master chief in Washington, DC, who doles out assignments) while I sat and listened. I heard a lot of "uh-huhs" and "yeah, I see" before Tony finally put his hand over the phone's receiver. He told me the detailer was fresh out of boats, and since I was due for sea duty, I would have to call back next week when new assignments were available.

However, as Tony was saying goodbye, he received an offer for me. "The detailer wants to know if you'll extend your enlistment for nine months and take the USS *Midway* home-based in Japan."

"Senior Chief, I'm not extending for any boat," I said.

Once again, Tony received another offer, one that made him smile. Tony asked, "He wants to know if you'll take orders to NAS Cubi Point, the Philippines."

I was speechless, literally.

Tony looked at me while talking to the detailer. "He's pissing all over himself, so I guess that's a yes."

I had just pulled off the biggest coup in Whiting air traffic control history. Not only had I gotten out of going to a boat, but I had orders to one of the choicest duty stations in the navy. Life for the past two years had been pretty damned good, but my naval experience was about to get a whole lot better.

Postscript

Merlyn Eldred Albert went to the USS *Saratoga* and completed his navy obligation around April 1980. He was hired by the FAA after the 1981 air traffic controller strike, attended the FAA Academy, and spent his FAA career at the Milwaukee tower/TRACON. He and his absolutely wonderful wife, Dawn, raised two daughters who attained college degrees and still live in Wisconsin. After retirement, he and Dawn sold their Milwaukee house and built a new house in their native home of Fond Du Lac to be close to family. I heard a story of an administration assistant at the Milwaukee airport who needed a kidney. She found a donor. I can't *say* it was Eldred; he'd be upset if I did. But I do know he's light one organ. I've met some special people in my career. The list isn't terribly long, but they are all close to my heart. Eldred and a few others are at the top of that list. I'm fortunate to know him.

Mark Bachand went to the *Saratoga* with Eldred and Steve Hall. According to Eldred, Mark got off the boat, was discharged, and told Merle he was going back to sell roses on a street corner in his home town of Dudley, Massachusetts—very Mark. He had shown up at work one morning with a shaved head, long before shaved heads were in vogue. While at Whiting Field, he bought a Yamaha 500 motorcycle despite never having ridden one in his life—crashed it three times learning. The first crash happened in the parking lot of the dealership, while the salesman taught him the fundamentals. I heard Mark went into the computer industry and was working as a system administrator, having married and had a daughter. Our Heavenly Father, please look over Mark's wife and daughter. They need you. Bachand was an endless source of cheap entertainment and is on that short list of people I am fortunate to have known.

Steve Hall also went to the Sorry Sara. I hooked up with him twenty-five years later in Syracuse, New York. He was identical to the way I remembered him. We had dinner and caught up on old times, and I learned that he had written software with some friends for doctors' and lawyers' offices. I don't know how much he made, but he cashed out and did financially very well. This doesn't surprise me. Steve is a very sharp guy, but you'd never know it from sitting down and having a beer with him. He has a great sense of humor and is very light and easygoing. He loaned me his ski jacket to go to Wisconsin that winter at Merle's. As of this writing, he's still in the FAA working as a senior adviser to a district manager in the Northeast. Once again, I'm not surprised.

Despite my best attempts, I have not been able to find Kyle Goon. I have no idea where he went or what he did after being medically retired from the FAA. Kyle, if you read this, call.

David Dodd was hired by the FAA in 1981 and sent to the Los Angeles tower. From there, he went to LA TRACON; Sacramento TRACON; Washington, DC, headquarters; and too many upper-level management positions to mention. He raised two incredible daughters, Jaime Kay and Jillian. Dave is also at the top of that short list. Referring to someone as your "best friend" indicates that there can be only one best friend. Never one to play by the rules, I have two best friends: Don Scott and David Dodd. Both were there whenever I desperately needed a friend. I've tried to pay back the favors Dave has done for me, but I am confident I still have a few IOUs out there. He retired a few years ago after a very distinguished career and went to work as a contractor in the Washington, DC, headquarters of the FAA. We talk at least once a week and do not see each other nearly as much as I would like.

4
CUBI POINT, PHILIPPINES

"I love you. No shit. Buy me air-conditioned helicopter."
—*Albert (Tippy) Ensell*

Two years of total immersion in the reality of air traffic control at Whiting Field was the best preparation imaginable for life at Cubi Point. For some reason, I believed that leaving behind the pilot training environment and dealing now with experienced fleet pilots would calm the experience of "oh crap, I can't believe that happened" a bit, but that proved to be a fantasy. Despite my best efforts to avoid those aviation realities, they tracked me down like an ex-wife on payday.

Having grown up on the Gulf Coast, I thought I knew about heat and humidity. That all changed when I got off the Flying Tigers contract DC-8 at Clark Air Force Base. I arrived in the Philippines in late June, just in time for the beginning of the monsoon (rainy) season, and quickly realized it would've been easier to breathe with my head in a bucket of water. A few months later, I witnessed the environmental effects of extreme humidity firsthand when, in preparation for the end of the rainy season and the start of softball season, I removed my favorite baseball glove from the closet of my non-air-conditioned house. Rainy season had magically transformed my closet into a warm, dark, clammy petri dish, and my baseball glove had mutated into a fuzzy, moldy, green wad of leather. But I'm jumping ahead.

There were twenty or thirty sailors on my flight, all of us heading for Olongapo City, ("Oh-long-a-poe") about two hours away. Upon departing the plane, we grabbed our seabags, loaded them into a panel truck, and boarded a school bus. A number of the other sailors had been stationed on ships that had made port calls to the Philippines a few times, and as we left Angeles City, driving into the countryside, they let out a coordinated "whoop," emphasizing their joy at being back in the Philippines. I had heard good things about the Philippines, and this was a very good sign.

The Philippines reminded me of every Vietnam war movie I had ever seen, probably because most of them had been filmed in the Philippines. The rice paddies out the bus window were a contrast of bright green stalks and muddy water, filled with Filipinos wearing the familiar pointy, dome-shaped hats, bent over and planting rice in preparation for the rainy season. With water buffalo pulling plows and the mist-shrouded mountains in the background, I genuinely believed I could not have been farther from Conroe, Texas, if I was on the moon. The comfort of the Florida Gulf Coast was replaced by the very real thrill of adventure. I had no idea what to expect, and I looked forward to seeing new places, meeting new people, and doing things I had never imagined.

As with my first two years in air traffic control, the reality of life in the Philippines struck early and often. Our bus driver, a Filipino, was passing cars on a two-way, two-lane concrete road with no shoulder by simultaneously pulling into the oncoming lane, flashing the headlights, and honking the horn. According to Filipino traffic laws, the first vehicle to do this had the right of way. The whoops increased as the game of Filipino chicken progressed, culminating with rambunctious cheers as we pulled into Sandy's, the midway point between Clark Air Force Base and Subic Bay Naval Station.

Sandy's was like a Filipino Stuckey's, consisting of a small kiosk whose primary objective was to sell beer out of a very large open-air building housing fifteen or twenty picnic tables. Being good sailors, we disembarked intent on contributing to the local economy and practicing good ambassadorship. I enjoyed my first beer in the Philippines, a San Miguel. Fortunately, San Miguel was a good beer because it was the national beer and the only one sold in the Philippines, so buying a beer

CUBI POINT, PHILIPPINES

was very easy. When asked, "What do you want to drink?" the only answer was beer, I learned. You were getting a San Miguel, and that was that.

My fellow sailors and I selected a table in the limited sun—it was the beginning of the monsoon season, so there was still some sunshine—and when we were asked what we wanted to drink, the other sailors each replied, "Three beers!"

"Why three?" I asked.

My closest tablemate replied, "That's about how long we'll be here."

Okay, three beers it was! I was half-finished with my second San Miguel when reality dawned. At the next table sat our bus driver and the driver of the truck transporting our worldly goods, drinking beer—three beers each, to be exact—and I concluded that my first road trip in the Philippines was about to get more interesting. With our initial contribution to the welfare of the San Miguel employees complete, I resumed my front-row-seat view of Filipino chicken. Luckily, after several spectacular near misses, we all made it to Subic Bay. I figured that the philosophy of "I drive better after I've had a few" had merit and that my safe arrival was proof.

The navy had several bases in the Philippines, two of them at Subic Bay: the Subic Bay Naval Station and the Cubi ("Cue-bee") Point Naval Air Station. Subic Bay was surrounded by mountains, with the naval station located immediately inside the main gate, and Cubi Point was located a few miles up and around the bay. The runway and airport at Cubi Point had been created during the post–World War II buildup and consisted of roughly half the side of a mountain directly adjacent to Subic Bay. The navy Seabees had literally dynamited the mountain, bulldozed it into the bay, and piled up enough land to make a runway and ramp large enough to accommodate hangars and other facilities necessary for airport operations. The entire airport was surrounded on three sides by water. Quite a sight.

Navy ATC was a small world, so it was with no surprise that I met my friend Scotty again. After leaving air traffic control school, Scotty had spent his one year of isolated duty on Diego Garcia (the rock) and then, in accordance with navy protocol, had been given his pick of orders. He had returned to the States for a thirty-day leave and visited me at Whiting Field. Being an avid tennis player, Scotty had twisted a knee while on the rock, tearing some ligaments and requiring a medevac trip to Clark Air Force Base, Angeles City, Philippines. While visiting me at Whiting, he told me of his two weeks of rehab and described the Philippines as a sailor's Disneyland and his next duty station as an easy pick. Believing at that time that there was an aircraft carrier with my name on it, we stayed in touch, and I hoped to see Scotty while I was on shore leave in the Philippines. As it turned out, he picked me up at the base operations building the day I arrived.

Scotty had a three-bedroom house in Olongapo. One of the rooms was vacant, so I moved in immediately. We shared the house with a Filipina woman, Lorna, whom Scotty called "Doones" after the Lorna Doone cookie girl.

Doonesy was the absolute best! She was sweeter than a peach pie and cute as a bug, and we became very good friends. That first evening, as the three of us sat upstairs watching an air force babe deliver the daily news on the Armed Forces Radio and Television Service station, Scotty asked Doonesy if she would get us some beer. Happy to help, she agreed, and as she walked downstairs, Scotty yelled, "And don't pay more than three pesos each!" Laughing, she called Scotty "kari put," or cheap. In that instant I had learned two things: my first term in Tagalog (the predominant language of the Philippines) and that Doonesy was very perceptive—because Scotty was indeed cheap. Still is. He calls himself frugal. When Scotty buys anything, he buys the best at the lowest price.

After finishing three more San Miguels and with the rain coming down in buckets, Scotty decided it was time for dinner. I showered, changed into shorts and flip-flops (or ICBs—Israeli combat boots—as Scotty called them), and headed out for my first Filipino meal.

The first stop was a money exchange. I changed twenty US dollars for Filipino pesos at eight pesos to the dollar, and Scotty made sure the teller gave me the last peso instead of a pack of Juicy Fruit gum. The Filipino economy was completely void of a middle class. Therefore, locals came up with some very ingenious ways to separate sailors from their money. Some were just plain illegal, but some were very creative and even benign. Exchanging a pack of gum for the last peso at a money exchange was one of the more benign scams. The pack of gum probably cost the teller fifteen centavos (there were one hundred centavos to a peso, and a peso was worth about thirteen cents US), so exchanging it for a peso meant an eighty-five-centavo profit margin. Not bad. Most sailors didn't blink an eye at the deficit, but Scotty wasn't the average sailor. If he wanted a fifteen-centavo pack of gum, he'd buy a fifteen-centavo pack of gum.

My second reality check in the Philippines came as I took my money and Scotty stepped up to get his. I turned to find five or six kids, street urchins, between the ages of four and seven surrounding me with their hands out, asking, "Peso? Peso?" I had some centavos and a few ten-centavo coins (dimes, essentially) in my pocket. I felt sorry for them, so I started doling out the coins. Scotty shouted at the kids, saying something in Tagalog that got their attention, and ran them off.

"That wasn't nice!" I said.

"Bird," Scotty said (Scotty and a few other close friends have always called me Bird), "you need to learn right now you can't feed all the homeless kids in Olongapo! Besides, look at your watch."

Noticing that the band on my dive watch was partially undone, I looked up at him in disbelief.

"Did you feel them poking you in the side?" he asked.

"Yes."

"Four of them were distracting you while the fifth was trying to steal your watch. You've got a lot to learn. The good news is you have me to teach you. Your first lesson will cost you a pitcher of beer and a pizza!"

It was one interesting pizza because the cheese was made with buffalo milk. Of course, Scotty shared this tidbit of information after I had eaten my share. It wasn't bad. I didn't bother to ask what the pepperoni was made from. Don't ask, don't tell. Boudin (Boo-Dan) is sausage made on the bayou. It's great! But don't ask.

I dutifully paid for my first lesson, and with bellies full of water buffalo cheese and something that looked like pepperoni, we headed out for a night on the town. I followed Scotty down Magsaysay (Mag-sigh-sigh) Boulevard, the main street in Olongapo, to his favorite bar, The Big Together club. Don't ask me because I have no idea what the thought process was or what the meaning behind such a title would be, but I found this bastardization of words to be the case from time to time in the Philippines. Looking back, I can only deduce that it stemmed from a desire to accommodate English-speaking patrons without a complete grasp of the English language. Filipinos routinely swapped Ps and Fs, turning Pepsi into Fepsi and Filipino into Pilipino, for example. However, the population of Olongapo was around one million, and during my eighteen months there, I never met a single person who didn't speak English conversationally. But the decision to name a rock-and-roll bar "The Big Together" still puzzles me.

Arriving at the bar, Scotty immediately recognized three controllers: Scott Twombley (Squatty), Chevis Barry Smith (variously known as Chevis, Barry, or CB), and Kurt Mayo. I had a hard time getting a good look at Kurt that night, not because the club was dark and smoky, but because he was facedown on the table with beer still in hand. Scotty had trouble too. He introduced Squatty and Chevis but drew a blank when he got to Kurt.

Chevis picked up the slack by saying, "That's Kurt; he's got the midwatch tonight."

We all laughed, except Kurt, and I immediately surmised that there was less adult supervision here than at Whiting. I had my work cut out for me.

During the Cold War era, the United States had a patrol aircraft (in this case a P-3) on station in the Philippines constantly, looking for Soviet submarines. A P-3 Orion, like the one that famously took out that Chinese MiG driver in 2003, was used as a submarine hunter and a general eye-in-the-sky looking for Russian "fishing trawlers."

Two days after arriving in the Philippines, I was in the radar room when a P-3 that had taken off with a full crew for an eleven-hour look-see developed major troubles shortly after leaving Cubi's radar range.

The P-3 had four turboprop engines numbered 1 through 4 from left (port) to right (starboard). According to the incident report, the number 4 propeller came off, causing the number 3 engine to overheat from compensating for the loss of power, resulting in a small fire and forcing the crew to shut down the number 3 engine. P-3s stay airborne for a long time and do this by shutting down two engines once they

CUBI POINT, PHILIPPINES

have been airborne long enough to burn off fuel. But, to stay airborne for 11-13 hours, they need a lot of fuel. This one had just taken off, so it was loaded with gas, and with only two props operational on one side of the airplane, a bad situation turned into a really bad situation.

The ill-fated flight limped home to Cubi, but shortly after lowering the landing gear in preparation for landing, the aircraft rolled hard right and impacted the water 1,400 feet from the end of the runway, killing five crew members. I watched the crash from atop the operations building.

The day after the P-3 crash, as I walked past the ATC offices down the hall from the radar approach control room, I recognized the distinct sound of an air traffic control tape machine playing taped controller instructions. I stuck my head in the office, drawing the attention of a chief I had yet to meet, Bruce Herman. Herman saw me, introduced himself, and suggested I come and learn firsthand what not to do at Cubi Point.

As Chief Herman played the tape, he explained that an S-3, a twin-engine, carrier-based antisubmarine warfare jet aircraft, had departed Cubi a few days earlier, opting to fly under visual flight rules, or VFR. In the case of the Cubi S-3, the pilot opted to depart VFR, making a left turn over the mountains surrounding the airport and remaining under the cloud deck en route to the aircraft carrier. Unfortunately, the base of the cloud deck had dropped below the tops of these mountains, preventing pilots from seeing the peaks.

Bruce played the tape, and I heard the two controllers discussing the amorous talents of a local bar girl, describing their relationship with her to anyone with access to the tapes. The headsets used at Cubi had a button on the handset that the controller could lock, allowing the use of the foot pedal to transmit instructions to aircraft. Without locking this button, the controller was required to squeeze the button and step on the foot pedal to transmit. The convenience of locking the button came at a price: every word spoken was taped—not transmitted to pilots, but taped all the same.

One voice belonged to Scotty, but I had not yet met the other person: Tippy Ensell. Tip cleared the aircraft for takeoff, authorized a left turn, and instructed the pilot to contact the Cubi radar departure controller. With the frequency change accomplished, Scotty and Tippy resumed their conversation, oblivious to the disaster about to occur. Arriving rain showers totally obscured the mountain peaks, making the aircraft invisible to the tower but not the flash from the impact.

"Whoa, did you see that?" one of them said.

"Yeah, must be the marines bombing Green Beach again."

Their conversation resumed and was once again interrupted, this time by a call from the radar room. "Tower, did you switch that S-3?"

"Yep, aren't you talking to him?"

"No. I don't have him on radar either. Do you see him?"

A pause on the tapes indicated that the controllers had just put two and two together. "Uh-oh" was the last remark before both buttons were unlocked.

One crash had occurred a few days before I arrived in the Philippines, the other immediately afterward, and I remember thinking, *So this is how it's going to be.*

Aviation is an inherently dangerous business. Military aircraft are designed to push the tolerances of aerodynamics and physics. Human fallibility and Mr. Murphy are variables in the equation. However, Mr. Murphy is an accomplished mathematician. The frequency of crashes at Cubi Point was lower than at Whiting Field, but this was mostly due to the experience of the pilots. During my time at Cubi Point, I would see many experienced pilots safely land their aircraft in dire situations emphasizing their talents, skills, and abilities. However, as with the S-3 incident, even experienced pilots make flawed decisions.

I learned quickly that my professional life at Cubi Point was not going to be any easier than at Whiting. For some reason, I thought I had already been indoctrinated into the brotherhood of air traffic control and had been relieved of the responsibility of proving myself again. That was before I met Chief Bruce Herman.

Bruce Herman was from the Chicago area, and he had started his naval career as an E-1, eventually rising to the rank of O-5, a full navy commander. In the navy, an enlisted member who crosses into the officer ranks is referred to as a "mustang." Mustangs are well-respected, and the title is worn proudly.

Herman, also known as "Mad Dog," was believed to have a

photographic memory, loved air traffic control, and proved it by quoting entire verses from the air traffic procedures manual word for word. There was a joke among the controller workforce: "How do you know when Herman has been reading the air traffic procedures manual? The pages are stuck together."

Bruce was a spit-and-polish sailor. I don't know which he enjoyed more, being a sailor or being an air traffic controller. Squatty once encountered him in the office, and Herman asked, "Petty Officer Twombley, what is your main objective in life?"

Squatty replied in a somewhat condescending manner, "To be the best air traffic controller I can, Mr. Herman."

"Being a squared-away petty officer should be first," Herman replied. "Being a good controller is easier."

Herman didn't do anything halfway. He had earned the name "Mad Dog" for the uninhibited manner in which he participated in debriefs. By the time I got to Cubi, Herman's remaining time there was short. He was awaiting notification of selection into the officer program. As a navy chief, the lowest member of the upper levels of enlisted management, he needed to show more discretion when it came to extracurricular activities, and officer standards were even more stringent.

"Growing old, but refusing to grow up" is a popular attitude routinely sported at Jimmy Buffet concerts. But like parrot-head hats and beer bongs, that attitude is best tucked away safely in the back of a closet on Monday morning when it's time to put on the coat and tie required to pay the mortgage. Herman knew this. By the time I met him, he had a wife and two small children, so the frat house lifestyle was relegated to his memories—well, almost. I did experience the old Mad Dog just once before he retired his alter ego.

The controller workforce took him out for one last wingding. Herman had been selected for officerdom, was about to receive his commission as an ensign, and his wife, Linda, had given him a "shore leave" one last time. I don't know if an enlisted man can ever completely purge the enlisted out of his soul, or if one would ever really want to, but we were determined to sand down what few rough edges our officer-to-be had left and leave the shavings in as many Olongapo bars as possible. It was an exorcism of sorts.

That night I learned new and interesting ways to have fun, one of which was playing helicopter. Playing helicopter required the right number of sailors (a dozen or so) consuming copious amounts of San Miguel, a light sprinkling of bar girls, and the addition of one Mad Dog spending his last evening as an enlisted chief. Then you had to find the right bar, pretty much any on Magsaysay Boulevard, locate a stage large enough to accommodate the shore leave party, and follow the leader—in this case, Mad Dog. We lined up on the stage with Mad Dog Herman, lowered our skivvies (except Tippy, who never wore skivvies), and rotated our hips in a constant circular motion conducive to turning our ding-dings just like the rotor blades on a helo. What fun! The bar girls loved it.

Except for the time David and I went skinny-dipping in the Black Water River with a crowd from a biker bar in Milton (biker chicks are cool), I hadn't been naked in public since I was two. I have never before or since expressed myself in such a flagrantly exposed manner. Suddenly, standing naked on a stage in a bar with a dozen drunken sailors had a whole new meaning. Controller camaraderie had risen to a new level—or descended, depending on whether you were in the audience or on the stage. The other patrons, drunken sailors mostly, cheered and laughed, so a good time was had by all.

I must point out a very important detail. Although the majority of the controller workforce was composed of young, single men, some were married. I can honestly say that I never witnessed any married men participating in behavior contrary to their vows. I heard of occasions, but I was never privy to them. Besides, I associated with Tippy, Scotty, Squatty, Chevis, Skeeter, and many others of my ilk. Very rarely did we conspire with the married guys. They lived on base, and we lived off base. In the end, Mad Dog received a proper send-off, and we all behaved in a manner appropriate to our marital status.

Back at work, I started out in the tower but was quickly reassigned to the radar room. With my coming from Whiting and the heavy traffic we worked there, the tower was a natural fit. However, I had certified at Whiting on a piece-of-crap precision approach radar (PAR)

CUBI POINT, PHILIPPINES

unit used strictly for the helicopters, and the Cubi radar room was very short of radar controllers. There is a major distinction to be made here. The Cubi approach control room was divided into a PAR section and an approach control section. The approach controller radar identifies aircraft and vectors them to a point ten miles from the runway, where the aircraft are handed off to the PAR controller.

The PAR controller is then responsible for directing an aircraft to the runway. The approach control training process is very long and difficult. I had never worked in an approach control environment or attended approach control school, so I really didn't know much about it. Besides, I was a tower controller. However, the navy is an authoritarian environment, and my pleas to work in the tower fell on deaf ears.

I went to the radar room and certified on the PAR while hoping for the arrival of some newcomer whom I could train and pass my PAR duties to while moving up to the tower. But nine months into an eighteen-month tour, it was obvious that I was destined to become a radar controller, and my dreams of a tower certification were just that.

I certified on the handoff position, one that assists the approach controller, which required a detailed understanding of the airspace, procedures, and policies of the approach control. The training and test were much more difficult than anything I had done at Whiting; as difficult as Whiting Tower had been, it wasn't nearly as complicated as radar. The approach control had more airspace, more aircraft, and more variables. I struggled in the radar room for a few reasons. First, there were no training facilities at Cubi Point for approach control. As far as I'm aware, all the approach controllers had come to Cubi after attending approach control school in Memphis. There may have been a few who didn't follow this path, but to my knowledge, everyone did. Second, there was a new, inviting world outside the main gate and a bunch of guys with which to share it. Third, having less than a year left on my enlistment and no intention of reenlisting, I was a short-timer. Why bust my ass getting certified just to leave Cubi and the navy a few months later?

Ironically, about the time I decided that the navy was paying me to talk to airplanes and that I had an obligation to buckle down and commit myself to certifying throughout the approach control room, word came from the office that my request for approach control training had been denied. The chiefs had done the math and concluded what I already knew: I would certify and then leave the navy, which made no sense. There were new arrivals who had two- and three-year tours ahead of them, and the navy would greatly benefit by concentrating its efforts on training and certifying them. My career progression at Cubi was never really in my hands. I certified on PAR and then sat on my hands waiting to go to the tower, and by the time I realized that wouldn't happen, it was too late to train and certify in the radar room. Oh well. I'd had fun anyway.

My career progression had stopped, but the airplanes kept coming. One monsoon day, the shit really hit the fan. A carrier—I believe the *Kitty Hawk*—was pulling into the Philippines for a port call. When carriers pull into port, they fly the carrier air group (CAG, all the airplanes on the boat, approximately sixty-five) off the boat and onto the nearest naval air station such as Cubi Point. The naval air station receiving the aircraft gets very busy very quickly. Add to that the monsoon downpours, and things can get interesting.

I was working PAR when both the A-7 squadrons, consisting of twenty-four aircraft, arrived. A-7s are short and fat with one engine under the belly of the aircraft and the main landing gear spaced closely together. This configuration creates a very unstable environment when combined with a wet runway and with tires overinflated to accommodate carrier landings. Imagine driving on the freeway at seventy miles per hour in a car with tires inflated to ninety pounds per square inch instead of thirty-two, turning them into balloons. Add an inch or two of water to an already slick concrete surface, and you have the perfect recipe for trouble.

Normally, there would be twelve inches of rubber in contact with the runway, but in a carrier configuration, rubber on the runway was minimal. On a dry runway, A-7s routinely blew tires because the pilots unknowingly locked the brakes, grinding the tires down to steel belts in seconds. The explosion and shower of steel were pretty cool, and the tower windows made a distinctive "thump" as the sound wave hit them, but blown tires created real headaches for the crash crew who had to pick up the debris. Whether the conditions were wet or dry, during

CUBI POINT, PHILIPPINES

A-7 operations, Mr. Murphy was home! With his feet kicked up on the ottoman, a cold San Miguel in his hand, and a Filipino bar girl on his lap, he just sat back and watched the show. Amusing as A-7 operations might have been, a blown tire closed the runway to all other traffic while the mess was cleaned up and the disabled aircraft was removed.

CAG recoveries were a combination of mission necessity and get-off-the-boat-itis. Pilots carried enough fuel to shoot a couple of approaches at Cubi and still make it to a suitable divert field, assuming that an incident such as a blown tire prohibited landing. But variables in the equation such as a month or two at sea and dreams of a cold San Miguel with hot bar girls encouraged bold pilots to force a bad hand. Nobody bets the pot while holding a pair of deuces, right? Especially when everyone at the table knows Mr. Murphy is holding three aces, queen high. But unlike the air force, navy carrier pilots routinely bet the pot. It comes with the job.

As I sat at the PAR scope, nursing a soda and a hangover from the previous night's activities, Chevis lined up the A-7s for arrival. I accepted a handoff for the first A-7 and checked in with Tippy in the tower at eight miles, who reported that the weather was very bad. A large squall with heavy rain and gusty winds had blown in through the mouth of Subic Bay, resulting in a couple of inches of water on the runway and a severe crosswind.

I relayed the weather information to my first A-7 pilot while calling for our favorite radar technician, Rob Coggins, to come and adjust the reception, hoping to get a better target. Coggins worked his magic, and the radar filtered out rain a little better than before, but I knew the tolerances were being pushed. If the storm didn't let up, I'd be guessing at aircraft positions soon.

The weather got worse, a lot worse, to the point that even Coggins threw in the towel, stating that he could do only so much with what he was given. The good news was that this was the first landing attempt for all of the A-7s, and they had enough fuel for two more approaches before declaring minimum fuel. "Minimum fuel" indicated enough fuel to reach their divert airport, Clark Air Force Base, make it back to the Shitty Kitty, or try one more approach at Cubi before declaring emergency fuel. "Emergency fuel" indicated that the pilot had enough fuel for just one more approach, wherever he was. In the case of emergency fuel, divert field options were no longer options, which meant landing at Cubi or ditching. What happens when the pilot declares emergency fuel and doesn't land? The pilot points his aircraft toward the South China Sea and ejects outside of Subic Bay. A planned ejection is also known as "ditching." Bad juju, baby.

The first squadron arrived, and most landed on the first approach, but I noticed that adjusting all the buttons, switches, and filters on my radar had no positive effect. In desperation, I called for Coggins. He admitted to being out of options. The second approach had just put all but two aircraft on the deck safely when Chevis announced the arrival of the second A-7 squadron. The last two A-7s landed successfully, and with the entire first squadron safe on deck, I checked in with Tippy in the tower. He confirmed further deterioration of the weather situation. I checked the big picture on the surveillance (a radar located between the PAR scopes, exactly like the approach control radar, depicting the entire airspace) to my right and saw more of the same weather on the way. Chevis was up to his ears in airplanes, breaking flights of four into single-ship arrivals, four miles behind each other, and setting them up for the PAR.

Since the A-7s had overinflated tires, landing and rolling out to a stop on a wet runway was not an option. Therefore, they trapped, meaning their arresting hook caught the arresting gear just like on the carrier. The problem was that trapping required the arresting gear boys to get the aircraft out of the gear and off the runway before the next aircraft arrived, approximately thirty to forty-five seconds later. Cubi had two PAR scopes and two PAR controllers, allowing us to run aircraft four miles behind one another. The second squadron arrival went pretty much as the first: most aircraft landed on the first pass, and the majority of leftovers landed safely on the second pass. Then the situation took a big turn for the worse. With five aircraft left, the wind picked up, the rain intensified, and as Chevis vectored the aircraft in the pattern for another approach, each aircraft, one at a time, declared minimum fuel, indicating enough fuel for two more approaches. Chevis passed the information to Skeeter, the other PAR controller, and me.

Dan "Skeeter" Englund is one of the most mellow people I have ever met. He could perform the duties of a controller with no problem, but it was obvious to all of us that Skeeter was not cut out for air traffic control. They say a bitching sailor is a happy sailor, but not in Skeeter's book. When we'd bitch about the navy, Skeeter would stare at us over his bifocals and calmly ask, "Why'd you sign up?"

After receiving the potentially fatal news from Chevis, Skeeter glanced in my direction with his "Why'd you sign up?" philosophy firmly intact, shrugged his shoulders, and continued tinkering with the filters, hoping to get a better picture. The declaration of a state of minimum fuel was not common, but it did happen. Besides, what were we supposed to do? We gave the best approach information to the pilots, and they took it from there.

When all five aircraft "went around," or didn't land because they couldn't see the runway, we knew the situation was not just bad but real bad. The PAR controller lines up aircraft on the runway centerline by issuing headings to the pilot. It's called the "precision approach radar" because the information is extremely accurate (precise), and the radar gives a controller the aircraft position in relation to the runway centerline, but also in relation to the optimal "glide slope" to the runway. Controllers use radar information to tell the pilot if the aircraft is right or left of the runway centerline and above or below the optimal glide path to the runway, and the pilot makes adjustments accordingly. When the aircraft reaches a point referred to as "decision height" (typically a quarter mile from the runway), the controller informs the pilot, "At decision height. If runway and runway lights not in sight, execute missed approach." At this time, the pilot looks away from the instruments and out the cockpit window for the runway. If the runway is in sight, the pilot lands; if not, a missed approach procedure is executed.

After missing the last approach, the five airplanes were in an "emergency fuel" situation. The next approach would be the last for all five aircraft irrespective of the outcome. If they landed, great. If not, they would climb to a specified altitude, turn to a specified heading, fly a specified number of miles, and eject into the South China Sea.

Chevis's voice jumped into my headset. "Eight miles, November Foxtrot four-zero-five, A-7, heading zero-four-five, button 3."

I responded, "Radar contact, November Foxtrot four-zero-five."

"Take button three," said Chevis. "And he hasn't been given ditch information."

Wonderful, I thought. But Chevis was saturated and doing a great job in very difficult circumstances. As I confirmed that proper communications with the aircraft had been established, the supervisor, Mark Grossman, slid a piece of paper in front of my radar console, and I read it silently.

Keying the mike, I read it aloud. "November Foxtrot 405, missed-approach procedures. Turn left, intercept the Cubi Point 265 radial, and proceed outbound for planned ejection. A search-and-rescue helicopter and the boat pool have been advised; both are en route."

A single word—"Roger"—was the pilot's reply.

Once again, it was no longer fun and games. I was familiar with the planned ejection instructions but had never had to issue them to a pilot. I think everyone in the radar room heard the instructions, and the normally noisy radar room became quiet. We all took our jobs seriously, but in that instant, things changed. Knowing there was a fair chance that at least one of these five aircraft would go around, dooming it to Davy Jones's Locker and greatly reducing the chances the pilot would be enjoying a San Miguel with his wing mates, caused a sobering sense of reality to invade our minds. We had all seen this before.

Even if the first aircraft landed safely, a flameout on the runway at the wrong place would effectively close the airport, and other aircraft would not even have the chance to shoot an approach. Controllers and pilots routinely butt heads. Pilots do not like to be told where to go and what to do, and as we've seen, controllers have a tendency to rub everyone the wrong way. But in situations such as this, controllers and pilots become brothers-in-arms, supporting each other as though we were born and raised together. Losing a pilot was one thing, but losing a pilot because a controller didn't do their best was completely different.

Having issued the planned ejection information, I took a deep breath and talked my pilot to the ground. Information was spotty, but Coggins was there opening the electronics drawer under the radar display, tweaking this and turning that to give me the best presentation possible. I called "four miles" to Tippy in the tower, and he replied, "Cleared to land." I almost asked him for a weather report, but I had wind indicators a foot from my face and decided additional weather information would be meaningless. We all knew how bad things were. These five pilots had nothing to lose by violating naval air regulations and would press on well past the mandatory missed-approach point of decision height, so existing weather conditions were irrelevant. However, in accordance with the book (I knew Herman would review the tapes no matter the outcome), I issued the wind conditions and cleared the aircraft to land. To my right, I could hear Skeeter talking to the second A-7 four miles behind mine and giving missed-approach procedures. Once again, he turned to look at me, tilted his head, gazed over his bifocals, and shrugged. The guy was one cool cucumber.

When the green dot on my radar reached decision height, I said, "At decision height. If runway and runway lights not in sight, execute missed approach." I unkeyed the mike and waited. Dead air. And more dead air.

I heard Skeeter call Tippy, informing the tower that the second of five aircraft had reached four miles. Tippy replied, "Continue."

A click in my headset announced that Tippy had information to share. "He's on deck in the first gear."

Immediately, the pilot spoke. "Cubi final, four-oh-five is in the gear. I think it's the first one—I can't tell—but I've flamed out," the pilot said before electrical power was lost.

Tip's voice immediately jumped into my headset and confirmed the information, adding that the arresting gear boys were hooking up a tow truck to remove the aircraft from the runway.

"Tip, there are four more, all of them four miles in-trail. They'll never tow him off the runway in time," I said.

Tippy replied, "They're not towing him to a taxiway, Binski." (Tip and Goon called me "Robinski.") "They're pushing him into the mud."

Good idea.

Immediately, Chevis initiated my next handoff for aircraft number three, and I heard Mark Grossman telling Skeeter to relay the following information to his pilot: "Tell him to take the first gear if at all possible. The lead aircraft flamed out and is in the mud off the runway, and his wing mates are close in-trail."

Hmm, are they thinking what I'm thinking? I wondered. *Or more accurately, am I thinking what they're thinking?*

Mark Grossman passed the game plan along. Cubi Point had a ten-thousand-foot runway with four arresting cables (gear): one at the approach end of the runway, two spaced a few thousand feet apart, and the last one at the departure end of the runway ("abort" gear), used in the event of an aborted takeoff. The hope was that the second aircraft (Skeeter's) would catch the number-one arresting gear closest to the approach end of the runway, leaving three other arresting gear available to the other aircraft. Of course, the worst-case scenario was that the arresting gear boys were using their only tow for the first A-7, and if Skeeter's aircraft flamed out on the runway, the next aircraft would be forced to land over it. One aircraft landing over another is strictly prohibited, but even Herman couldn't fault us for this one. When the A-7s declared emergency fuel state, the book had gone out the window.

Skeeter's A-7 landed safely, taking the second gear and posing a real problem. If the arresting gear guys couldn't clear the runway quick enough, I would have to tell my A-7 to take the third gear, leaving only one other chance for him to safely stop by taking the abort gear. At four miles, as expected, Tippy instructed me to continue. At two miles, the radar took a turn for the worse, and my target disappeared. I called for Coggins, who was standing behind me, and he immediately accessed the electronics.

Skeeter's aircraft avoided flaming out and taxied off the runway on its own power. Two down, three to go. Tippy advised me that we had a clear runway and gave me clearance to land. Once again, I issued the clearance to my pilot and instructed him to take the first gear if at all possible. And he did—right before he flamed out. Once again, the pilot told me he'd flamed out just before his radio quit. I relayed the information to Tippy and Skeeter. It looked like our luck was running out. I heard Tip tell Skeeter that the arresting gear boys were struggling with the tow in the mud, and it was painfully obvious that they weren't going to get my A-7, the third, off the runway in time. Skeeter passed the information to his aircraft, the fourth, as Chevis interrupted and handed me the fifth and final A-7.

Mark Grossman, our supervisor, was only a few years older than we were but was wise beyond his years. He was married with kids and lived on base, covering for us whenever a situation made it difficult for us to get to work on time. I think we might have tried Mark's patience once or twice, but we never intentionally took advantage of his good nature. He didn't party the way we did, and I can remember only one instance of his participation in a controller debrief. Mark was the yin to our yang. He kept us in balance and could easily be described as our adult supervision. This situation was bad, and we were handling it, but with one A-7 flamed out in the first gear, an insightful decision was needed, and Mark came through.

As I took control of the fifth A-7, Mark tapped me on the shoulder. "Have your A-7 land on the right side of the runway," he said.

"That's assuming he can see the runway," I replied. I looked back at Mark for a second, thinking about his instructions, and it hit me. It was bold, yes, but a very smart call. Without asking, I concluded that Mark was assuming the worse. Skeeter's A-7 would flame out in the second gear, so to maintain some manner of safety, Skeeter would instruct his A-7 to land on the left side of the runway while mine would land on the right side and have access to the third and fourth gear. If everything went to hell and we wound up with A-7 parts all over the runway, at least Herman could speak well of us at the naval aviation inquiry.

As if the participants were reading from a script, it all happened as Mark thought. Skeeter's A-7 took the second gear at about the time the arresting gear boys cleared the first gear. That must have been exciting. The weather was so bad that the arresting gear crew could not have possibly seen the landing A-7 until it passed them at 140 knots. Runways are two hundred feet wide, and since the fourth A-7 did in fact land on the left side of the runway, it must have passed within feet of them.

The fifth approach went routinely, and as I called "four miles" to Tippy, he cleared my A-7 to land, saying the weather was beginning to let up. But the second gear was fouled, and the fourth A-7 had flamed out on the runway. I passed the information along to my pilot and advised him, if at all possible, to land on the right side. He'd be passing a wingman on the left side in the second gear, flamed out.

Once again, the response was simply "Roger." My target, now more clearly displayed, passed the decision-height mark.

I issued final instructions once again, and the fifth A-7 responded,

"Four-zero-two, runway and wing mate traffic on the runway in sight," seconds before taking the arresting gear. It was music to my ears. Tip in the tower said it was a sight to behold: two A-7s in the mud and two in the arresting gear, one on the left side of the runway in the second gear and one on the right side of the runway in the third arresting gear.

Is it any wonder that the Apollo 11 mission commander and first man on the moon, was a navy pilot? Call it hero worship if you want: I am in awe of navy pilots.

We unceasingly bitched about the navy but could always tell who would reenlist. The guilty dog barks loudest. Unlike our Soviet counterparts, we were well-fed and had great jobs and good health care—for the most part. I had already had a taste of socialized medicine in boot camp, but I got a real scare while in the Philippines. If it weren't for our flight surgeon, Commander Speed, I wouldn't have an appendix.

Gastritis in the Philippines was common. However, the morning I awoke doubled over and in excruciating pain, it was time to forgo the antidiarrheal medicine and go to sick call. A bus trip to the dispensary took about fifteen minutes, but it seemed like days. Every bump in the road was another kick in the stomach. I checked in and told the corpsman that I was a controller and needed to see the flight surgeon, Lieutenant Commander Speed. He said I'd see the physician's assistant, a Filipino, like everyone else. In no shape to argue, I figured I'd do as I was told and plead my case with the physician's assistant. Guess again. The physician's assistant was certain I had an appendix on the verge of rupturing and ordered me sent up the hill to the hospital for immediate surgery.

As I was wheeled out the door on a gurney and loaded in an ambulance, Dr. Speed (no kidding, his real name) walked up and asked, "Robin, where the hell are you going?"

"Ask Dr. Wu there. He wants to operate."

The physician's assistant attempted to explain his diagnosis, but Speed would have none of it. "He's a controller. Controllers see flight surgeons, and I'm the only flight surgeon here!" Speed turned to the ambulance drivers and barked, "Take him to my office!"

CUBI POINT, PHILIPPINES

Thank you, God! I thought. *And Godspeed, Commander Speed!*

Commander Speed was one cool dude. Not only was he a flight surgeon, but he also flew in one of the best airplanes ever made, the F-4 Phantom. Commander Speed had a plank of Filipino mahogany hanging on his wall. The top half was a carved picture of an F-4 climbing through the clouds. The bottom half was inscribed, "Yea, though I fly through the valley of the shadow of death, I shall fear no evil, because a clean F-4 is a fast son of a bitch!" He also had a killer wife. Whew! She didn't come into base operations enough for us.

Speed took one look at me in the fetal position, poked around my belly, and said, "That's one bad case of gastritis you got there, Robin."

No fucking shit, I said to myself. "Yes, sir, Commander," I replied aloud. I told him that all the water I drank was base water (filtered).

"It doesn't matter. Someone stole the filters from the water filtration plant, and half the base has severe gastritis," Speed explained.

You've gotta be kidding me, I thought. *Who would steal water filters?* Filipinos.

Speed gave me some industrial-strength antidiarrheal stuff and some pain pills and sent me home for two days. Between the two medications, I was feeling good in a few hours and caught up with Chevis, Scotty, and Tippy after the day shift.

Speed gave me some level of confidence in navy medicine, but nothing compared to what I saw on a 11:00 p.m. to 7:00 a.m. midwatch. Walking through base operations one night for the midwatch, I noticed a flurry of activity out the doors to the ramp. Investigating, I asked the drivers of an ambulance for the straight skinny. Apparently, the USS *Midway* had been working just off the Cubi coast when an airman hooking up the catapult bridle to an F-4 slipped and was run over by the nose wheel. More accurately, his head was trapped under the F-4 nose wheel. The *Midway* skipper had opted to pull into port and medevac the poor guy to the States. I don't remember all the particulars, but those in charge had decided it was better not to fly him off the flight deck in a helo, choosing instead to port the *Midway* at the Cubi dock, build a ramp to the flight deck, load him into an ambulance, and drive him to the medevac C-9 on the ramp in front of base operations. Apparently, he was in bad shape.

I was scheduled for a midnight shift on the base operations desk that night, so I had a front-row seat for all of it. In as little as a few hours, the Seabees built a ramp fifty feet high to the USS *Midway* flight deck, and the ambulance boys, the same guys who had almost carted me off to the hospital, drove up to the flight deck, loaded him into an ambulance, and drove back to the base operations building, waiting for the C-9 to arrive from Clark Air Force Base. While they were waiting for the C-9, I had a chance to check out the patient. His head looked like Goon's hand, wrapped so completely in gauze that it was five times its original size and soaked in blood. I could see half his face, and it struck me that he could've been any one of us. He was a generic sailor to me, but I'm sure he was one of a kind and special to some people stateside.

As I stared at him, two things occurred to me. First, this was not a game. I watched planes crash and, on a few occasions, pilots die, but always from a distance. Unlike a movie when Arnold kills eighty bad guys and gets the girl in the end, exploding body parts were not merely some form of latex with a lot of red liquid. This was the real deal, and I couldn't help thinking this guy was done. He was alive, but that was only a technicality. I just could not picture him sitting at another Thanksgiving dinner saying grace with his family. Second, the lengths the navy went to for one sailor were amazing. Sometimes bad things happen to good people, and in this case the inevitable was obvious, at least to me. But the navy was determined to throw all its available resources at the situation in trying to save him.

The C-9 arrived, and the crew collected this prone personification of hope. I watched it take off, sad for him but rather content to know that we were all in this together and there were many good people on my side. Our acceptance of crashes and the resulting casualties had been unintentionally nonchalant, but staring at him, I knew that I would never again view the loss of a pilot or aircrew's life the same way. It was an important moment for me.

The next afternoon, Scotty told me that the man had died en route to Hawaii, somewhere near Guam—one more casualty in the defense of the Constitution. I never even knew his name, but sometimes, for no reason at all, I think of him and can still see his face.

While at Cubi, many guys fell in love and took home a Filipino bride. Just when I thought I'd escape the country unhitched, I met Remy. She and her sister had been raised in Manila and had to find out for themselves whether Olongapo was everything they had heard. So they told their mom they were staying with their older sister and snuck off one weekend. Remy was an accountant for a big company in Makati, the business district of Manila. I met her and her sister at the same pizza place Scotty had taken me on my inaugural evening. Remy was beautiful, and I do mean beautiful, and college-educated, and her dad was the first engineer on a West German freighter. In other words, her folks were wealthy. Just before leaving the Philippines, I popped the question, and I went back to the States a "spoken for" man.

Life in the Philippines was great fun. Although it was a young man's dream, it was also a cultural treat. I've met people who consider themselves to be worldly and well-traveled, but my time in the Philippines made me realize what it was like to really experience another country. I lived there for eighteen months, off base, among the Philippine people and learned a lot of the language, much of which I still remember today. It was a wonderful experience.

But as great as it was, there was a dark side too. With only two classes of people, the poor were very well represented and took every opportunity to separate sailors from their money. Sometimes this came in the form of thievery. A sailor had to assume he was a target 24-7. Consequently, whenever I walked down the sidewalk, I would constantly glance nonchalantly across the street, looking into plate-glass windows for the reflection of a would-be pickpocket sneaking up on me. I regularly, discreetly swept my right hand across my back pocket to ensure my wallet was not hanging out.

Dealing with the obvious wasn't easy, but it was sometimes fun. Ne'er-do-wells routinely approached us on the street, hand outstretched looking for a shake, and asked, "Hey, buddy, remember me?"

This was the setup for a scam, and at first, in accordance with my

Scotty training, I simply avoided them, but as my confidence grew, I would play the game. "Yeah! I remember you, you son of a bitch!" I would say. "You're the asshole who stole my watch!"

"No! No! Not me. My brother maybe?" was the standard response.

However, there were times when I just wasn't in the mood, and I would say, "Get the hell away from me!" That always did the trick.

I didn't realize how much the Philippines had changed me until I returned to the States. While walking through the San Francisco airport, I was approached by some poor, long-haired, dumb-ass con artist wannabe with a Bible in one hand and a rose in the other. "Have you heard the word of God today, brother?" he asked.

My response was automatic. "Get the hell away from me!"

The soft-spoken Jesus guy immediately disintegrated. "Sorry, dude, whatever you say."

I don't know which one of us was more surprised.

Postscript

Chevis Barry Smith went on to work for the FAA at LA Center, LA TRACON, Guam approach control, Las Vegas, and a few other locations, retiring in San Diego. He is a husband and father to a son, as well as a good friend.

Kurt Mayo also worked at LA TRACON, Guam, and Honolulu TRACON, retiring in San Diego. To my knowledge, Kurt never married and never had children. We stay in touch through social media.

Skeeter came back to the States, realized what we all knew—that although he could do the job, ATC was not for him—and became a navy diver. He retired as such, and I'm not sure where Skeeter ended up.

Squatty returned to the States, retired as a senior chief at Point Mugu, California, and earned a master's degree in education. He has a beautiful wife and still works at Point Mugu approach control.

This chapter is dedicated to Tippy Ensell, one of the kindest, most considerate, most loving men I have ever been fortunate to know. My first Christmas in the Philippines, Tip invited all Cubi orphans (single controllers) and all the controllers on the carrier in port—the *Kitty Hawk*, I think—to his home for Christmas dinner. He had two turkeys, two hams, and all the trimmings. I walked through the door and was given a gift. Everyone got a wrapped present—everyone. Mine was a book, *Jonathan Livingston Seagull*. I still have it.

Before Tippy transferred back to the States, we took him out sailing on Subic Bay—me, Tip, Chevis, Squatty, and Kurt. While we were in the middle of the bay, Tip stood up, stated that it was hot, and dropped his drawers. Except for Kurt, we all followed suit. Shortly thereafter, now naked as the day he was born, he walked to the stern, grabbed the line, and jumped in the bay. Being towed by the boat, he exclaimed, "This is nice!" Naturally, we followed suit again. I held Tip's ankle, Chevis held mine, and Squatty held Chevis's. Kurt, the only person on the trip who didn't know how to sail, was at the helm. Then, in typical Tippy fashion, Tip let go of the stern line. Tip had pulled some dandies in his time, but this was truly memorable. As we tread water, watching Kurt sail away, Tip let out a belly laugh.

"What's so funny?" I asked.

Tip replied, "I'm imagining the look on my mom's face when she reads about four drunk sailors who were found naked on a Subic Bay beach and sees my name!"

In 2007, I took a job in Atlanta, and Tip, working at Atlanta TRACON and living in Peachtree City, put me up for a few months. His son, Palmer, gave up his room for me until I could find an apartment.

Sadly, we lost Tippy Ensell in August 2014. He and his brother-in-law took off from Peachtree City airport early one morning in his Cessna 150, headed for what was soon to be his retirement home near Savanna. The weather turned bad, and Mr. Murphy took over.

Tip was a great man, a great husband, a great father, and a great friend. There were over three hundred people at his service. Even Scotty drove up from Jacksonville to attend. I stay in touch with his wife, Tanya. Sometimes, out of the blue, I decide to call Tip. Then it dawns on me that he won't answer. I miss my friend.

5
GUAM

Timing is everything, and my timing sucked. I was twenty-four, and I had moved back to Houston and taken a job laying tile for a major pool company, which was probably the worst job I ever had. It was a crappy job that involved long hours (on the road at 4:30 a.m., home at 7:00 or 8:00 p.m.), working in the hot Texas summer sun for fifty dollars a day, no furniture, no breaks, and no time off (I worked Monday through Saturday and then mowed Dad's yard, five acres, with a tractor and a brush hog on Sundays for seventy-five dollars).

Remy showed up in early May, and we were married by a justice of the peace shortly afterward. Our marriage wasn't off to a terribly good start, which made the navy look a whole lot better than it had just a few months earlier.

In late July 1981, just about the time I decided I'd had enough of the working-for-a-living lifestyle, there was light at the end of the tunnel. I had taken the FAA exam, scored in the nineties, and now I was biding my time, waiting for a call when I found out there was unrest in the FAA air traffic control ranks. Robert Poli, the Professional Air Traffic Controllers (PATCO) union president, was on TV stating his claims, demands, and threats. I watched with great interest, not really believing that they would strike and Reagan would fire them, opening the door for new talent like me, but hoping all the same. Hoping for someone else's misfortune may seem like a crass, self-centered attitude, and it is, but I knew their course of action was illegal. And I had seen just enough to know that I wanted a job talking to airplanes.

My life was so bad that I had taken a physical and spoken with the navy recruiter, laying the groundwork for reenlistment. Still, I was hoping the PATCO situation would work out to my benefit. Finally, Robert Poli, PATCO president, announced there had been an agreement with the FAA, and I thought that was that. I didn't know that the PATCO members had to approve the agreement, with a vote scheduled for the following Saturday, August 1, 1981. Believing my fate was sealed, I abandoned my career as a tile guy and drove into downtown Houston, the main recruiter station, determined to once again relinquish control of my life to the US Navy.

Knowing I had been considering this for some time, my dad would set his alarm for 2:00 a.m. and routinely call me, shouting into the phone, "Don't do it!" He was intent on preventing his number one son from making a mistake. Dad was the reason I had enlisted in the first place, but I guess he figured I had paid my debt to society, done my time, and another hitch was the first step down the slippery slope of careerdom—not a bad career, but not Tommy's son's destiny. Remember—my dad was a controller at heart.

I've always been hardheaded, and I think even God was trying his best to stop me from reenlisting. At the downtown Houston recruiter station, I spoke by phone with the newly arrived navy air traffic control detailer, the guy who cut orders, and it was none other than the chief who had taught me CTO in air traffic control school—the same guy who had driven a two-seat convertible and had been sleeping with our cute blond class member who went to Guam. We shot the breeze for a while, and I reminded him of our previous brief relationship. Understandably, he didn't remember me. Hundreds of smiling air traffic controller faces floated through the academy every year, and remembering one airman over the rest was not realistic. He didn't even remember the blond, or at least he believed it prudent to claim no recollection. He did remember our class party, though.

Getting down to business, we discussed my situation and possible orders to some tropical paradise for the next four years. It was an unbelievably short conversation.

"I have the USS *Saratoga*, USS *Midway*, USS—"

"No, no, no, Chief, I'm reenlisting, and I'm not reenlisting for a boat!"

"Look, you're up for sea duty, and I'm offering you some good ships here," he replied.

A "good ship" was destined for the Caribbean or the Mediterranean with a Panamanian registry and did not have "USS" painted on its stern. "Thanks anyway. I'll call back some other time," I said with finality and hung up on him midsentence.

After slamming down the phone, I walked into the entryway. The recruiter asked what had happened. He had the same look on his face as a father walking his pregnant daughter down the wedding aisle. Just calling the detailer had led the recruiter to believe he was going to make his quota for July: reenlistment no less, the mother lode.

I said that I would not talk to that jackass again.

"No, no, no!" he pled. "Let me get him back on the phone, and we can work something out!"

I agreed to one more try, and the recruiter called me into his office a minute later. Handing me the phone, he begged me to be nice and work things out.

The first words out of the detailer's mouth sealed the deal for me. "Nobody hangs up on Frank—"

Click, buzz, was my answer. Once again, the recruiter's jaw dropped as I walked past him, headed for the parking lot. One option down and none to go. I had just broken a cardinal navy rule and pissed off the detailer. My attempt at a second enlistment was off to really bad start.

Evidently, Frank, who had never been hung up on, had just accepted the detailer position. The outgoing detailer, a master chief who had insisted on being called Peaches, was a good guy whom I had met a few years earlier. He was still in Washington, DC. I told the recruiter I would talk to Peaches, but other than that, we had nothing to discuss. Low and behold, minutes after I got home, the phone rang, and it was Peaches. We had a good conversation and agreed on orders to Guam if I raised my hand the next afternoon. Peaches had a goal to meet also. Monday was another month, and he'd rather close out July with a reenlistment than open August with one.

So the next morning, I drove back into Houston, and the doctor performed a quick physical to make sure I still had ten fingers, ten toes, and a penis that, at the very least, *appeared* to be operational (after the Philippines, I wondered myself) and certified me as "re-enlistable." With all the t's crossed and i's dotted, only the hand raising and swearing-in ceremony were left, and that was scheduled after lunch, which the recruiter offered to buy. Lunch consisted of a sandwich and a pitcher or two of beer, each of which violated a whole bunch of Uniform Code of Military Justice rules. The recruiter figured he could justify it as ensuring his career progression by preventing logic from catching up with me. Being a sailor at heart and offered free beer, I was at a disadvantage.

I reenlisted Friday, July 31, 1981. On Saturday, August 1, 1981, PATCO voted down President Reagan's offer and opted to strike the following Monday. That Monday, Reagan offered them the opportunity to reconsider their actions, giving them a grace period until Wednesday. They stuck with the initial decision, and on Wednesday, Reagan fired approximately thirteen thousand FAA air traffic controllers. As I stood there watching it all on TV, I had my reenlistment papers in one hand, my FAA air traffic control exam test results in the other, and the beginning of a headache that would last for a very long time, brought on by a self-inflicted case of depression.

Other than the headaches and depression, things weren't so bad. Remy was tickled pink to be going to Guam, a three-hour flight from the Philippines, and I was going back to the South Pacific. I had fallen in love with the South Pacific and was happy to be returning. The lifestyle—beaches, clear water, fishing, and diving—was heaven on earth. Before leaving, I spent thirty days in Orlando being "reindoctrinated" into the navy, getting my records up to date, and learning how to be a squid all over again. We loaded up my little Celica GT and pointed it west to San Francisco, stopping off in Jacksonville, Florida, on our way to spend a few days with Scotty and Tippy.

Guam is an eight-hour flight west of Hawaii and, as mentioned previously, three hours by plane from the Philippines. It is the largest (thirty miles long, eight miles wide) and southernmost island in the Marianas chain, and I could see both sides of the island from the tower. Guam is an American territory, which means Guamanians use the US dollar for currency and have US citizenship but not voting privileges. Like residents of the District of Columbia, American Samoa, and Puerto Rico, they have a representative who has no voting privileges either.

After arriving in Guam and settling in, I got to work certifying at the tower and PAR unit. It took me all of one month. I had seen more action at Cubi on the midwatch than I saw in an eight-hour shift in Guam. I certified in the tower in two weeks and had to spend one midwatch under the watchful eye of a supervisor, Les Carriel. Les met me in the tower at 11:00 p.m., pillow under one arm, sleeping bag under the other. I quickly figured out who'd be pulling the bulk of the load. Ironically, Guam was busiest during the midwatch. Japan Air, Korean Air, Northwest, and a few others landed between 2:00 a.m. and 4:00 a.m., leaving between 4:00 a.m. and 6:00 a.m., in time to arrive in Tokyo around 7:00 a.m. All the aircraft were "heavy jets"—Boeing 747s, DC-10s, or Boeing 707s.

Immediately after we arrived in the tower, Les told me he could be found on the floor underneath the runway and taxiway lighting panel in his sleeping bag. He would keep one ear open, turning the lights on when necessary, and I was responsible for working the traffic. Around 3:00 a.m., after a number of Japan Air 747s had arrived, refueled, and swapped a load of pasty, fish-belly-white Japanese tourists for tanned, hungover Japanese tourists, one aircraft called for taxi: "Guam tower, Japan Air 143 heavy, ready for taxi to runway 6 left, departure to Narita" (Narita being the Tokyo airport). Because the northwest taxiway was closed, the aircraft would have to cross runway 6 left, back-taxi down runway 6 right, and then turn right onto the taxiway to runway 6 left.

Since I had cleared Northwest 256, a DC-10, to land on runway 6 left, I replied, "Japan Air 143 heavy, Guam tower. Hold short of runway 6 left. Landing traffic."

The pilot's response confused and concerned me. "Japan Air 143 heavy, roger. Request taxiway right."

Although I really couldn't see what was going on at the international ramp, since it was over a mile from the tower, or see Japan Air 143's relationship to the runway, I knew the northwest taxiway would be directly to his right. I replied, "Japan Air 143 heavy, that's the northwest taxiway, and it is closed."

His reply made things even worse. "Japan Air 143 heavy, roger. Request taxiway right."

Without an accurate picture of Japan Air's location, I was becoming very concerned that he might be on runway 6 left, the runway Northwest was about to land on, or just as bad, the Japan Air B-747 was about to taxi onto the northwest taxiway, which was unable to support a Boeing 747. The aircraft would literally sink into the pavement, and I was certain that somehow I would be held accountable. Panic set in. Fearing the worst, I decided that the time had come to wake Les. I kicked the sleeping bag, and Les jumped up, groggy, asking, "What? What?"

I quickly explained the situation with Japan Air repeatedly asking for the northwest taxiway.

Les looked out the window and saw the lights of the Northwest closing in. "Who's that?"

"A Northwest DC-10. He's cleared to land on six left."

Les keyed the mike and asked, "Japan Air 143 heavy, say again your request?"

"Japan Air 143 heavy, request taxiway right," he reiterated for the fourth time.

Les understood immediately and shouted to me, "Lights! Lights! 'Right' is Japanese for 'light'! The taxiway lights aren't on!"

I spoke Texas redneck, navy, enough Spanish to order a beer and find the toilet, and sufficient Filipino to get around the country, but absolutely no Japanese, until now. With things returning to normal, we laughed, and Les crawled back into his sleeping bag, adjusted the pillow, and assumed his midwatch position. Nobody scraped paint, so I was certified to work a midwatch in the Guam tower. I was so proud.

The day I certified in the PAR unit, completing my training, I followed my instructor Les, into the operations office and signed the paperwork. As I finished the last signature, the leading chief slid a piece of paper in front of me. It was the watch schedule for the month of November, and at the top of section three was my name, with seven others below it.

Confused, I looked up and asked, "What's this?"

"The watch schedule for November. You're the section three supervisor," he replied.

"No, no, no, I'm a controller, not a supervisor. I've never been a supervisor and don't want to start now," I pleaded.

"The strike bled us dry, and you're the senior second-class petty officer, so you get a crew. We'll help you with anything you need," he insisted. Yeah, right. Famous last words.

I had the next two days off, and the more I thought about the situation, the more appealing it became. If they wanted me to be a supervisor, I'd be a supervisor. I'd take all that David Dodd, Mark Grossman, and Bruce Herman had taught me and capitalize on it. I could very well become their worst nightmare.

Although I was a supervisor in the tower, while walking the halls, I was a petty officer with many superiors. "Military bearing" is a term routinely used to describe the degree to which one conforms to military rules, regulations, and protocol. If I didn't know better, I would swear it was a term created by Bruce Herman. I had dropped my military bearing in San Francisco before boarding the airplane for Guam. Oops, my bad. The navy's enlisted working uniform consisted (then) of a dungaree shirt and bell-bottom dungaree trousers. Your name was stenciled above the left shirt pocket and above the right rear trouser pocket. The shirt stencil was black and lasted forever, but the trouser stencil was white and faded after a few washings, requiring re-stenciling routinely. The effects of the strike had settled in, and I decided my second enlistment was a big mistake, the navy would realize soon enough, and make things right by issuing me an A1 navy "early out." This didn't happen, of course, but for some reason, I considered myself an unwilling participant in a four-year daydream and decided I would voice my opinion in, discreet ways, one of which was the trouser stencil. After all, why did my trousers need to be stenciled at all? I knew everyone, and they knew me.

My stencil deteriorated to nonexistence, and I was beginning to wonder how long it would take for someone to say something when finally, in the hallway on my way to the tower stairs, our division officer, a lieutenant, cornered me.

"Petty Officer Smith, turn around," he said while checking out my butt. "You're a section leader and a facility watch supervisor, aren't you?" he asked.

"Yes, sir," I replied.

"Those trousers need stenciling and have for a while. I strongly recommend you present yourself in a manner appropriate to your responsibilities," he said.

Did you learn to talk that way at the academy? I thought. "Yes, sir," I replied to my superior officer and walked away. Now what?

Unwilling to conform, I found my air traffic controller training kicking in, and I figured out a workaround: my checkbook. The trouser patch pockets were small and barely held a wallet, but a properly positioned checkbook artfully concealed my now completely absent name stencil, keeping my futile, imbecilic, and adolescent attempt at nonconformity intact, for a while at least. Eventually, the lieutenant caught me and had me pirouetting in the hallway again and removing the facade. With a great deal more emphasis, he suggested I act in a manner commensurate with my position and responsibilities. And I did. Damn it!

It may seem that this was a foolish course of action, but I was dealing with issues. I had come from very busy facilities, in a time that had been completely dominated by the message "be on time, do your job to the best of your ability, and play the navy game when forced to." My first tour had been less like the navy and more like a job. With the turn of the decade and the arrival of the eighties, everything had changed. Practically overnight, the attitude had changed from "work, fun, navy" to "navy, work, and more navy." Being a supervisor—or more accurately, a babysitter—made things even worse. I now had to deal with day-to-day issues I previously never even knew occurred. Making position assignments, ensuring my crew was properly attired, being responsible for my crew's performance in personnel inspections, and writing annual performance appraisals were among the many duties and responsibilities I inherited. Supervision sucked. I just wanted to talk to airplanes.

During personnel inspections, if one of my crew took a hit, I answered for it. If one of my crew got in trouble off base, I answered for it. If a working party needed a warm body, I had to assign one of my crew and suffer the consequences of being the messenger. There were good times too, though. I had a third-class petty officer named Carol who was one sharp cookie. Carol was very athletic (a surfer chick, very cool), she could match tequila shots with the best of us, and even without trying, she was a seven or eight on a scale of ten. Tall, tanned, and with short blond hair and an ever-present smile, Carol wasn't just a good controller and watch supervisor; she was also a good friend. I had a great deal of admiration and respect for her. Shortly after transferring to the island and joining section three, she attended an evening debrief, and we decided to watch *Young Frankenstein*. Carol could recite a great deal of the dialogue word for word, and I immediately knew she was a good fit for my less-than-controllable controller crew. After her certification, although she wasn't the next-senior person to me, I recommended and received approval to certify her as a facility watch supervisor.

The facility watch supervisor certification allowed Carol to run the shift and assume all duties and responsibilities when I wasn't present. A few of my crew took exception to this because they were senior to her and believed their seniority should have taken precedence. Remember—this was the military, where rank and seniority were the controlling authorities. As with the trouser stencil, I once again was bucking the system, but I got my way this time. The decision was a very good one, and an incident a short time later confirmed my judgment to the powers that be and the naysayers within my crew.

I was taking night classes, working on a computer science degree, when I was scheduled to work an evening shift during a class. I had coordinated with the office and received approval to attend classes, leaving Carol in charge, as long as I was on immediate recall with a portable radio. One problem: radios in the computer room interfered with the main frame computers and were prohibited. So I had a decision to make—I could leave the radio on and risk screwing up the mainframe computer or turn it off and violate the agreement allowing me to take classes. I told Carol that I was going to turn it off and that she would be on her own if anything happened. She shrugged her very confident shoulders and with her ever-present smile replied, "What can happen? We're in Guam." Famous last words.

I attended class that night well aware that I would be held responsible if something went wrong, but it *was* Guam, and I had complete faith in

Carol. The class was held on the second floor in one of the squadron hangars, so I walked down the flight ramp to get there. Three hours later, as I was leaving the classroom, walking through the hangar toward the ramp and the runway beyond it, I saw red and blue flashing lights reflecting off the silver metal hangar walls. My heart dropped into my stomach.

Running to the ramp, I saw a Continental DC-10 between the runways, surrounded by emergency vehicles, with passengers disembarking through extended emergency inflatable exits. "Oh shit!" I exclaimed. Immediately, I turned on the handheld portable radio I had agreed to monitor, but there was so much chatter that I got no sense of the situation, and I ran to the tower.

Climbing the steps into the cab, I saw through dimmed lights a tall blond standing in the back, arms crossed, quietly but insistently, issuing orders. "Cross the ambulances now! Tell the crash captain he has runway 6 left." Occasionally, Carol would write something on a pad of paper while pointing left at another controller, whose duties were nothing other than to type entries of events in the official tower log. She glanced in my direction and stuck her finger in the air, indicating "one moment," and answered the phone.

A brief conversation later, she hung up and leaned in my direction. "Captain Butterfield is in base operations and on his way up," she whispered, handing me her notepad.

I read the notes quickly while Carol continued to issue instructions. I soon realized that the Continental DC-10 had been taxiing out for takeoff when a bomb threat was called in. She had taken the call from Continental base operations, instructed the ground controller to position the aircraft between the runways on the correct taxiway, and followed emergency procedures to the letter.

A knock at the tower door indicated that Captain Butterfield had arrived, and Carol quickly instructed the controller manning the tower log typewriter to enter the following: "CC [her operating initials] off, RS [my operating initials] on, watch checklist complete." Carol turned to open the door and descend the stairs, but I immediately countered her order and told her she was in charge and would brief Captain Butterfield. Carol hesitated for a second, smiled, and agreed. I knew

Captain Butterfield personally—we were on the base running team and had participated in numerous fun runs together around the island. Occasionally, on an evening shift, he'd pop into the tower unannounced, and we'd shoot the breeze one sailor to another instead of base captain to petty officer.

When he arrived, Captain Butterfield immediately looked to me and asked for the situation. I deferred to Carol, and he looked at me quizzically for a second before turning to her. Carol handled the situation at least as well as I would have, and I felt almost smug about my decision to recommend her as my go-to—my executive officer. I put her in for a letter of commendation, but she was given only a letter of appreciation. The first carried a great deal of weight, and the recipient was awarded points on the next promotion exam; the latter merely stated things everyone already knew and looked good in a personnel folder. I asked Captain Butterfield later about the issue, and he said that the letter had come across his desk as a letter of appreciation. He agreed that Carol's actions warranted more, but he was in no position to second-guess the air traffic control officer.

As proud as I was of Carol, the confidence I gained was immeasurable. I had made a controversial decision, one that I knew was right, and had taken the heat for it. The experience I gained would serve me well throughout my career. If you believe in something and are convinced it's the right thing to do, do it. Even if you're wrong, most people will respect you for standing up for something you believe in and for taking responsibility for the outcome whether it's good or bad. Fortunately, the outcome of this decision was good. Not all of my decisions would turn out so well.

Due to the lack of air traffic, incidents were thankfully hard to come by in Guam. Amazingly, I had become comfortable with the high-energy lifestyle of Cubi and Whiting and found myself missing it. So when the office wasn't finding ways to keep me occupied, I found my own ways.

Section three—"Robin's crew," as it was known all the way up the chain of command—was too often the focus of attention. With Carol certified and perfectly capable of running the show, I decided that my responsibilities for adult supervision could be shared. So I shared them. I didn't tell Carol she was picking up some of my duties and responsibilities, but she was smart and figured it out on her own.

By now, my crew was all handpicked, and what a crew we were. Dan King, all six feet three inches of him, was a huggable bear. I never hugged him (danced with him once), but he looked the part and was as creative as I when it came to finding new ways of entertaining ourselves. One day, Dan and I were the only people in the tower when a squadron of marine A-6 Intruders, twin jet-engine, two-piloted, carrier-based attack aircraft, arrived on a trans-Pacific trip. The marines routinely rotated squadrons from Hawaii to Japan on six-month detachments. To get there and back, the squadron and all its administrative personnel were loaded into two C-130 Hercules aircrafts, four-engine turboprop transports, for the trip. They routinely landed in Guam for a day or two of rest en route to Japan or on the way home to Hawaii.

The squadron, twelve A-6s and the two C-130s, landed uneventfully, parking on the ramp directly in front of our tower. With nothing else to do, Dan started dancing to a Stray Cats tune blaring from the tower radio, and unable to contain myself, I joined in. The next thing I knew, Dan grabbed me, one arm around my hips, the other over my shoulder, and took the lead. We danced completely oblivious to nearly one hundred marine eyes staring up at us from the ramp. The song ended, and we congratulated each other on our moves and then turned to see the entire marine squadron staring up at the tower. As they began to clap and cheer, Dan turned to me, knowing we were thinking identical thoughts, and simply asked, "Shall we?"

Without a second thought, we jumped on the tower communications console, turned our asses toward the ramp and our now appreciative audience, dropped our drawers, and pressed our bare cheeks to the windows. The cheers turned to a roar, and everyone went away happy, almost everyone anyway.

I still don't know who complained, but I quickly found myself on the lieutenant's carpet, unable to explain the lapse in supervisory judgment and promising to do better before being dismissed—or more accurately, before being thrown out of his office. As I was leaving, he barked another reminder: "And stencil your goddamned trousers!"

Believing I would score points and ease his pain a little, I turned my now trousered ass toward him, removed my ever-present checkbook, and revealed a bright white and obviously fresh stencil, which pissed him off even more.

Dan and I were a perfect match. One night on a midwatch, we were bored to tears and decided to hop in the tower jeep and tour the airport. While at the approach end of the runway, watching Japan Air B-747s land over the top of us, I noticed a slight movement in the grass. Curious, we grabbed the flashlight and found scads of field mice hopping from one hole to another. Jumping in the jeep, we drove around checking out our nocturnal friends, and with Dan at the wheel, we decided they were just quick enough to be challenging. So Dan tried to run over them—and failed. And failed and failed. It quickly became personal. Dan figured out their system after nearly an hour and a quarter tank of gas, he finally nailing one. We got out, checked the flat little mouse body, and asked, "Now what?" The answer was "do it again." And again and again. We returned to the tower just before dawn, parked the jeep in its usual spot, and left the day shift with a field-mouse body count on the front seat.

Called on the carpet and reprimanded, I left the lieutenant's office, trouser stencil proudly displayed, with orders that it would never again be hidden by a checkbook. Dan, on the other hand, didn't slow down. To punish him for getting me in trouble, I assigned him a few midwatches on the flight dispatch desk in the base operations office.

On one wall of the base operations office hung a large plexiglass board that we used to keep track of VIPs coming to Guam. We normally got notification from the communication shack a few months in advance, and the day before a VIP arrival, a call sheet was filled out, and everyone from the base captain to the chow hall (which provided finger sandwiches and coffee to the VIP lounge) was called and notified. Among the names on the VIP bulletin board was a captain named Beck. Over the next few weeks, the name was gradually changed to "Geck" and then "Gecko." Geckos are small lizards native to warm climates and prevalent in the South Pacific, so much so that our enlisted club was named El Gecko.

Over the next few weeks, I watched the transition with amusement, truly believing that the individual responsible for making calls on the

VIP call sheet would recognize the joke and consult the VIP movement message, correcting the name before the joke went too far. Guess again, dumb ass.

The day came, and ironically, section three, Robin's crew, was on duty. We had a person who volunteered to work the flight dispatch desk Monday through Friday because he wasn't competent enough to work the traffic (which was nearly nonexistent). He was competent only enough to realize he wasn't competent. Sad. Well, he proved to all of us exactly how incompetent he really was by calling in the VIP name as it was listed on the VIP board without consulting the VIP movement sheet. Even the crash crew captain, responsible for putting out the big, decorative, three-foot-tall bullets, a red carpet, and the name board welcoming "Captain E. L. Gecko" to NAS Agana, Guam, missed it. Amazingly, no one caught it—well, almost no one. Specifically, Captain Butterfield caught it. Apparently, he had attended the Naval Academy with Captain Beck (E. L. Gecko), and he caught the error as we walked out of base operations to meet his old classmate. As he read the name on the "Welcome Aboard" sign, I watched as his expression turned from confused to startled to panicked and, finally, to angry. With the VIP aircraft making its final turn off the taxiway and stopping abeam the red carpet, he realized there was no time to correct the mistake, and he simply turned the "Welcome Aboard" sign around. He looked at me, confident he knew who was behind the prank, and I immediately knew our next sailor-to-sailor conversation was going to be more like a ringknocker–to–enlisted puke ass-chewing.

Other than that, the event went as usual, and I thought I might have dodged a bullet. But a few hours later, I was in the tower when the supervisor phone rang and the senior chief said, "Come to my office now and bring Dan with you!"

I grabbed Dan and told him his little prank had just landed us in a lot of hot water. He insisted he hadn't done it over and over again. He was so convincing, I almost believed him. That gave me an idea. I knew that although there was no evidence Dan and I were responsible for the prank, I was never going to convince anyone otherwise. This situation was going to require a completely different approach, one that I had never tried before and one that was a one-time good deal.

We walked to the air traffic control office door, and I stopped Dan. "Stay here," I said.

"No, I'm going with you," Dan replied. "I didn't do it, Robin!"

"No, stay here!" I insisted. I took a deep breath, straightened my gig line (an imaginary line formed by shirt seam to belt buckle and fly seam—another Hermanism, I'm sure), put on my best pissed-off face, and walked into the office.

Turning right and finding the senior chief seated behind his desk, I exclaimed, "Senior chief, I know why I'm here, and I'm pissed! I don't know who changed the captain's name, but I'm the practical joker around here. I didn't do it!" I continued my indignant monologue, getting louder and madder and ending it with a very bold pounding of my fist on his desk.

Astounded, he simply stared at me. "I don't know why, but I believe you. Now get out of my office," he said.

I walked out and grabbed Dan, and we were almost in the tower before we started laughing our asses off. He never did admit to it.

During my naval career, I met a number of people who had profound effects on my life. Herman, Dave Dodd, Tippy, Scotty, and a few others were among them, but Senior Chief Jim Smith really emphasized the responsibility that came along with my supervisory duties. Smitty checked into Guam when I had about a year and a half left on my tour, and I'll never forget the day I first met him.

I stood in Guam base operations looking into the air traffic control offices and watched as he unpacked plaques and awards, carefully hanging each one in its proper place on his "I love me" wall behind his desk, and I thought, *Here we go*. Smitty was tall, slim, and clean-shaven and wore a crew cut. The guy was more Herman than Herman, except he loved being enlisted. As I watched the unpacking ritual and his obvious admiration of these physical manifestations of his accomplishments, I realized this guy was navy first and air traffic control second. I knew it was going to be only a matter of time before we mixed it up, and I would very likely come out of the encounter with a hurting unit. I could easily see Smitty taking my crew from me, in which case I would wind up working for one of the other "lifer" section leaders, making my last few months more miserable than the day I stood in front of the TV, FAA exam in one hand and enlistment papers in the other.

Just when I had him figured out and had plotted my first attack on his authority, Smitty screwed everything up. The last item he unpacked was a piece of wood—Philippine mahogany if I wasn't mistaken—that looked like a nameplate. He lovingly polished it, and deciding it didn't shine bright enough, he sprayed more wood polish and rubbed a little more, making me think, *This guy is really full of himself.* Finally, content with the attention to detail, he turned the nameplate, which was not a nameplate at all, to face outward from his desk, and it read, "I Am They." Instantly, everything changed, and I thought, *We're going to get along just fine.*

Smitty turned out to be the exact opposite of my first impression. He was navy to the core and referred to his wife as "a long-haired mess cook," but after exposure to Herman, I took this in stride. In the morning, Smitty was a bear until he had his first pot of coffee. I don't know which he liked more, his coffee or the unfiltered Lucky that was always in the hand opposite a coffee mug.

Smitty and I saw eye to eye on all but two occasions. The evening crew was responsible for cleaning the air traffic control offices, and Smitty routinely left a paper clip or small piece of paper lying indiscreetly on the floor. He used these as indicators of the thoroughness with which we cleaned the office. This process is used on aircraft carriers during walk-downs for foreign object damage, or FOD: screws, nuts, bolts, and so on that vibrate loose and fall off airplanes. Foreign objects get sucked into jet engines, causing hundreds of thousands of dollars in damage, so FOD walk-downs are performed to pick up these jet killers. A specific nut or bolt is placed on the flight deck, and a walk-down is performed until that particular nut or bolt is found, ensuring a thorough check was performed. I'm sure Smitty saw this process as an avenue to ensure the job was done properly, but I personally believe he took some degree of glee from calling the section leader into his office and presenting a paper clip that had been missed.

One night when my crew had the evening shift, I sent two junior controllers to clean the office. The next day, Smitty, very uncharacteristically, walked into the tower, asked whom I had sent for cleanup the evening before, and proceeded to dress down one of the guilty controllers who was working ground control. I interrupted, only to be told to take a seat in the back of the tower. And I almost did. Knowing this was a turning point in my career, I jumped in even more insistently this time and forced the issue.

After a fair amount of shouting between Smitty and me, we agreed to discuss the issue in his office. I gave the shift to Carol and left a now very quiet section three in her charge. In his office, Smitty closed the door, sat behind his desk, and ordered me to attention. He was so furious that he couldn't utter a word. When he finally did, he asked succinctly, "What do you have to say for yourself?"

"Senior Chief, the chain of command works both ways. It was my responsibility to have the office cleaned. Obviously, I failed to meet your standards. Discipline me, and I will discipline my crew." As I spoke, I realized that I had become *way* too navy. But they were my crew, and I had to stick up for them.

Once again, Smitty was speechless. I could tell by the look on his face that he knew I had a point. He had broken the chain of command and made an ass of both of us in front of my crew. Smitty sighed deeply, pushed his chair back, told me to sit down, and thought about what I had said. Moments later, he said, "I owe you an apology. You're right."

I was right, but I felt like shit. It had never been my intention to embarrass Smitty in front of my crew. Without another word, he dismissed me, and we never discussed the issue again. He did remember the event, though, and the next time section three screwed up, the wrath of Smitty came down upon my pointy head and narrow shoulders with all his authority. Fair enough.

The second event was frustrating for me. I went to work on an evening shift and, as usual, checked my mailbox. In it was a notice instructing me to show up for training attached to a one-year detail with the "security" department. *Whoa!* I thought. *I'm a controller, not a security guard!*

I immediately protested to Smitty, and he replied, "It's a one-year detail, and you've only got nine months left. It's the air traffic control division's turn to contribute to the security detail, and we chose you."

From a strictly pragmatic point of view, the decision made perfect sense. All the others in the air traffic division were lifers. They were committed to a career in the navy, and a one-year detail to security would be a slap in the face, potentially pushing one of them into the open arms of the FAA.

It wasn't the first time the division had screwed with me. Although my days of piling mouse bodies in the tower jeep, pressing ham on the tower windows, and playing hide-the-stencil with my checkbook and "guess the real name of the VIP" were long gone, the powers that be had not forgotten the stress I had caused.

A year before, I had been assigned to the "burial detail," a misnomer for the Honor Guard. Each year, Honor Guard responsibilities were passed from one navy base to another, and it was NAS Agana's turn. Fortunately, a fellow section leader had been assigned to the team as the leading petty officer and gave me the option of rifle team or pallbearer. I chose the rifle team. The intent of my one-year collateral duty detail, I am convinced, was to screw with me the way I had screwed with my superiors. It backfired, badly. I performed in an uncharacteristically stellar manner, earning letters of appreciation and letters of commendation out the wazoo. We performed Honor Guard duties for World War II heroes and Medal of Honor awardees among others, receiving letters from wives, mothers, fathers, children, and grandchildren praising our performance during the final sendoff for their loved ones.

The icing on the cake, though, came when we buried a former Guam congressional representative. Ben Blas, a marine corps general of Guamanian descent, attended the ceremony and was so impressed that he personally wrote a letter of commendation for the team and invited us to parade the colors at the next marine corps ball. Needless to say, we were extremely honored but could not accept the offer. The navy parading the colors at the marine corps ball just wouldn't be right. We compromised, sharing the opening ceremony duties with our marine counterparts and leaving the closing ceremonies to them. Jarheads and squids will fight over the color of the sky, but some things are sacred, and the offer was greatly appreciated.

During that year, I met some very interesting people and developed a real respect and understanding for the people of Guam. Like many Pacific islands, Guam is predominantly Catholic, and funeral wakes are but one of their traditions. The entire Honor Guard detail was invited to every wake. Wakes consisted of more food than could be eaten in three days and fifty-five-gallon drums filled with bottles of beer. Of course, family and friends from the youngest to the oldest attended the internment ceremonies and the wakes, which were more like parties than anything else. One of our duties as the Honor Guard was to meet and greet the immediate family, expressing our condolences before enjoying the festivities. During a few of these greets, I met older Guamanians who had been on the island during the Japanese occupation. They had incredible experiences to share.

At one wake, I noticed an older woman who seemed to be in pain. Her face was contorted, and her jaw drooped, almost to the point of opening but not quite. I walked up to her, bent down to her height, offered my hand, and introduced myself. She took my fingers ever so frailly, opened her mouth, and with her free hand, took a lit cigarette out of it. She was very old, easily in her eighties, and I asked the reason for the unusual manner of smoking a cigarette.

She explained that during the war a light could give away your position, and therefore, they had learned to smoke with the ember in their mouths. The whole concept so surprised me that I didn't even think to ask the logical logistical question: "How do you not burn your mouth?" As amazing as this was, it only began to illustrate the hardships these people had endured.

After that, I actively sought out Guamanian elders at these wakes. The stories they told were equally fascinating and horrifying. Japanese occupiers would ignore local villagers living in nipa huts deep in the jungle for months, only to march in unannounced, gather the entire village together, take pigs and chickens, and then, to emphasize their total control, randomly select a person who was forced to his knees and beheaded.

By my time there in the 1980s, Guam had become a favorite destination for Japanese vacationers. Guam was only three hours by air from Tokyo, with beautiful beaches and clear, warm waters, perfectly suited for a two-week getaway during cold, snowy Japanese winters.

Consequently, Japanese visitors constituted the vast majority of income for an island dependent on tourism, making it all the less palatable for elders who still lay wreaths at headstones of beheaded mothers, fathers, sisters, and brothers.

My one-year burial detail ended, and I was asked to remain a member of a now-abbreviated Honor Guard team responsible strictly to the naval air station. Our duties were to parade the colors at official ceremonies—no more pall bearing or meeting family members. The entire detail left me with not only a sense of pride in a job well done and a number of family and friends comforted that their loved ones were retired respectfully, but also a sense that I had performed my collateral military duty to the best of my ability. My collateral duties were now complete, or so I thought.

Although the decision to now send me to security sucked, the office hadn't beaten me yet, and I wasn't going down without a fight. Another supervisor, Steve Phillips, had crossed into the air traffic control occupation from a radioman job. The FAA strike had hit us hard, and the navy had actively recruited from within to replenish the midlevel air traffic controller ranks, from which controllers had defected to the FAA. "Phil" was one of the most unlikely candidates for air traffic control I had ever seen. We carpooled to and from work and played softball together, and he was as much an instigator in some of the screw-the-office antics as Dan or I. Phil came to my rescue. The afternoon after I got the news, he walked into the tower, and I told him what the office had done this time. Phil's response was "Hell, I'll do it!"

"You'll go to security for a year?" I asked.

"Hell yeah. Why not?"

Cool, I had found my replacement. There was only one problem: the office didn't want me replaced. I discussed it with Smitty, and he just said no. So I threatened him. Seriously.

In the navy, if there is a disagreement, in certain situations a "chit" could be submitted requesting captain's mast. As mentioned earlier, the term "captain's mast" comes from the old days of the navy in which the captain held nonjudicial court at the main mast. This court addresses violations of the Uniform Code of Military Justice, but it can also be used to resolve disagreements among the crew. In this case, I had been assigned a detail that I did not want, and I had a completely agreeable replacement.

I told Smitty I would submit a chit requesting Captain's Mast, and I meant it. He knew that although I routinely got crossways with the division officer (the lieutenant), I was tight with the operations officer and definitely with the captain (all had been forgiven regarding the Captain E. L. Gecko incident), one of whom would decide my fate. He also knew that if an issue of this nature escalated out of the air traffic division, it would be an embarrassment.

Smitty discussed the matter with the powers that be (the lieutenant), and they decided, without the benefit of the formal Captain's Mast process, that they would give me an audience with the operations officer. Smitty, the lieutenant, Phil, and I walked into the ops boss's office and pled our respective cases, and the ops boss just stared at us.

"Now let me get this straight. Someone has to go to security. Robin was chosen but doesn't want to go. Phil wants to go, but you won't let him. They are equally qualified, both watch supervisors and section leaders, so losing one or the other is moot as far as the operation is concerned. Am I right, Lieutenant?" he said.

"That's all correct, Commander."

"And you're here for me to resolve the issue?"

"Yes, sir," replied the lieutenant.

"Fine. Phil, pack your bags; you're going to security for a year. Robin, I'll see you in a few months for a reenlistment talk. Now all of you, out of my office."

Whew! The score was now Robin 252, air traffic control office 0. Three and a half years and I was still undefeated. No hits, no runs, no errors, and never been caught. Phil was thrilled. Why, I do not know, but he was. For most people in the navy, security is a place to go when no one else wants you, but not Phil. And I soon found out why.

Phil really didn't like air traffic control that much and had transferred into the job because the sea/shore rotation for a controller was three years at sea, five years shore duty. Radiomen, on the other hand, spent three years floating followed by two years on shore duty. Phil had been in the navy for ten years and was tired of being haze-gray and underway. He was also very laid-back and easygoing. To him, a year in security would look good on his promotional paperwork showing diversity. Since the early 1980s, the navy had become a lot more navy and, except to people like Herman and Smitty, a lot less fun, concentrating on shoe shines, haircuts, and career diversity. Phil was career navy and knew he had to play the game, so the detail was good for him. Everyone was happy, almost. I really don't think Smitty cared. He too was playing the game, but the lieutenant was calling the shots and had once again been outshot by me.

I saw Phil quite a bit while he was keeping the naval air station safe. He conscripted an airman as his partner in crime, and the two of them were inseparable. The poor dumb-ass kid was young and impressionable, following Phil's lead dutifully. They visited base operations when my crew had the midwatch on a number of occasions.

One night, each of them had a grocery sack full of single-serving beanie weenies, chili, and chili mac and a variety of other heat-and-serve cans. These were sold in barracks vending machines, which kept them hot, and both bags were full of still-warm cans of goodies. There were probably forty or fifty cans in all, and I asked Phil where the hell he'd gotten them.

"The barracks," he answered.

"No shit. How?"

He put down the empty (hopefully) .45 pistol he was cocking and pointing long enough to show me a vending machine key.

"You've got the key to the vending machine?"

"Yep!"

"Which machines?" I continued.

"All of them. This is a master!"

So section three ate beanie weenies, chili, chili mac, and an assortment of other complimentary single-serving meals that evening and a few other evenings as well.

Not unexpectedly, one of the most memorable midwatches involved covering for Phil. He and his delinquent conscript burst through the doors of base operations around 2:00 a.m. one night. Phil was in a panic, and his shadow was about to piss his nineteen-year-old pants. Catching his breath, he insisted we all agree that the two of them had been in base operations for the past hour. Dan and I agreed and asked what they had done that was so bad. Phil was mischievous but not criminal. In the navy, acquiring certain items necessary for civil existence is not stealing; it's referred to as "comshawing." The beanie weenies had been comshawed, not stolen.

Apparently, there had been reports of a stray dog, a German shepherd, roaming around base housing getting into trash cans, and Phil had decided to hunt the animal down himself. Having keys to the armory and being the only two security officers on watch (no parental supervision), Phil and his sidekick comshawed a tranquilizer gun and a few darts in the quest for the rogue canine. With his faithful conscript driving, Phil searched the alleys of navy housing that surrounded the airport and stumbled upon the poor animal. Drawing a bead, Phil shot the shepherd, which immediately leapt three feet in the air, howling at the top of its lungs, and desperately tried to run away. Tried, being the operative word. Neighborhood lights came on as it became painfully obvious why Phil's quarry was unable to retreat into the darkness. The dog was chained to a fence, as any pet would be. Phil and his partner hauled ass to the only refuge Phil knew, base operations. Dan and I were questioned by the lieutenant, and we did what we did best: lied.

One of the things I really appreciated about Phil was his ability to take as well as he gave. Although he was detailed to security, he was technically attached to air traffic control, so when it was time to call for orders, Smitty made the call. I don't know what Phil was thinking. He had been in the navy long enough to know better, but he really pushed the detailer's patience when he called for orders. That opened a door for us to have some fun at his expense.

Phil was due to rotate back to the States shortly before I got out of the navy, and he came into base operations at midnight to call the detailer. Remember—we were on Guam, "where America's day begins," and midnight on the island was around 8:00 a.m. in Washington, DC. Phil sat down with Smitty, and Smitty made the call, describing to the detailer Phil's first, second, and third choices. Phil asked for three different duty stations and, after some negotiations, got exactly what he asked for—all three times, on three separate occasions, three separate nights. Each time Phil reneged and told the detailer he'd call back in a few days. The third time, Smitty was hot and rightfully so. I asked what the problem was, and Phil told me he wanted to go one place and his wife wanted to go another. I then quoted an old navy line: "If the navy wanted you to have a wife and kids, you'd have been issued those in your seabag." He smiled, agreed he had probably pushed the detailer too far, and said he would call back a few nights later, confident he could still get what he wanted.

In the navy, a set of orders may as well have descended from the mountain on a stone tablet. Orders are a done deal, and it's very tough to get them changed. The process of authorizing them requires a number of stamps, signatures, and various other authentication devices. Phil, being a former radioman and dealing with this stuff every day, knew all this. What he didn't know was how resourceful Dan and I could be.

The boys in our communication office knew Phil and liked him. They also knew he was a former radioman and figured he'd enjoy a good practical joke. So I approached them with my plan, and they agreed that it would be tough to pull off—many of the stamps were logged and had to be accounted for—but it was doable. My crew had the midwatch, and the comm shack boys worked their magic during the night. My crew stayed past our midnight shift the next morning to watch the show. I didn't even let Smitty in on the plan, and we watched while he sorted through the nightly communication traffic.

As expected, Smitty found the authentically falsified orders for Phil, read and reread them over and over, and then called me into the office. As the watch supervisor, I was responsible for ensuring that an hourly run was made to pick up communications traffic and for reviewing comm traffic for anything important throughout the night. Smitty asked me about Phil's orders, and I said I'd seen them but hadn't looked closely. I said I figured Smitty had spoken with the detailer and resolved their differences. Playing dumb, I looked shocked to learn that Phil had received orders to the USS *Tarawa*, a west San Diego–based "gator" boat. Gator boats are smaller than aircraft carriers, carrying only helicopters, and are filled with marines. Phil had fulfilled his sea-time obligations on Guam and was due for five years of shore duty, but he had orders, compliments of Robin, Dan, and some enterprising comm shack boys, to a gator boat. Smitty sat back and finally let out a laugh that could be heard upstairs in the captain's office. Smitty figured the detailer had had enough of Phil's games and cut him orders to the *Tarawa*. He picked up the phone, called the security chief, and asked to have Phil report to base operations as soon as possible. This was going to be good!

By the time Phil showed up, the base operations office was filled with pilots filing flight plans, aircrews getting briefings, and most importantly, the base chaplain searching outbound flights with space available to Hong Kong or Singapore. Smitty handed Phil the orders in the middle of base ops, and after Phil read and reread them, he blew a gasket. Phil used words that even after eight years as a squid, I'd never heard, and he shouted them at the top of his lungs. He had really hit his stride when I grabbed him by the shirt to get his attention and pointed out the cross on the chaplain's shirt.

"Oh, shit. Sorry, Father," he said apologetically before resuming his tirade under his breath.

It was beautiful, a true work of art. I've pulled a few dandies in my time, but this one topped the list. I let Phil stew for a few more hours, constantly reminding him that he shouldn't have pissed off the detailer. Then I left for home and stopped off at his house to tell his wife it was all a prank. She was laughing nearly uncontrollably as she beat my arm for putting her through it all. Phil showed up at my house later that afternoon, still believing he was screwed. We told him the truth, had far too many beers, and eventually agreed that our prank had been well executed.

As his last act of defiance on Guam, Phil called a local pizza delivery service and ordered five large pizzas for a 10:00 p.m. delivery to the lieutenant's home. Just good clean fun.

Things between Remy and me had started out badly in Houston and hit a plateau in Guam, but then they got worse. We didn't get along very well. She wanted children, and I refused to have them until I got out of the navy, got hired by the FAA, and got certified at my first facility. I was determined to have some stability before having children. Three years after we married, we divorced. She is a good person, and I think things didn't work out because we just weren't ready to make the adjustments that needed to be made.

I would leave Guam and my crew in Carol's very capable hands. At the time, I viewed my time as wasted because, other than some college credits, I didn't believe I had achieved anything professionally.

When I first arrived in Guam, small things such as a home phone outage ticked me off. A year later, if my home phone was out of order, I shrugged my shoulders, content to know my parents wouldn't be calling me at two in the morning (midmorning their time in Houston). I learned to catch, cook, and eat octopus and developed a taste for sushi and kimchi. Tuna boats operated out of the Agana harbor, and fresh tuna sashimi was offered in bars as a free appetizer. Same with kimchi—beer nuts, South Pacific style.

Despite a lack of air traffic and the consequences that came with it, I grew up in ways I never imagined. During my time at Whiting and in the Philippines, life had been fun and games. Although my colleagues and I were adults, some with spouses and children, and we had jobs that required us to act in a responsible adult manner, we still found ways to rebel and push the envelope of authority. I remember one afternoon in the Philippines when Tippy walked into work wearing red Christmas socks. Management went nuts, and Tippy could not understand the reasoning. It was a pair of red socks for Christ's sake! What's the big deal? Good order and discipline—that's the big deal, a lesson I learned in Guam.

Before I became a section leader in Guam, being told to get a haircut was usually met with "Yeah, yeah, I'll get one," and it usually took two or three warnings and a threat for me to do it. As a section leader, I always had a haircut, polished shoes, and a pressed uniform. What about the stencil? It was my way of staying in touch, ever so slightly, with my former life while proving to my crew that I was still one of them at heart and not management. It was a delicate balance that I thought I pulled off, but as I look back on it, I really wasn't fooling anyone. Refusing to grow up and fully accept my new position in life probably did more damage than good. I'm confident that my crew saw me as management and that the office saw me as a boy in a man's body. The navy forced me to grow up, and I was not happy about it. But as Skeeter would say, "Why did you sign up?"

6

OXNARD

Arriving back in the States, I had nothing to do but wait. It was late 1985, the strike had occurred four years earlier, and the FAA was on its feet, but just barely. Hiring had slowed to some degree. The important change, for me anyway, was the FAA's strict policy of sending all newly hired air traffic controllers to the academy screen.

During its inception, the FAA Academy screen was a very accurate way to assess a newly hired controller's abilities while weeding out potential training failures. The screen was comprised of training and scenarios using nonradar air traffic control, and it was brutal. The washout rate was anywhere from 30 to 50 percent. Some classes performed better than others, but each got the same welcome-aboard speech on the first day: "Look at the people on each side of you. One of them will not be here for graduation, and there is a fair chance neither of them will be." As with the navy, a 70 percent score was needed to graduate from air traffic control school. The FAA, however, had taken matters one step further by employing mathematicians to write algorithms that fine-tuned the grading process. On the day of the final exam, the halls were filled with grown men crying their eyes out because their final academy score was 69.95 percent, and they were now unemployed. Worse, most of them never got another chance at the academy, so they went back to the military or learned to hang sheetrock. Or so I heard.

I went to the academy but not for the screen, thanks to my gang of angels or dumb luck. I chose to believe it was the result of good clean living and the karma that came along with it, but I can't say for sure.

During my four years living in Guam, I returned to the States just once and spent only five days in Houston while in the States. So when I left the navy and Guam, I returned to Houston and visited friends and family for exactly one month. This, coincidentally, was the same duration of time it took my car to be shipped from Guam to Los Angeles. Dave Dodd had been picked up by the FAA immediately after the strike and was working at LAX tower. I decided I'd shared myself with my family long enough, and it was his turn to enjoy my company. Besides, that's where my car was. Dad was a little perturbed when I told him I was going to LA without plans to come back, but I think he understood. Remy and I had separated and she had left Guam for San Diego a year earlier, so I was now single, had money in the bank and was on the FAA's list to be hired in the western Pacific region (California, Arizona, Nevada, and Hawaii).

While still in Guam, after Remy left, I met Kathy, another navy controller, and we fell in love. Well, I fell in love. Until Kathy could transfer back to the States, I lived with—or more accurately, mooched off—David and his wife Wanda (or Wander, as we called her—you don't get to pick your nickname) for a couple of months and then moved north to El Segundo, where I mooched off my uncle, a federal judge, for a month. Just as I was wearing out my welcome there, Kathy arrived stateside to take a job in Oxnard at Naval Air Station Point Mugu, a research, test, and development base. Whew! Close one. I almost had to get a job.

We rented an apartment in Oxnard (well, she rented an apartment, and I mooched), and at a controller get-together, I ran into Squatty and Chevis. Squatty had transferred from the Philippines to Point Mugu, and Chevis had left the navy after his enlistment ended, opting for the FAA, which hadn't worked out. He had made it through the academy and then had been assigned to Los Angeles Center in the middle of the desert. Chevis could not have possibly been more miserable.

An air route traffic control center, often referred to simply as "the center," is more like a factory than an air traffic control facility. I've never worked at a center, thankfully, and have never met anyone who will admit to enjoying working at a center. Typically, centers are divided into four areas, which are divided into four sectors. A controller certifies in only one area, and it is not uncommon for controllers to spend their entire career in that area. Centers may have as many as three hundred controllers, so it is possible for two controllers to work in the same center for twenty years and never meet. Because I came from the tower and approach control world, where everyone knew everyone and where we were like a big family, this concept was totally foreign to me. Controllers were members of a brotherhood, and for controllers to work in a building for twenty years without knowing one another was contrary to everything I knew to be true.

Chevis hated Los Angeles Center at least as much as he hated the desert. He loved the ocean, and we had spent our days in the Philippines snorkeling, diving, sailing, and swimming. He and I would finish a midwatch at 7:00 a.m., have a few beers at Mariposa's on Magsaysay Drive, and go to the beach. It didn't surprise me that Chevis spent less than a year at the Los Angeles Center before quitting the FAA. Everyone hated the center so much that it was impossible to transfer out. Once you were there, you were there. The only way out was to quit.

During the early years immediately after the strike, the FAA was hurting so badly that controllers assigned to a facility like LA Center would quit and reapply in another region, hoping to get a tower or approach control assignment. The FAA caught on to this scheme and established an unwritten rule of not rehiring a controller for six months. When I ran into him, Chevis was doing his time in the penalty box working for the Department of the Navy as an operations test conductor at Point Mugu. He scheduled, conducted missions, and debriefed tests on missiles such as the Phoenix. It was a low-level GS-7 job, but it was on the beaches of Southern California (Ventura) rather than in the middle of the desert. Chevis suggested I go to work with him and set up an interview. A month later, in early January 1986, I did.

Working with Chevis again was like old times, only better. We didn't have the restrictions of the navy. We dressed the way we wanted, showed up, and did our job, and the rest of the day was ours. Typically, we had a mission at 5:00 a.m. and another at 2:00 p.m. Quite often, the afternoon mission would be canceled due to mechanical problems with an F-14 or because we were short a pilot or for some other reason out of our control. Life was good. Chevis and I were both hanging out, waiting for the FAA to come to its senses, realize it was short two highly qualified controllers, and hire us.

Then things changed. Our program analyst, responsible for logging miscellaneous bean-counter information associated with the programs we supported, accepted another position. The job was boring but very necessary to our operation. When Chevis was initially hired, the program analyst position had been vacant, and he had been assigned the collateral duty. So he had done his time in the barrel. This time around, I was the junior man, so guess who got the nod?

Once again, a crappy job turned out to be a blessing. One day, I finished entering mission-critical bean-counter data a little early, and tired of waiting for the FAA mountain to come to me, I decided I would go to the FAA mountain. I looked up the phone number for the nearest FAA tower, Oxnard, and contacted the facility manager, Bruce Troyer. We talked for a while, and he suggested I come in and see him. When I arrived, Bruce showed me an FAA air traffic controller advertisement for a direct hire. In other words, if I met the minimum requirements (and I did), the FAA could hire me off the street, avoiding the dreaded academy screen.

I applied and, after making several phone calls to convince an air traffic specialist in the Los Angeles regional office that I was indeed qualified, received an offer of employment with the FAA at the El Monte airport not far from Burbank, about fifty miles from Oxnard. But Kathy and I were pretty happy, and I didn't want to relocate to the San Fernando Valley, so I called Bruce and pled my case. His response was simple: "Take it and worry about the other stuff later." So I did accept the El Monte tower offer. A few days later, Bruce called to tell me a controller at Burbank had washed out and was being reassigned to Oxnard. The washed-out controller didn't want to relocate, so he offered to swap orders with me and take El Monte if I would take Oxnard. Um, okay. I swear I have a gang of angels, not just one, taking care of me. In June 1986, my dream came true, and I went to work for the FAA.

Oxnard was located in the Ventura/Santa Barbara area on the north side of the Canejo Grade. This probably doesn't mean anything to those not familiar with the LA area, but it is extremely important. The Canejo Grade separates the San Fernando Valley and Los Angeles from the rest of California. It's like a barbed wire fence. Although there are areas of LA that are the exclusive property of the wealthy, such as Beverly Hills and the hills of Malibu, the real money is in Santa Barbara about eighty miles north of LA. Oxnard is immediately adjacent to Ventura (two or three miles), which is a close second to Santa Barbara. The Oxnard airport is right on the Pacific Ocean. At the west end of the single runway is a road. On the other side of the road are the sand dunes and the Pacific Ocean. It was a home by the sea, my home.

I had never lived in California, and I fell in love with it immediately. Oxnard was a perfect location. It didn't have the crime, traffic, or smog of LA, but LA and all the goodies that came along with it were only forty-five minutes away. Two baseball teams, two football teams, a jillion things to do, and my best friend David were all right there.

Kathy soon realized we weren't cut out for each other, and she gave me my walking papers. It was for the best; she was six years younger than me and hadn't experienced life the way I had. At least that's what she told me. She married a year later, so it's quite possible she found greener pastures while grazing in mine. In any event, I've been dumped in worse ways, and the consideration was appreciated. Kathy was and, I am told, still is a very good person. I'm better off for knowing her.

With emancipation papers in hand and a good FAA job talking to airplanes, I moved to Ventura Beach, literally. My new home was a half block from the beaches of the Pacific Ocean and stumbling distance from three bars, one of which had a blues band on Friday and Saturday nights and a reggae band every Sunday. Conveniently sandwiched among them was a sushi bar. Life was good. There was only one exception: training. I had some very good air traffic experience under my belt, but nothing prepared me for civil aviation.

Military pilots are extremely experienced, even at the junior officer level, because of the training they receive, and they fly airplanes that are, by and large, compatible. Civilian pilots, on the other hand, can have experience that varies a great deal, from commercial pilots logging thirty hours a month to VFR (visual flight rules—not required to be instrument-rated) Cessna pilots who fly only once a month. Airplanes vary just as greatly. Cessnas and Piper Cherokees do not mix well with twin-engine turboprops such as Beechcraft King Airs, much less with Learjets. However, all these aircraft constituted the daily makeup of our traffic at Oxnard. I hadn't experienced anything like it before and was initially overwhelmed—or more accurately, blown away. It was a big transition and a difficult one.

I slogged through training for a number of good reasons. First, I have always been a slow learner. There, I admit it. For me, grasping and understanding essential elements usually required repeated illustration before I got the point. Don't believe me? I've been married and divorced three times. Although all my ex-wives were good people, we just weren't meant for each other. I felt it before I proposed yet proposed anyway. Fortunately, my learning problem at Oxnard was a speed bump and not a complete blockage.

The second and most debilitating problem was a result of the other: I began to question my own capabilities and talent. The cocky, bulletproof facade I had created at Whiting Field was beginning to show signs of wear. Worse, this was my first FAA facility, and it was a very low-level one at that. My dreams of working LA tower or approach control were becoming questionable. I believed I would certify at Oxnard, but because I was working a type of traffic I had never seen before, it was not going to be a walk in the park. Eight months passed. I improved slowly but surely until operations became routine, and I could clearly see trouble before it happened. I was recommended for certification, and Bruce certified me, which proved to be the real beginning of my education.

Controllers go through a steep learning curve during training, but the real schooling commences immediately after certification. Once a controller certifies, there is no instructor looking over their shoulder pointing out a missed turn or a late clearance for takeoff. Attention to detail during this period is at its peak, and mistakes create tools that are discreetly stored in our bag of tricks. Events occur that, if unnoticed by other controllers, generally go unmentioned forever. This is a building period, not just for the controller but also for the controller's coworkers. Building confidence internally is just as important as instilling it in coworkers and management. Without both, a controller can easily become labeled the "weak link" and be treated as such. In general, controllers have thick skin but typically have one vulnerable spot: credibility. An attack on a controller's credibility is met with an enthusiastic response. Credibility is directly linked to ability, and as with other career fields, a person's credibility carries a lot of weight and could mean the difference between reaching the next rung on the career ladder or not.

Ironically, during my time in training, I didn't witness a single crash. Maybe the air traffic control gods had pity on me. After I certified, things went back to normal—not Philippines or Whiting normal, but normal for a small civil airport.

The Oxnard tower was open from 7:00 a.m. to 9:00 p.m. seven days a week. The first controller was on their own until 9:00 a.m., and the last controller was on their own between 7:00 p.m. and 9:00 p.m.. Early one morning, as I sat alone in the tower reading the newspaper, a Long Easy called fifteen miles east of the airport for landing. Long Easy planes are single-engine aircraft that are very small and very fast. A Long Easy has only two seats, one in front of the other, with the engine and propeller in the rear of the airplane. The Long Easy has one retractable gear, the nose gear, and its main mounts (wheels under the wings) are fixed (welded in place) and do not retract.

I issued instructions for the Long Easy to report a five-mile final and buried my head in the morning *Los Angeles Times*. He called again at five miles, and I looked out the window—and looked and looked. Finally, he reported two miles, and I saw him with the binoculars, very, very, low, but with all three wheeels down. Controllers are taught from day one, when the words, "Cleared to land" are uttered, we do two things, every single time. No exceptions. Ensure all three wheels are down and scan the runway to ensure a truck or other vehicle hasn't wandered on the runway.

I cleared the Long Easy to land and watched the Long Easy land. Everything looked normal until the aircraft settled onto the runway—and kept settling, until his wings were on the runway. I watched in complete disbelief as the Long Easy slid down the runway from side to side, screaming to myself, "Don't hit the runway lights!" He slid left and right and back again but somehow always managed to keep the miniature aircraft on the runway.

When he came to a complete stop, I uttered one of my top three most moronic "fuckin' Ernie" lines of all time: "Long Easy two-three-echo, do you need any assistance?" *Of course, he needs assistance, you idiot*, I said to myself. The aircraft had no main mounts, the propeller exploded when it struck the runway, and the aircraft was sitting on its belly. Immediately, I keyed the mike and said, "Long Easy two-three-echo, the crash truck is on the way."

Since the Long Easy has welded main mounts, I could not understand why the aircraft was sitting on its belly. Aircraft with retractable landing gear land from time to time with their wheels up (when the pilot forgets to put them down), but there was no way for the Long Easy to retract its main mounts even if the pilot wanted to. I started filling out the crash report, called the FAA regional duty officer in LA, and was logging the crash when the second controller came in for the day shift. I passed the tower operation to him and went downstairs to talk with the crash crew.

This pilot was a real piece of work. First, he was qualified only as a student pilot, meaning he was not certified to pilot an aircraft that carried passengers, and he had one in the backseat. Second, he wasn't qualified to pilot a high-performance or retractable-gear aircraft. The Long Easy is small and very, very fast and has a retractable nose wheel that, in this case, was down and locked. No main mounts were anywhere to be found, but the nose wheel was in the down and locked position. Third, and this is the best part, his passenger was his eighty-year-old mother-in-law, whom he was taking to Ventura for a cardiologist appointment. Apparently, she'd had a heart attack the week before and needed a follow-up visit. Seriously.

The big question, though, was "where are the main mounts?" They were nowhere to be found—not on the runway or off the runway in the grass. Nowhere. The mystery was solved a week later by the FAA maintenance guys. Remember when I had to look low for the Long Easy? He was so low, he hit the approach lighting, taking off the main mounts and wiping out two rows of lights. The lights give pilots a path to follow at night or in bad weather and are elevated seven or eight feet off the ground. The maintenance guys were performing routine checks when they found his hardware. Amazing.

Events such as this generated a lot of paperwork, but since nobody died, they were more of a pain in the neck than anything else. Some were actually humorous. I was the second controller one morning, arriving at 9:00 a.m. to a completely "socked in" airport. Oxnard was a half mile from the Pacific Ocean, and the marine layer, a thick blanket of fog, moved in regularly, completely obscuring everything. The fog was so thick that even the first row of parked aircraft were not visible, and in aviation, this condition is referred to as "socked in." Translation: no one was going anywhere. We sat and read the newspaper or went next door to the Red Baron for breakfast, waiting for the fog to lift.

Around ten thirty on this morning, the fog began to burn off, slowly revealing the taxiway leading to the one runway. As more fog burned off, I could see the runway. Then, when the far side of the runway was visible, I noticed that runway lights were missing and trenches were dug in the broccoli field surrounding the runway. The Oxnard airport was surrounded by fields that were farmed nearly year-round. Celery, broccoli, and a few other vegetables were planted and grown right up to the runway.

I told the controller in charge (we didn't have a supervisor, so we assumed the responsibilities through the FAA designation "controller in charge"), and he told the crash crew, one of four guys who drove a one-ton pickup truck loaded with firefighting equipment and emergency medical stuff. Except for the Long Easy episode, I never saw the crash crew in action, and with only one emergency worker (firefighter, emergency medical technician, and ladder man all rolled into one), I always wondered which was their higher priority, stopping a bleeder or putting out a fire.

The crash crew, all one of him, went out to have a look-see and radioed back, "Tower, you're not gonna believe this one." After the Long Easy, anything was believable. About that time the fog burned off to reveal a twin-engine Cessna in the broccoli and three bodies lying around it, two on the wing and one in the broccoli. They were not dead bodies—pickled maybe, but not dead. Apparently, these three clowns had decided to take off the night before after the tower closed (which is legal), and they lost an engine, ran off the runway, and stopped in the broccoli field. The fog was so thick that they had decided to overnight right there and just happened to have a shit-pot full of airline liquor bottles, which now were everywhere, empty, of course. Although it was highly suspected that they had been flying, or attempting to fly, intoxicated, there was no proof, and it was decided that a broken twin Cessna was enough punishment and therefore "no harm, no foul."

There was one instance in which bold pilots did not become old pilots. The Camarillo airport is located fifteen miles east of Oxnard, and two pilots departing Camarillo died one night trying to get back home to Northern California. As I understand it, they had flown a buddy to Camarillo that afternoon and developed what turned out to be serious electrical trouble along the way. They had dinner and decided to hand-crank the prop just like in the old days of aviation. I didn't know that would work, but evidently it does because the engine started. However, as they added power and took off, the electrical problem became fatal, and the Cherokee lost all power, crashing just past the end of the runway. Their burned-out hulk was found the next morning, and they were identified by dental records. Old pilots, bold pilots. Sad.

Camarillo was a source of numerous exciting and entertaining events. The traffic load at Camarillo was picking up, and the FAA decided it was time to look into installing a control tower. Bruce was tasked with performing a traffic count, which required a controller at the airport from 7:00 a.m. to 7:00 p.m., seven days a week, for two weeks. Camarillo duty was cool. We were given a portable radio that plugged into a car cigarette lighter to monitor traffic. Uncontrolled airports such as Camarillo are much more common than you'd think. As a matter of fact, the majority of airports in the United States are uncontrolled because they do not accommodate enough air traffic to warrant a control tower. So at uncontrolled airports, how do airplanes keep from hitting each other?

Uncontrolled airports are assigned a frequency, which pilots dial up to broadcast their aircraft number, type of aircraft, position, and intentions. For instance, "Camarillo airport, Cherokee two-three-bravo is twelve miles east, straight in, full stop, runway 25." Other aircraft on the frequency will report in and coordinate their position and intentions. The concept of "control" is placed squarely on the shoulders of the pilots, and they operate in self-separate and sequence mode.

To acquire traffic count information that would be used to determine the necessity of an FAA tower at Camarillo, we positioned ourselves on the ramp adjacent to the midfield taxiway, yet out of the way of taxiing aircraft. As we monitored the frequency, we logged touch-and-goes, departures, arrivals, and transitions over the airport, all of which in a busy airport fall under the watchful eye of an air traffic controller. Bruce was a very easygoing boss, and his relaxed attitude was even more relaxed when it came to the traffic count at Camarillo. His policy was simple: count airplanes and don't get into trouble. So we did. One day I waxed my car in nothing but a Speedo (I had just come from Guam, and that was our rugby team's standard beach attire—besides, I had the physique back then) while drinking Coronas, two of which I shared with the crash crew guy (yeah, yeah, yeah—pay more and get better help). Some controllers did their time in lounge chairs, covered in suntan oil, while reading a book and listening to a boom box.

Although we had very little problem entertaining ourselves, the locals did provide specialized entertainment from time to time. I arrived early one morning to find the airport completely socked in. However, as I set up camp and turned on the radio, I heard an airplane engine overhead. I assumed it to be an aircraft that was attempting an approach in the prohibitive weather and couldn't see the runway at decision height, until I saw it fly over the runway. Confused, I turned up the radio volume, heard nothing, and switched to the Point Mugu approach control frequency, figuring the aircraft would be talking to them. Again, no luck. The pilot should've been talking to someone but wasn't. As the engine sound grew louder and I saw the aircraft pass by me on the runway once again, I realized this clown was in the pattern, performing touch-and-goes. He stayed very low, which was the only way he could possibly keep the runway in sight, and performed another touch-and-go. This was insane. If another aircraft commenced an instrument approach, there was no way for this guy to know it was about to land, and in the fog, a midair was very likely.

About the time that I decided something needed to be done and was preparing to call Bruce, the crash crew guy rolled up to my car. We exchanged pleasantries (we knew all the crash crew guys; they worked at both Oxnard and Camarillo airports), and I asked what the hell was going on with this guy. He laughed, explaining it was just Bob. Bob was a local who flew an old Piper Cub with no radio. He'd come out early in the morning and shoot touch-and-goes when no one else was in the pattern.

"What if an aircraft lands?" I asked.

"No problem. See that truck over there?" he asked.

I looked over and saw an old Ford pickup next to the runway. "Yeah, so?"

"That's Bob's wife, Edith. She's monitoring the frequency, so if an aircraft checks in on an instrument approach, she just flashes the headlights and Bob lands," he stated matter-of-factly.

Simply amazing. The crazy part is that it made perfect sense, and I decided to cancel my hazardous-situation phone call to Bruce, opting instead to pop a breakfast beer and watch the show. The crash crew guy joined me.

Without a doubt, though, the wildest incident happened one sunny afternoon with two Cessnas in the pattern executing touch-and-goes. One pilot was either learning or just methodically safe, and the other was young and bold. Neither, however, had any patience for the other, and both seemed to be spoiling for a fight. As they coordinated their intentions on the common frequency, one pilot chastised the other for flying too deep on the downwind before turning base leg and asked to be allowed to turn inside of the other pilot. In other words, Mr. Young-and-Bold was pissed because Mr. Methodical was flying an extended pattern, resulting in wasted time. In the air, time is money. Airplane gas is not cheap. Getting no cooperation from Mr. Methodical, Mr. Young-and-Bold took matters into his own hands and turned inside Mr. Methodical. Words were exchanged on the frequency, and things heated up. On the next pass, Mr. Young-and-Bold pulled the same stunt again, and things got very interesting, only this time names consisting of only four letters were hurled. With beer in hand, I was content to watch. This had the potential to be good. The third time was a charm, and the option to resolve the dispute man-to-man on the taxiway was offered and accepted.

They landed, taxied to the taxiway directly in front of me, shut off the engines, deplaned, and commenced duking it out right there on the taxiway. I had free front-row seats to the Camarillo Smackdown. Priceless! This was small municipal airport activity at its best. Definitely uncontrolled. Just as they were really getting into it, rolling on the ground, fists flying, the crash crew guy rolled up, dove into the middle of the fray, and separated them.

I thought for about half a second about jumping in and helping out but remembered what Bruce had told us about staying out of trouble. This situation had trouble written all over it. In an instant, I pictured myself standing in front of Bruce, in nothing but a Speedo and with beer breath, explaining a bloody nose and black eye, and quickly decided that my best course of action was to be a passive observer. The pilots cooled off, took their split lips and bloody noses back to their aircraft, fired them up, and taxied back to their respective hangars, deciding to call it a day.

A few years later, the Camarillo airport got its control tower.

Life at the Oxnard tower continued as usual. The FAA was still short on controllers, and we were working a lot of overtime. It got to the point where I just wanted time off to spend all the money I was making. A typical month consisted of three six-day weeks, many of which included ten-hour days, and the fourth week had a two-day weekend. By law, the most a controller can work is ten hours a day and six days week, so we had that going for us. Since we were so shorthanded, vacation time was very hard to come by. We compensated by taking a sick day in the middle of the week. If you think about it, that was probably a major part of the reason that we were working six-day weeks. It was a vicious cycle.

However, there was just enough amusement occurring daily to break the monotony. One Saturday morning, I answered a call from another municipal airport informing me that a drunken pilot was inbound. It was around 10:00 a.m., and this guy was toast. Somehow, he flew into Oxnard and landed, and we had two sheriff's cruisers waiting for him. He didn't go without a fight, though, and used his airplane as a weapon. The sheriff's deputies, using their cruisers, cornered him on the midfield taxiway, and one cruiser approached the airplane with its propeller still turning. The drunken pilot gunned it, and both deputies abandoned their vehicles, running for ditches next to the taxiway. To this day, I don't know how his prop didn't hit one of the vehicles.

One afternoon a Cessna full of people landed—well, sort of. If an aircraft doesn't "flare" (in which the pilot pulls back on the yoke just before touching down so the rear wheels, or main mounts, touch down first), it lands nose wheel first and "porpoises." In this case, the aircraft continuously bounces back up into the air, flying ever so slightly before losing enough airspeed to land again. Porpoising is hilarious to watch but must be scary as hell if you're in the aircraft.

This Cessna porpoised over and over again, much worse than I had ever seen, and finally bled off enough airspeed to stay on the ground without running off the end of the runway. It taxied to the ramp in front on the tower, and we all had to get a look at the responsible party. Both doors opened, and a few people got out. Then a few more. Then a few more. It was like watching thirty clowns get out of a miniature circus car. They just kept coming. Old women, kids, more men. We were laughing so hard that no one thought to do a head count.

Oxnard was located about thirty minutes down the road from Malibu, making it a prime arrival and departure point for movie stars. I once met Steve Perry, the former lead singer for Journey. Whoopie Goldberg came up to the tower one night, and she was very relaxed. She explained that she didn't care for flying too much and was on medication. I believe her; many people don't fly well. But I bet she did enjoy that trip. Kurt Russell soloed from Oxnard. His home airport was socked-in the day he was scheduled to solo, so his instructor flew them to Oxnard. He did fine.

There were many more celebrities, but in most cases, they flew in, a limo pulled up to the jet and loaded them and their luggage, and they were gone.

A favorite memory of mine didn't involve an accident, an incident, or a movie star. I was closing on my last night in the tower when the phone rang. It was a Cessna pilot who'd been practicing approaches and touch-and-goes for most of the afternoon and evening. He explained that it was his airplane and his dad had just retired from one of the airlines as a Boeing 747 captain. His dad and mom were taking his aircraft on a cross-country spring tour the next day, and he was "checking out" his dad in the airplane. It sounded funny to check out a B-747 captain in a Cessna, but I guess it had to done.

I asked how his dad had done, and he replied, "Fine, except he kept trying to flare at forty feet." A B-747 is so big that the pilot must flare forty feet above the runway. We laughed, and I posted a note on the board for the morning crew to wish his dad and mom a happy retirement and a safe trip.

Although time off was hard to come by, I was like a moth to a flame, and I had just enough of it to meet and marry my next ex-wife. I met Karen on the beach next to my house. She was a tall brunette and very outgoing; we hit it off from the beginning, and before I knew it, we were exchanging rings. I did love her, and she loved me, but once again, it just wasn't meant to be. The marriage was a tumultuous one for a lot of reasons, and before I knew it, we had reached an impenetrable impasse. Once again, my angels, or whoever it is watching out for my dumb ass, intervened, and I was selected for transfer to a tower and approach control in Tucson, Arizona.

7

TUCSON

March 1989

Tucson was not my first choice or even in my top ten choices, but I wanted to get to a level-five radar room and was told a level-three tower with a radar room attached was the way to go. In the FAA, air traffic control towers and terminal radar approach control (tower and TRACON) facilities were designated a level from one to five in accordance with the number of air traffic operations. The rating system changed in early 2000, but the principles are still the same. Air traffic operations include arrivals, departures, touch-and-goes, and overflights (aircraft transitioning or flying through a particular piece of airspace). The more operations, the higher the facility level rating, and controllers are paid in accordance with the annual traffic count.

Typically, terminal facilities east of the Mississippi were combined, meaning tower and TRACONs were considered one facility. A controller certified in both the tower and TRACON before being considered a "full performance level" controller. At facilities such as Atlanta, Dallas / Fort Worth, Chicago, and Los Angeles and many of the other busiest airports in the world, not only was certification a very long and drawn-out process, but also it was difficult for controllers to maintain currency between the tower and TRACON. Controllers must maintain currency on all positions in both the tower and TRACON by working a minimum number of hours (around eight) per month on each position. In the prestrike days, towers and TRACONs were co-located, with the TRACON a floor or two directly below the tower cab. As airports grew busier and equipment changed, controller staffing requirements grew, and more space was needed to accommodate updated equipment and more bodies.

Many older towers did not have the space available to accommodate either more bodies or more equipment. In the case of the Los Angeles airport, for example, space in a coast guard hangar was acquired, creating logistical problems. The hangar was located a stone's throw from the tower, but fifteen or twenty minutes by car. Accordingly, controllers were assigned to work in one place or the other for a full day. Although LA tower was by no means an easy place to work, certifying in the TRACON required much more time, and the washout rate was much higher. Why? This is going to piss off all the dedicated tower flowers, but the following is undeniable: TRACONs encompass a great deal more airspace than towers by their very nature. They typically provide radar services for, generally, a twenty-five-mile radius surrounding the host airport—sometimes more, sometimes less. And, provide ATC services to a number of airports, not just one.

Los Angeles TRACON fell into this category, providing radar services for Hawthorne, Santa Monica, Torrance, and a few other airports. Controllers must have a detailed understanding of all of the approaches, frequencies, and minimum altitudes and a host of other particulars for each airport to certify at LA TRACON. Los Angeles tower controllers, on the other hand, are fundamentally concerned with LA tower. Because of this, towers are easier to work than TRACONs. There! I said it, and I can already hear the furious howls from all the tower flowers who never worked in a TRACON. I am not saying that Los Angeles, Chicago, Dallas / Fort Worth, and many other of the largest and busiest towers in the world are easy to work; they are just not as difficult as their TRACON counterparts.

However, I am told that many controllers certify on the tower or local position (responsible for clearing aircraft for takeoff and landing) before training on ground control at LA and Chicago because ground control is so complex. A popular belief is that more controllers wash out on ground control at these two facilities than on local control. Whether it is myth or fact, I don't know. I do know many controllers who have worked at these two towers, and this information comes from them. I'm sure they'll use this fact to justify their argument that towers are every bit as difficult to work as TRACONs. They are wrong, and I'm right. So we'll just have to leave it at that.

Once the towers and TRACONs were physically separated, and the need for radar instructor controllers was so high, maintaining currency at both facilities became prohibitive, and the FAA decided it was best for all concerned to separate them. For reasons I still don't understand, this attitude was prevalent throughout the western states but gradually diminished the farther east a facility was located. As of this writing, the Atlanta tower and TRACON were just recently separated even though the TRACON, located in Peachtree City twenty miles south of the airport, had been in operation for quite a while.

En-route or center facilities are designated as levels one through three. But who cares? They're center pukes. The controllers there know only a few bits of phraseology, such as "Good morning, Captain. How's your ride?" or "Roger, altimeter two-niner-niner-two." When the shit hits the fan and they know not what to do next, they utter, "American 243, contact Los Angeles approach or Chicago, or one of the other busiest TRACONs in the United States for your sequence," effectively putting all the hard work on the TRACON's very large shoulders.

Just kidding. The center folks earn their money and do a great job pulling a very heavy load, but the en-route environment is a mystery to most terminal controllers. Because of this, there is a rivalry of sorts, and as with most rivalries, it's good-natured. Overall, very few controllers are cross-rated between the center and terminal. It's a big transition, and as I've stated before, most controllers who know better don't want to go to a center.

Until recently, all controllers at level-five towers and TRACONs and level-three centers were paid in accordance to the general schedule (GS) at the GS-14 level. Most controllers had no upper-level education, and their being paid a GS-14 salary (approximately $70,000 in the late 1980s) really pissed off doctors, lawyers, and engineers who were also in government service. Most controllers, however, would reply, "Grab a headset, Mr./Ms. Doctor, Lawyer, or Engineer, and plug in. Let's see if there is any lead in your pencil." Of course, this attitude only served to piss off the doctors, lawyers, and engineers even more, but controllers were doing a job that wasn't meant for just anybody, and they earned their money.

Level-fives were GS-14s, level-fours were GS-13, and down the line. Oxnard was a level-two tower, so the next logical step for me was to transfer to a level-three tower/TRACON, and I bid every one of them with an opening. Finally, Bruce walked into the Oxnard tower and asked, "What are you going to do with all that beach and no breakers?"

"What are you talking about?" I asked.

Pat O'Sullivan, the Tucson manager, had called and informed Bruce that I had been selected for transfer. I had really become spoiled living on the beach of Ventura, California. I didn't have an air conditioner because the summer temps never exceeded eighty-five, and I was not looking forward to 110-degree summers. But this was an excellent opportunity to get into a busier tower and get a TRACON ticket (certification) under my belt, so off to southern Arizona I went.

I arrived in late March 1989, did my training, and checked out in the tower by midsummer. Tucson tower was a hell of a lot of fun. It hosted the 162nd Fighter Group, a wing of the Arizona Air National Guard, which had around sixty F-16s. They flew twice a day, and it was just like the old days at Whiting, only twice as good because the F-16s were twice as fast. We had airplanes coming out of our ears! The struggles I'd had at Oxnard were long gone, and air traffic control was fun again. There was no less a mixture of airplanes and capabilities than at Oxnard, but we had three runways at Tucson and just sequenced the slow airplanes to a separate runway.

As usual, aviation was aviation, and Mr. Murphy executed his duties when the time was right. Early one evening, just before I went home, he showed up, unexpectedly as always. It was late December 1989, and for all practical purposes, I had finished my 11:00 a.m. to 7:00 p. m. shift and was biding time in the back of the tower, shooting the breeze with the supervisor. The controller on local announced he had to pee, and with me out the door in a matter of minutes, the supervisor offered to watch the position for just a second or two, which was against policy. He was signed on as the supervisor and therefore not allowed to work another position. An America West B-737 had been cleared to land on runway 29 right and was on a one-mile final. The approach end of runway 29 right was over a mile away from the tower, so we really couldn't accurately judge the aircraft's landing speed—until it passed the tower at forty miles an hour. We all stood there, mouths wide open, watching the Boeing roar past us, slowing but not quite stopping, until it ran off the end of the runway. As it left the pavement, the nose wheel collapsed, and it came to a stop just short of Valencia Boulevard.

The crash crew was on top of it before the emergency chutes hit the ground. The controller returned from the restroom to the tower cab just about the time passengers were sliding down the chutes, and when he figured out what had happened, he told the supervisor, "It's all yours."

The supervisor argued that he hadn't cleared the aircraft to land and was signed on as the supervisor (again, it was illegal to work two positions at one time when staffing was available), so he wasn't responsible. The controller argued that he had been in the toilet when the incident occurred, so he wasn't responsible. I snuck out the door when no one was looking, having been around enough crashes to realize I wanted no part of this one. Fortunately, other than a damaged nose wheel and a huge round of blame, everyone was fine. It turned out that a cable in the wheel well had been stripped, and a hydraulic line was leaking. A spark in close proximity to hydraulic fluid had caused a small fire and rendered the brakes useless.

Tucson has two parallel runways (side by side) and one intersecting runway. We used the intersecting runway quite a bit, but it did have a tendency to create conflict where there should have been none. Some supervisors would tell the local controller to stop using it when things were busy. Many of us looked on this as a violation of the Maginot Line between controller and supervisor, but in hindsight, it was a good call.

Errol Porter was not one of those supervisors. "Do what you want; just don't let them scrape paint" was his motto. Errol also liked to watch college football on Saturday afternoon—in the tower. Officially, the TV was a prohibited item in the tower, but the David Dodd approach of "break any rule you want; just be prepared to deal with the consequences" seemed to be in effect throughout the air traffic control world.

Errol's favorite game of the year was pretty much whichever game he could get with the rabbit ear antennae; however, he was fired up when Notre Dame played the University of Southern California. I was working local that afternoon, and Errol was oblivious to the operation until a commercial came on. He looked around and saw that I had six bug smashers (Cessnas) in the touch-and-go pattern and a fair number of commercial arrivals and departures at the other runway. Errol asked if I needed any help. I told him, honestly, "Nope."

Errol returned to the game, and I continued working traffic. Then it got really busy. With two more bug smashers added to the touch-and-go pattern, a string of commercial arrivals, and a stack of departures at the end of the runway, I began to get a little antsy. Deciding it was time to simplify the operation, I shut off intersecting runway operations- after these last two. Just two more, and that was it.

Suddenly, Errol screamed, "Did you see that?"

My mind went into overdrive, checking the end of all three runways for aluminum showers; back to the final approach, I counted all my Cessnas like fingers and toes; then looking back to the runways, I shouted, "What, Errol? See what?"

"That catch! Holy shit! That was amazing!" Errol screamed.

I was sure I had pushed my luck one airplane too far, but it was just Errol being Errol. His excitement was over a fantastic USC football catch apparently. I almost killed him.

My year in the tower went quickly, and I found myself attending radar school at the FAA Academy in Oklahoma City, Oklahoma. Oklahoma City in February of 1990. Three weeks of misery. Just before I left for the training, I was told I would come back to the tower for a few weeks and then go on to the TRACON and would not return to the tower at all. When I bid Tucson, it was a combined tower/TRACON facility. However, the TRACON was located at Davis-Monthan Air Force Base (just twenty minutes away), and there was a fairly high TRACON washout rate, which had caused the FAA to decide to split the two facilities. It made sense. The tower folks who didn't certify in the TRACON returned to the tower and did not want to relocate to a tower in the Phoenix area. The FAA didn't want to pay to move them either, so it all fell into place, and everyone was happy. In the meantime, the TRACON traffic load had increased to the point that we were bumped up to a level-four TRACON, which meant a nice pay raise for me.

To say I was not a naturally gifted controller would be an understatement. I studied the airspace, procedures, and policies nightly, but my certification in the TRACON took a while. It's safe to say that until the day Pat O'Sullivan signed my certification paperwork, it could have gone either way. Fortunately for me, I had a group of instructors who cared whether or not I successfully completed the program. They were some of the most dedicated, colorful, and loyal people I have ever had the pleasure of knowing.

Some of the best supervisors in my career were at Tucson, and CJ Idlewine was one of them. If CJ had been an inch taller, she would have been round. She had positively white-blonde hair, had breasts that entered a room long before she did, and was—how do I put this?—less than attractive. CJ was either in a cranky mood or happy as hell to be alive. She had two little dogs, including one named "LS"—not "Ellis" but "LS for "Little Shit." That was CJ being CJ. There was no in between. Ceej was a good sport, and we all loved her. Ceej had two not so great habits. She had a severe sweet tooth and picked her nose no matter where, when, or who was present.

I once walked into the radar room with a fist full of Red Hots.

"Whaddya got?" CJ asked.

"Red Hots."

"Where'd ya get those?"

"My locker."

A few minutes later, Ceej was munching on my Red Hots. By the time the shift was over, the bag was empty. I know because she left the empty bag in my locker. Throw it away, Ceej? Next time, I guess.

A communications room was located directly behind the supervisor desk in the TRACON, and a telephone in the communications room had its ringer permanently set on "ungodly high" because the radio connectors made a *very* loud clacking noise every time a mike was keyed, and there were probably a hundred of them. Sometimes the telephone company, looking for one of its technicians, would call, letting the phone ring for five minutes at a time, and CJ hated it. One day, as I was leaving the office, headed for a pilot briefing, I stopped to get JJ, a fellow controller. He was on the phone and stuck his finger in the air, indicating for me to wait a minute. Finally, he hung up, laughing, and explained that he had answered the communications room phone one time and gotten the number for the phone (the phone wasn't labeled with the phone number, so we had no way of knowing it) from the caller. Every now and then, when CJ was the supervisor, he'd call and let it ring for ten minutes or so, knowing it would drive CJ nuts, and this was what he'd been doing when I came by. Beautiful.

However, being a prankster meant getting as well as you gave, and JJ got his one day. Mark Pickerel was our resident genius, with a degree in physics, and he programmed our new break-room television to switch to the Playboy channel at a particular time. The channel was scrambled, so there was no video, but the audio wasn't scrambled. Ironically, it switched on this day at the same time JJ, who was raised by a Presbyterian minister father and still followed the good book to the letter, walked through the TRACON door. JJ would have taken it all in stride, except that day he had his wife and two kids with him. Fortunately, there was no picture, but the moans, the groans, and a female voice verbally admiring two guys' manliness were enough.

"Give me both of them! I want both of them!" I'll never forget those words. Just good clean fun.

Lon Chaney was always right there, ready to lend a hand, when the other hucksters took the day off. Chaney and I were leaving the tower one day when he looked out the tower window and saw Mark Nelson running across the parking lot to catch the elevator. Nelly was consistently on the time bubble for his shift. Every single day, he would hustle his backside across the parking lot, through the terminal, and to the elevator in a desperate attempt to make it to the tower cab without being late. Nearly every day, he made it. On this day, though, I noticed Chaney watching the parking lot with enthusiasm. Our shift ended at the same time Nelly's shift started. Just as I signed out, Chaney grabbed me and said, "Wanna have some fun?"

Stupid question, Lon. "Sure, why not?"

Chaney pointed toward the parking lot, at Nelly doing the "I'm late for work hustle." We got in the elevator and descended to the first floor. Just as the door opened to the terminal, Chaney pushed the button for each and every floor all the way up to the tower cab, ten floors in all. We got out, Nelly got in, the door closed, and he screamed our names interlaced with obscenities, realizing the elevator would stop at every floor and he would be late today.

They say, "We wouldn't screw with you if we didn't like you," and Nelson fell into that category. He and I were good friends, taking regular trips to Las Vegas when he wasn't going back to San Francisco to visit his wife. He had met his wife while attending Arizona State University. They married, and she pursued a career in broadcast journalism, eventually earning a position with one of the big three networks in San Francisco. Mark and I traveled a lot. And I mean a lot—on airlines, for free. How? We asked.

Before 9/11, there existed a "familiarization" program that allowed controllers to ride in the cockpit of commercial airliners, exposing them to the operations and duties on the flight deck. The program, referred to by pilots and controllers as "fam trips," was very regimented, with the number of flights per year restricted to a dozen or so, no more than two per year on any one airline, and authorization from the facility manager was required. Rules, rules, rules. We were controllers. *We* make the rules. For most of us single folks, the airlines were a national taxi service. It was beautiful. The only other people authorized to ride in a jump seat were other pilots and a few mechanics who were certified to taxi the aircraft, severely restricting the competition for a free ride. In other words, all other airline employees rode "nonrevenue" (nonrev) or free, fighting over a seat in the cabin of the aircraft. Even if the airplane was full and nonrev employees couldn't get on board, chances were the jump seat was open. This policy kind of pissed off some airline employees, but it was all part of the controller experience.

As far as authorization paperwork was concerned, the airline had all the paperwork we needed: a jump seat pass signed by the pilot in command. How did we get it without paperwork from the air traffic control manager? Simple. We asked. The new and improved fam program was called "flash and dash." We simply walked up to the gate, flashed our FAA badges and jump seat authorization, and asked for a jump seat request. The gate agent took it to the captain and returned with a signed pink copy for our records. We usually boarded before old women and children and put our bags in the first-class overhead bin, which didn't go over too well with the well-to-do.

The pilots were great! They had no problem letting us mooch a ride. On one trip, the pilot bragged about having the title of "Jump Seat King." Apparently, after the Reno Air Show, he had authorized over forty jump seat vouchers on one trip. There was risk with the flash-and-dash program: getting caught. If you were caught, the FAA dictated a two-year suspension from the program, but enforcement of the penalty was up to the facility manager. Nobody I know was ever caught, and I really couldn't see Pat, our manager, suspending anyone's privileges.

I did come close once when an FAA flight inspector wound up on my flight. Part of a flight inspector's duties is to review all the documentation associated with the aircraft, including the passenger manifest. When boarding the aircraft, controllers who were jump-seating checked in with the pilot and were routinely asked if we had ever jump-seated before.

"Yeah, more than a few times, Captain," was my standard answer and one that nearly always earned me a seat in first class. Even in big aircraft, the cockpit is small and cramped. It's noisy, cold, and boring. Yes, boring. The first few trips were fascinating, but the routine quickly became old. In the cockpit, alcohol in your bloodstream was strictly prohibited, and it was one rule we never, ever violated. But if the flight was the last leg of your trip, the pilot decided the cockpit was cramped enough already and the controller was not going to become more familiar with cockpit operations, why not let him or her sit in first class and enjoy an adult beverage? When I was offered a chance to sit in first class, my pat answer was "It's your aircraft, Captain. I'll sit wherever you tell me."

This trip with the flight inspector on board nearly put an end to my flash-and-dash days. After checking paperwork, he realized there were two jump seats authorized: me and him. When asked where the other jump seater was, the captain pointed at me—in first class. There I was, comfortable in first class, *Sports Illustrated* in one hand and gin and tonic in the other. The flight inspector approached me and started the question-and-answer routine. Just about the time I realized I was screwed, the flight attendant told him to return to the cockpit for taxi.

His last words were instructions to see him after we landed and before I deplaned.

"Sure, no problem," I said. *If your ding-ding is long enough to touch your sphincter, go screw yourself,* I thought. I didn't work for his department, so I was under no obligation to to answer any of his questions.

Midflight and, for me, a handful of gin and tonics later, the pilot came back and told me he'd delay the flight inspector after landing so I could make a getaway. Fortunately, I was landing in Atlanta, not Tucson, and I always signed my jump seat requests "A. Smith." My middle initial is A, so I wasn't lying. But I was sure there were a lot of A. Smiths in the FAA. Tracking me down would be impossible. Phew! A close one.

I learned the initial trick from a fellow female controller, who was one of my favorite people in the world. She was known far and wide as the "fam queen." As a single man in Tucson, I flashed and dashed a lot, but nothing compared to her. Each time she fammed, she kept the pink slip, and she collected quite a few. She once bought an old formal evening dress from Goodwill, stapled all the pink slips to it, and went to a Halloween party as the fam queen.

She called me early one morning and said, "I've got to go to the beach. Wanna go with me?"

"Where we going? LA?"

"Nope. San Diego. Put on your sport coat and tie, and I'll meet you at the airport in an hour." We flew into San Diego, rented a convertible, spent the day at the beach, dined at a fantastic restaurant, and flew home—sort of. Our trip took us through Las Vegas and then Phoenix, and from there we were to fly on to Tucson. We landed in Phoenix at midnight and sat on the airplane waiting to go to Tucson. With all the paying passengers off the aircraft, the flight crew just stared at us, and I looked around to find a now empty airplane.

The fam queen finally asked, "Aren't we going on to Tucson?"

The lead flight attendant responded, "Normally, we would, yes. But we have no paying passengers going to or scheduled out of Tucson tomorrow morning, so this aircraft is spending the night in Phoenix."

Hmm. What now? Fortunately, I was in the company of the fam queen, so we jumped on a flight back to Las Vegas and caught a flight from Vegas directly to Tucson. While waiting for our flight in the Vegas airport, we dined on old pizza at 2:00 a.m. We still laugh about that.

Sadly, the familiarization program was already on the chopping block; 9/11 was merely the final blow. Some in Congress could not tolerate the fact that a few government workers were getting perks they weren't and started an inquiry into the program. I was jump-seating out of LAX one afternoon when a congressman standing three people behind me in line asked why I was riding in the jump seat.

The gate agent told him I was a controller, he was told there were two jump seats and one was available. He then insisted—nearly demanded—that he be allowed to ride in the second jump seat. I watched her handle this jackass as best she could while I stayed as much in the shadows as best I could. Fortunately, I was legal that time with all the appropriate paperwork. A short time later, he and those like him, forced the FAA to reevaluate the benefits of the fam program. But while it lasted, it really did bridge the gap between the cockpit and the radar room and promote good relations between controllers and pilots, seriously. But all good things must come to an end. Congress and the security concerns following 9/11 ended the program.

After certification in the TRACON, I worked for the mandatory one year before I was eligible to bid other facilities. The problem was no one was hiring. So, to expand my résumé, I bid, and was selected, for a staff position called "plans and procedures specialist." All facilities except very small ones have a staff of "plans and procedures" and "quality and training" specialists. The plans and procedures specialist is responsible for conducting airspace management, writing and amending letters of agreement, and planning and implementing changes to air traffic procedures. I accepted the position just as the Tucson tower and TRACON were de-combined at the management level. The facilities had been de-combined at the controller level shortly after I arrived in Tucson, but both facilities had continued to have the same manager, deputy, and administrative staff. When I took the plans and procedures staff position, Pat remained the TRACON manager, and the tower got its own manager.

Towers, TRACONs, and centers work hand in hand through letters of agreement. These letters are legally binding and dictate the manner in which each facility will interface. Operations such as handoff points, altitudes, and aircraft airspeed are all preset to prevent conflicts and facilitate traffic movement.

Remember Air Traffic Control 101? Ground control, local control, TRACON, en-route center, et cetera? The transition points (also known as "handoff" points because aircraft are "handed off" from one controller to another) between each of these environments are all coordinated, and to ensure compliance, they are written in letters of agreements.

The plans and procedures position was a learning experience. Our assistant manager, Monte Gillespie, was a real horse's ass. Just kidding. While I was the procedures specialist, Monte was my immediate supervisor, and every notice, memo, procedure, or research analysis I wrote had to go through him. Nine times out of ten, my work came back in short order with more red ink than the paper could reasonably accommodate—and thus with an attachment stapled to the original. Monte was the most frustrating person I had ever met, and I learned more from him during my staff time than I ever imagined possible. His standard response to every question was "What does the book say?" When I could quote the book, he'd ask, "What do you think that means?" Monte taught me to think about changes critically, and my writing improved dramatically. All written submissions were methodically taken apart and put back together again until they were bulletproof. If there was a hole in one of my procedures, Monte found it. Instead of pointing out the problem, he simply returned the document, saying, "It needs work." I had to find the hole. Working for Monte, I learned to research, analyze, and apply new and amended procedures to our operation.

When the tower and TRACON separated at the management level, all our letters of agreement became void and needed renegotiation with the signatories—thirteen of them to be exact. I, with the support of Monte's red pen, renegotiated them all. I learned more about how to protect my ass during this job than I had in all my time in the Philippines. Once signatories to the letters of agreement found out they were now void and open to renegotiation, they took advantage of my compromised position. I learned to tiptoe around the fact that the agreements were now void, telling signatories that I was updating the letters. Everyone, even the new tower manager, tried to take advantage, and we got wrapped around the axle quickly. Monte did come to my rescue on this issue.

The tower manager insisted that a particular operational issue was our (the TRACON's) responsibility, and I insisted it was his. He was trying to pawn off responsibility because the tower had already signed its now-renegotiated letter of agreement with the 162nd Fighter Group (Air Force F-16 squadron) and didn't want to reopen it. He pushed me too far, and after a heated exchange, I literally told him to kiss my ass. Can you say insubordination? Monte heard about the exchange before I made it back to the TRACON and asked for my side of the story. We discussed it, and he agreed to back me up by picking up the phone, calling the tower manager, and saying, literally, "Kiss our asses," and then hanging up. Monte supported me, and I really appreciated it.

To this point in my ATC career, I had worked for managers and supervisors who were stellar. Some of the best were at Tucson tower/TRACON. Our manager, Patrick O'Sullivan, embodied the philosophy of supporting the controller workforce, letting the controllers do their jobs, and being their wall, preventing crap from flying into the control room. More than once, when he was in his office with the supervisors behind closed doors, I heard Pat state, loudly, "Leave the controllers alone!" He was a controller's manager.

During my one-year tour in the tower, my supervisor, Jim "Pops" Kaiser, pulled me aside and asked how I was doing. "Okay, Pops. Why?" I was going through a divorce with Karen, who remained in Ventura, and it was frustrating to admit to myself that another marriage had collapsed. Pops saw this.

On one of my Fridays, shortly before the end of the shift, he took me to the back of the tower and told me to sign on as controller in charge. I did, and he left the tower and returned a short time later with a folder. Opening the folder, I realized immediately that it contained fam paperwork signed by Pat, yet none of the particulars were filled out. In other words, I had authorization to go wherever I wanted, in the jump seat, on any participating airline, and return when I wanted. Stunned, I just looked at Pops.

He calmly whispered, "Take a week off, go somewhere, and come back when your head is screwed on straight. Call me this weekend and let me know how you're doing. If you need more time, let me know."

"Jim, we're shorthanded," I said.

"Let me worry about staffing. That's what I get paid to do. Go, sort things out, and come back ready to work."

That's leadership. Pat's philosophy was simple: manage money, lead people. Our supervisors followed Pat's lead. I went to Jacksonville and spent a week with Scotty and Tippy. Spending time with them made a world of difference.

In the meantime, a military operating area (MOA) north of Tucson was about to be decommissioned when the Williams Air Force Base was closed. The 162nd Fighter Group used that MOA daily, but Williams Air Force Base was the designated owner of the MOA. So when Willy closed, the MOA would go away unless another group stepped up and assumed ownership. According to the rules, if the MOA was not renegotiated, certified, and activated in a certain period of time (six months, I think), it would disappear, and a new one would need to be created. Creating an MOA would mean years of environmental impact studies costing millions of dollars, so we were under the gun. It was a major project, and as the Tucson TRACON procedures specialist, I represented our interests during the restructuring. It was another enormous learning experience that got me a ride in an F-16. Some of us put in more than a few extra hours getting the job done, and to show his appreciation, the 162nd Fighter Group executive officer got us a ride. It was one that I will never forget. I pulled 9 Gs and got the "9 G" pin to prove it.

In accordance with standard FAA procedures, I attended "airspace management" school, a three-week course designed to teach prospective plans and procedures specialists everything they would need to know: airspace design, instrument routings, transitional routings, how to create holding patterns, how to create a standard instrument approach and standard instrument departure procedure. I learned how to write a letter of agreement, a notice, a memo and the differences among them. It was a very informative three weeks except for one little thing: I attended the class thirteen months after I had taken the Tucson TRACON plans and procedures specialist job and two months before I went back to the control room as a controller. I had already learned the entire curriculum by attending the University of Monte and could have taught the course with nothing but a red pen.

My time at Tucson was a hell of a lot of fun. I met some incredible people. Juan Fuentes was born and raised in Puerto Rico and had the accent to prove it. He also had a master's degree in airport management and was a very good controller, and I could easily see him in management. Juan wasn't known to be a prankster, but his mischievous streak showed up every now and then. One Thanksgiving Day, Juan, Tony, CJ, Lon Chaney, and I were holding down the fort. Since there was no air traffic to speak of, all the sectors were combined, and Chaney was the only controller actually talking to airplanes. An Aeroméxico DC-9 left Tucson heading south, and Chaney asked Juano how to say "Happy Thanksgiving" in Spanish. Juan explained that there really was no way to say it, but he came up with something anyway. Chaney practiced the phrase a few times, and as he switched the Aeroméxico to Albuquerque center, he uttered the words as best he could. With no immediate reply from the Aeroméxico, Chaney began to believe that something was up and maybe he'd been had.

Aeroméxico finally acknowledged the frequency change, although very hesitantly. Curious but wary, Chaney looked at a now grinning Juano and posed the inevitable question. "What did I just say?"

Juan said, "Well I *told* you, man, there is no way to say Happy Thanksgiving in Spanish."

"So what did I say?" Chaney repeated.

"Well, you said, 'Have a happy day, turkey.'"

When I first moved to Tucson, I lived in an apartment directly across from two women, Carol and Pam. We became good friends in every sense of the platonic word. One evening, Carol introduced me to Roseanne. Roseanne and I dated for five years before getting married, and we married then only because her boss frowned on our cohabitation, offering to give her the day off if we exchanged vows. So we did, in a downtown Tucson bar on a Friday afternoon while our brother-in-law, friends, and family toasted the union with shots of tequila. Very southern Arizona. Later that evening, the entire wedding party was "asked" to leave the bar. With a beginning like that, things could only get better. And for the most part, they did.

I inherited a medical condition from my dad, who inherited it from my grandmother. The condition, iritis (an inflammation of the iris), along with getting older, caught up with me. After ten years of a bad medical situation getting worse, the flight surgeon finally deemed me a hazard to aviation and pulled my medical certification. I discussed things with a few doctors, specialists in the area, and was convinced that my career talking to airplanes was over. I was nearly finished with college and had a good deal of experience outside of just talking to airplanes, so I accepted the situation as fate and moved on.

My tour at Tucson, as well as my career in the FAA as a controller, ended unceremoniously. I had lived an exciting and eventful life as a controller, but being a good sailor, I knew it was time to chart another course.

8

THE ACADEMY

The Headaches Are Gone, but the Voices Are Back

I didn't realize it at the time, but the FAA, outside of the field, is made up predominantly of contractors. Instructor duty at the Mike Monroney Aeronautical Center in Oklahoma City was my first experience working for the FAA but not as an FAA employee. I had been to the academy twice during my career: the Radar Training Facility and airspace management school. It's located smack in the center of the United States, Oklahoma City, Oklahoma, where the wind comes sweeping down the plains and logging chains double as airport wind socks. Nearly all of the FAA schools, some research and development, some flight-check folks, and the Civil Aeromedical Institute (now the Civil Aerospace Medical Institute) doctors are located at the academy. The Radar Training Facility had two parts: TRACON and center. There also was a division that trained tower controllers, but I was hired to teach the TRACON. Luckily for me, controller time was a fundamental requirement to be an FAA Academy instructor.

Step one was to certify at the academy radar facility, seriously. Just like in the field, all instructors had to certify at the academy radar facility before training to be an instructor. And there were a few who didn't make it. I mention this to controller buddies still in the field, and they laugh, but it was pretty difficult for some of the FAA retirees. Since most of the instructors were contractors, we were all retired

FAA controllers, no military. Some contract instructors had been in management for years before retirement and had worked at low-level facilities. With the combination of very little traffic at those facilities and minimal, if any, requirements to maintain up-to-date field training, it really shouldn't have been a big surprise that we had controllers who washed out while trying to become instructors.

Step two, certifying in the academics room, was a humbling experience. Most controllers, at one time or another, had stood in front of two or three trainees who had just arrived at the facility and taught air traffic control procedures and policies inherent to that facility. However, at the academy, there were twenty-four faces in a class, nearly all of whom knew virtually nothing about radar air traffic control, and the instructor had to teach from the book, which was the critical element.

Controllers in the field scoff at being intimidated by the experience of standing in front of a class and teaching, but they've always taught in the field and taught the local procedures. At the academy, all that changed. Instructors must teach the book, going by the letter of the book. And to do that, they must know the book inside and out. Most controllers learn the book while in training and don't open it again for extended periods of time after certification. Also, the book is complete and vast. Controllers in the field learn the portions that apply strictly to their operation and may never review other parts. Brain surgeons are not qualified to operate on the heart for a reason. At the academy, instructors had to learn it all and be familiar enough to speak intelligently on every subject. When the instructor was stumped by a student, the only intelligent answer was "Let's see what the book has to say."

It is popular in the field to say, "The book says this, but it's all bullshit, and we couldn't move traffic the way we do if we followed the book." In some cases that's true; in others, it's just idiots being idiots, and I will openly admit to being one of those idiots before my time at the academy. The point is, there has to be a standard of operation. Period. That's what the book is for. If a controller works airplanes by the book, he or she can never go wrong, no matter what happens. If a situation turns to crap because the book was followed, it's management's problem. They'll have to answer for it. Deviation from the book was standard practice in the field and was usually justified with an egotistical, smart-aleck remark. Very controlleresque. But, a controller could be burned by not following the book and a smart-aleck remark is not going to change that.

Certifying in the radar simulation room was another requirement. While training for certification in the simulator room, new instructors were also required to continue the normal classroom syllabus with a normal class of students. It was a good idea, and the intent was to refresh instructors while familiarizing them with the training syllabus. There is one point I want to emphasize about the FAA and the academy: I have never, ever met one single person who did not rank every class at the academy with highest marks. At the academy, during downtime, the FAA encouraged us to attend other classes. Very few took advantage of this opportunity, but I did every chance I got. Every course I took at the academy was top-notch, and I would grade them as A+ for content, instruction, and equipment. Every controller I know agrees with this assessment.

I completed training, took my check ride, and received an instructor certification. However, as with nearly all my air traffic certifications, the first class I taught without a net was rather humbling. This is a good time to address an issue that everyone brings up immediately after finding out I was a controller: stress. Previously, I used the teenager/McDonald's analogy to illustrate a stressful situation but not the effects: panic attacks. I spoke with a number of friends about panic attacks, so the following information is confirmed by many air traffic controllers.

Having complete control of an air traffic control situation is referred to as "having the flick." By the book, during a position relief (one controller taking over for another controller), the controller who is currently signed on and responsible for the position is required to follow a step-by-step procedure to ensure that all issues are addressed and that accurate and complete information is exchanged between controllers. Usually, the controller being relieved will follow a checklist and ask, "You got it?"—"it" meaning "the flick." If the answer is "Yep!" the relieved controller slides their chair back, allowing the relieving controller to belly up to the radar or tower position. The now-relieved controller will watch for a few minutes until everyone is comfortable with the situation.

What does having the flick have to do with panic attacks? Typically, a panic attack occurs when a controller loses the flick. A controller panic attack begins prior to the loss of the flick. And, on occasion, immediately following assuming a position brief. Sometimes this happens very slowly, and controllers refer to it as "going down the tubes" because that is exactly what it's like: slowly descending into a dark tube. A controller is ever so slowly overloaded with more and more airplanes and falls farther and farther behind until all control is lost.

Air traffic control requires a controller to stay two, three, even four steps ahead of the situation. When a controller has the flick, he or she is waiting for pilots to reply to instructions so that the next instruction can be issued. Things cannot happen fast enough. Staying on top of a very busy traffic session is exhilarating. The adrenaline rush is amazing and even addicting.

For the most part, controllers are egotists. Although this characteristic has mellowed with age, it is still persistent in me, so I know it is in others. Despite being egotists, controllers are open with each other about losing control. Some controllers have a natural talent and make it look easy, and I often wondered if these controllers ever had panic attacks. Amazingly, all controllers I have talked to, even the naturally gifted, have admitted to panic attacks at some time in their careers. The panic attacks generally occur shortly after certification, when controllers work by themselves for the first time. During this period, the comfort level is low. Controllers know they can work the heaviest traffic that even the busiest, most complex facility has to offer, but their confidence level is at its lowest at this time, which opens the door for panic attacks. Controllers must work traffic at the 80 percent level during certification. In other words, if the busiest traffic an airport handles is one hundred operations (arrivals and/or departures) in an hour, controllers must work at least eighty operations an hour during their check ride. Controllers routinely train on traffic levels of 100 percent prior to receiving a recommendation for certification, so the volume is nothing new.

Personally, I think panic attacks are rooted in confidence, and confidence is rooted in experience. A batter in the fifth inning of a baseball game will have a great deal more confidence than he had facing the same pitcher in the first inning. By this time, he has seen all the pitches in a pitcher's arsenal and has the ability to differentiate a fastball from a changeup by the spin on the ball. The key is to see the spin early and adjust immediately. It is the same with air traffic control. Recognizing a bad situation and adjusting accordingly is essential to handling the traffic and preventing a panic attack.

Panic attacks diminish greatly as time turns to experience, but they still raise their ugly heads on occasion. Controllers tolerate them but never get accustomed to them. Panic attacks are the worst part of the job, absolutely and without question.

With so many different schools at the academy, I got to see a number of old friends and made a few new ones. One of the new friends was Mark "High Speed" Washam. High Speed was attending a facility manager's class, and David Dodd called one afternoon asking me to find Mark and take care of him. David and Mark had met while working in Los Angeles tower, which was where Mark had earned his nickname "High Speed."

Large, very busy airports such as Los Angeles have taxiways that are angled, allowing landing aircraft to exit the runway at a higher rate of speed. The taxiways are aptly named "high-speed taxiways." Mark was training in LA tower on the local position, clearing aircraft to land and take off, when he loaded the runway with a departing aircraft while waiting for the landing aircraft to slow down and exit the runway—a squeeze play.

The key to a successful squeeze play is encouraging the landing aircraft to exit the runway as soon as possible, allowing time for the departing aircraft, now on the runway, to spool up and gain enough speed to become airborne. To ensure a squeeze play works, a controller will typically issue an encouraging reminder to the landing aircraft, such as "Turn right at the first high speed; landing traffic is on short final. Additional aircraft holding in position ready for departure." Although at airports such as Los Angeles and Chicago, this amounts to a statement of the obvious, it serves as a poke in the butt to the cockpit crew, emphasizing the fact that dawdling on the runway will screw another aircraft, and the next time, the screwee could be thee.

LIFE WITH A VIEW

I don't remember all the particulars, but despite Mark's best efforts, the landing pilot missed the first high-speed taxiway, and a now desperate and pissed-off Mark reissued the instruction, adding an extra adjective for effect. "Turn right at the next fucking high speed!"

David Dodd was the tower supervisor, and his gasp led a chorus of others—from everyone but Mark. Afterward, he honestly didn't remember uttering the word. Even after tapes were pulled and replayed, Mark refused to believe he had committed the foul. When asked what he had to say for himself, Mark replied in typical Mark fashion. "Well, he made the next *fucking* high speed, didn't he?" No one complained, so all was forgiven, and forevermore, Mark would answer to "High Speed."

Mark was only one of the good friends I made while at the academy. During my first six months as an instructor, nearly all classes were made up of PATCO rehires. Typically, they were rehired back to their former facility, spent a few weeks there taking care of paperwork and reorientation, and then arrived at the academy for radar school. Radar school was nearly three weeks long, with half the time spent in academics, learning policies and procedures, and the other half spent in radar simulation. Each class was composed of twenty-four students and was split in half during the simulation phase. Twelve students trained on simulation in the morning, and the other twelve trained in the evening (3:00 p.m. to 11:00 p.m.).

The PATCO folks gave me insight into the strike and, more importantly, the effects of the strike. I attended after-class reunions at a local watering hole and, like a fly on the wall, listened to them tell their stories while catching up on old times. For whatever reason, the FAA had rehired many of the PATCO controllers right back into their old facilities and pretty much all at the same time. The after-class debriefs reminded me of high school reunions, which is what they really were. The strike—or more accurately, the aftermath of it sent this brotherhood to all points of the earth. Air traffic control was the particle binding their lives together, and like a formula, an extra particle introduced at just the right time (the strike) had catastrophic results.

On that day in August 1981, as I stood in my living room, orders to Guam in one hand and FAA test results in the other, I could not have cared less about the PATCO strikers. To me, and to the majority of

Americans, they were unappreciative adults acting like spoiled children. Sixteen years later, they were grateful to have the opportunity to talk to airplanes once again, and the vast majority had learned valuable life lessons. Although many of them had struggled to survive during the sixteen years since the strike, some had landed on their feet and now had given up very fruitful occupations to return to air traffic control.

I don't know if all PATCO rehires returned under the same circumstances, but everyone I met had the same story. The FAA had rehired them as GS-11s at the bottom end of the pay scale. Those fired from LAX, Chicago, and comparable facilities had been GS-13s and GS-14s. That's a huge salary difference. They would soon be working side by side with controllers who were a lot younger and making a lot more money. Obviously, this didn't sit well with the PATCO folks, but it was only one of the bones of contention. The biggest was the stigma attached to being fired for striking. It followed them everywhere and still does. Many of them told me that getting a job had been nearly impossible when their résumé showed their last employer to be the FAA and last job to be air traffic controller. But of all the uphill battles they had fought in sixteen years, the biggest was still in front of them.

PATCO rehires reentered the FAA at the bottom of the pay scale, with virtually no seniority and no vacation or sick leave, and they had to conform to the powers that be, which included the new controller union, the National Air Traffic Controllers Association (NATCA). NATCA had taken over the duties of the now-defunct PATCO and had represented the controller workforce very well. In my estimation, the vast majority of PATCO rehires were content to go to work, talk to airplanes, and go home. But not all of them.

One afternoon, a former PATCO big cheese who had just been rehired returned to the academy to say hi to some instructors and offered to give a pep talk to a group of PATCO rehires attending radar training school. The Radar Training Facility's lead instructor accepted his offer, believing it would be beneficial to the rehires. But what followed was not a pep talk or even a briefing, but more of a fire-and-brimstone disaster. This guy had been one of the leaders of the PATCO strike from the West Coast, and he was one of those people whose attitudes and emotions about the strike had not mellowed with age. Rather, his feelings had simmered, boiled down, and fermented to a concentrated gravy of absolute hate, for everyone—the FAA, management, and especially those of us who had been hired after the strike.

He didn't sugarcoat his hate of the FAA in general, or of management in particular, stating that "they" had not changed in sixteen years. He was a teeny bit discreet when it came to the present-day controller workforce. Beginning with management, he simply asserted that it was composed of the same people who had ruined his life and that of every other honest, hardworking air traffic controller, which was only partially true. By this time, a large portion of FAA management, especially at the first and second levels, were poststrike controllers. Management who had stayed after the strike had moved up either into the facility manager ranks or into the regional office/headquarters positions and had been replaced by poststrike folks. The point is, his complaint was unfounded; we (the poststrike hires) *were* management. Members of the controller workforce who hadn't participated in the strike had become upper-level management. The ax he had to grind was with first-level management or supervisors, but the prestrike supervisors were mostly retired. He could have complained that the counterproductive principles leading to the strike were still there, but instead he focused on people who weren't involved.

The PATCO rehire effort commenced after I left the FAA, so I never experienced the rehire bitterness. But I was told there was some animosity among the poststrike workforce toward the rehires. I think it began as apprehension and evolved into animosity.

Under the administration of President Bill Clinton and the tenure of FAA Administrator, Jane Garvey, controllers were getting enormous pay raises. Controller staffing at historically understaffed facilities was at an all-time high, and management had been neutered by the Garvey administration. Yet something was aggravating controllers, and I couldn't put my finger on it. In the navy they told us that "a bitching sailor is a happy sailor." Maybe the controller workforce was just really happy.

Apparently, controllers were taking out their frustrations on each other. Our PATCO orator described situations in which a controller who had animosity for another controller would hand that other controller a "deal," or a loss of separation. Instead of recognizing conflicts and resolving the problem by issuing a speed adjustment, a heading, or an altitude change, the instigator just ignored it and handed the aircraft off anyway. This would have been absolutely inconceivable when I was in the field. There were controllers who didn't get along with other controllers, but the issues were always restricted to the break room.

Second, he claimed the poststrike controller workforce was anti-PATCO rehires. There might have been a degree of legitimacy to this claim, but for very good reasons. Many of the rehires tried to instill their way of thinking in the poststrike workforce. Their attempts were met with a great deal of pushback, logically. The existing controller workforce was not about to roll over and let PATCO assume control.

This PATCO controller started his speech slowly but built his rage and condemnation into a crescendo that would have made my First Baptist Church of Conroe preacher very proud. As bad as the rhetoric was, the foul language was the kicker. Evidently, some of the contract instructors who had known him during the good old days attended the speech with their wives. These women were not controllers and should have been given a certain amount of respect when it came to colorful language, but this guy was on a roll and had no control over his enthusiasm. I stood in a corner watching the display and began to look around the room at the FAA instructors and take notice of their responses, which were unanimous: sheer terror bordering on utter panic. Their faces all screamed, *What the hell have we done?*

This guy was a loose cannon, and at the end of his diatribe, which lasted about thirty minutes, the room was split down the middle: half of the audience wanting to put as much distance between themselves and this guy as possible and the other half ready to take up arms and finish the fight that had started sixteen years earlier. I was astonished and felt terrible for the lead instructor. This display, the accusations, the foul language, and the insinuations could very well have devastating effects if someone filed a complaint resulting in an investigation. I pulled the lead instructor aside later and attempted to discuss it, but he wouldn't, which was probably exactly the right response. I don't know what was said among the FAA instructors behind closed doors. I was a contractor and therefore was rightfully kept out of the loop on this one, but somehow, someway, the episode never saw the light of day. It was a dirty bomb that never went off. If it had, the fallout could have been far and wide. There was no way anyone who was present at that talk could write off the PATCO rehire's actions and words as merely an act of blowing off steam or as an innocent but overzealous illustration of the difficulties the PATCO rehires were about to face. This guy was spoiling for a fight and recruiting an army.

The incident blew over, and no mention was ever made of it again. I spoke with a female FAA instructor who was present, and she confided that she was very offended, but filing a complaint would have meant bringing charges against the lead instructor, who assuredly would have taken a big fall for his lack of insight. The FAA instructors were at the academy checking off a box in hopes of moving up in the agency and knew it was them against the world, so they stuck together. The wives didn't say anything because their husbands would be named in the investigation. Most of the students were just happy to be back in the FAA after sixteen years and were not going to do anything to rock the boat. As far as the contract instructors were concerned, "What speech?" Contractors were expendable and were routinely used as cannon fodder or scapegoats. When in doubt, fire a contractor. Everyone had a very good reason to keep their mouth shut. Last I heard, the instigator had gone back to Southern California and continued his campaign.

I spent two years at the academy, one as an instructor and the other as a consultant advising on training issues. It was time well spent, and I learned a lot about the FAA, air traffic control, and life in general. I watched a few of the PATCO rehires filter their way above the controller level, but I believe their decision on that day in August 1981 stayed with them, limiting career progression. I find it amazing that one decision could have such a profound and lasting effect on an entire life. They didn't commit rape or murder; they just had bad judgment.

Some people call controllers arrogant, and some call them confident. I must admit to wondering where the line is drawn.

9

THE NATIONAL AIR TRAFFIC CONTROLLERS ASSOCIATION

A Pit Bull Named Chardonnay

To accurately discuss and understand NATCA, we have to start with the air traffic controllers strike of 1981. I've researched the events, but as with most historic events, attitudes, opinions, and emotions, combined with the passage of time, have clouded memories and diluted some issues while concentrating others. Contrary to popular opinion, time does not always heal all wounds, and there are many that remain deeply embedded even after all these years, on both sides. I knew an FAA air traffic control facility manager who stated very clearly that he would retire before a former PATCO member walked back into his facility. And I believed him.

The Professional Air Traffic Controllers Organization was composed of a group of talented, hardworking, and dedicated people who, by and large, acted foolishly. They were not dumb or stupid but foolish. In the early 1980s, with the economy down, engineers with MBAs were working the drive-thru at fast-food joints. Meanwhile, the average PATCO controller was earning the same salary that an engineer would have, had engineers been employed as engineers, and yet most controllers possessed merely a high school education. Also, PATCO was led by a professional union guy who didn't understand the occupation, who didn't fully fathom the implications of what he was contemplating or the reaction of the general public.

Essentially, in 1981 the economy was in the toilet. The Carter administration had left Reagan with double-digit inflation, double-digit unemployment, and double-digit interest rates. Year after year, money was worth less due to inflation, so even if you had a job and got a pay raise, chances were you took a pay cut because the raise was less than the rate of inflation. A lot of people didn't even have jobs and gladly would have sacrificed a pay raise for gainful employment. For those who did have a job, a house was out of reach because of prohibitive interest rates. This information is critical in painting a picture of the public attitude.

Without public support and with the resulting pressure on Reagan and Congress, the strike was doomed to failure before it got off the ground. The fatal paper cut, though, was an overlooked (or ignored) law forbidding air traffic controllers from striking against the federal government. When controllers accept a job with the FAA, they raise their hand and swear to the Almighty above not to strike or support a strike under penalty of law. I know—I raised my hand and signed the paperwork that came with it. Hence, the union buffoon led his Kool-Aid-drinking followers down Reagan Boulevard, past the "road closed" sign, and off the cliff. Lemmings and swan dives just go together.

I write this in a somewhat condescending and seemingly unsympathetic manner, but in reality, the whole situation was sad. I applied to the FAA in 1981 and scored in the upper nineties on the exam. To this day, I thank God in my prayers every night that I wasn't hired before the strike and did not have to make the decision to strike or stay. If I had been hired, I probably would have been in training during that period, making the decision even more difficult. A controller's career is most vulnerable while they are in training. Instructors must recommend certification; therefore, certification is dependent as much on satisfying the instructor as it is on the controller's abilities. Instructors routinely tell controllers-in-training to work the traffic the way they want, not in a manner the controller believes will make the instructor happy (and cause the instructor to recommend the controller for certification). This concept is great in theory, but human nature dictates that controllers adjust their plans to accommodate the instructor.

For instance, while at Tucson approach control, I had two instructors whose techniques were completely opposite. Mike Dorso believed in sharing the big picture and his game plan with the pilots, resulting in a lot of transmissions. Mike Schrock believed in making only the minimum transmissions necessary and believed it wasn't important to share the big picture or his plan with the pilots. Consequently, when I trained with each one, I adjusted my technique to mimic theirs, believing they would be impressed and would recommend me for certification sooner.

There are two fundamental elements to air traffic control: (1) procedures—the rules and regulations in the book—and (2) technique, the manner in which a controller applies those procedures. Although it is strictly prohibited for instructors to critique technique, there is a David Dodd-ism that air traffic control instructors share with their trainees: "You have no technique, so until you get some, we're gonna use mine."

Being a trainee meant conforming at all levels. A trainee who rocks the boat is asking for trouble. It was not uncommon for a trainee to open their locker and find an application for a manager's job at a fast-food joint with a sticky note attached stating, "Don't buy a house." It was part of the indoctrination process, but for a trainee who was struggling, it was very intimidating. NASCAR fans refer to Dale Earnhardt Sr. as "the Intimidator," but air traffic control instructors could have taught him more than a few tricks. When you're working twenty airplanes, each filled with between 130 and 300 souls, all converging on one point in space, and you are watching your game plan fall apart, losing the flick—while your instructor calmly leans over and whispers, "How are you going to explain to ten-year-old Timmy why Grandma won't be visiting after all?"—you learn what intimidation really is. Driving a stock car at 180 miles per hour is not easy, but at least there's a roll cage. There are no steel bars between you and your instructor. The intimidation factor played a very important role in training. Not only was it a screening or weeding-out process; it also indicated to an instructor your ability to maintain sound judgment and make intelligent decisions while under extreme pressure.

The ability to work heavy traffic was only one critical element in the certification process. Equally important was situational awareness, or the ability to recognize your limitations by knowing when the traffic or other compounding situations were creating a hazardous environment, prompting you to ask for help. Many controllers viewed asking for help as a sign of weakness and refused to do it. I never had that problem. My favorite remark was "Hey, you! Not doing anything? Grab a headset, plug in, and coordinate for me before I kill someone!" Believe it or not, it is possible to have a loss of separation even with only one airplane. Violating a minimum vectoring altitude (MVA) restriction by descending an aircraft to eight thousand feet in a nine-thousand-foot MVA was just one way. But due to unrelenting foresight and a firm understanding of my limitations, I never lost separation with just one aircraft. No matter what any of my controller buddies say about my talent, or lack thereof, they can't take that away from me.

If I had been in the FAA during the strike, I probably would have been a trainee. If I had walked, I would have been fired too. Or if I had not walked, and things had turned out differently, I would have been perceived as a "scab," would have been blackballed, and never would have made it through training. So I ultimately would have been fired anyway. Sadly, these people really believed in the PATCO president and didn't think he would take them into harm's way.

The critical elements of the strike's failure are simple. One, it had no public support. Two, there was a new president who had shown support for PATCO during the campaign that had led to his election but who was known to be a hardliner when pushed. And three, the strike broke the law. It was a felony. PATCO was asking for, among other things, an across-the-board pay raise of $10,000 and a thirty-two-hour workweek, but it focused its appeal to the general public on the need for new and better equipment. Obviously, the FAA and the Reagan administration focused the attention on the money issue. Many Americans would have been happy to have a job and viewed the controllers as ingrates, not realizing how fortunate they were to have secure jobs while asking for an enormous (by 1981 standards) pay raise. Therefore, no public support. Love him or hate him, Reagan was a no-shit kind of guy. The Iranians were not intimidated by Carter but damn well feared Reagan. He convinced the Iranians during his presidential campaign that he would take serious, immediate action regarding the hostages, which resulted in their release on Reagan's day of inauguration. If that wasn't a "screw you" to Jimmy Carter, I don't know what would be.

Finally, PATCO swore not to strike and knew it was against the law to do so. How do you justify walking out when you agreed to the terms of employment? Reagan capitalized on this point by making public, over and over again. One PATCO controller refused to walk because, as he put it, he couldn't tell his kids to obey and respect the law if he broke it by striking.

I met a number of PATCO rehires while teaching at the FAA Academy. Their attitudes and poststrike stories ran the gamut. Most were tickled pink to be back and heading to the field to talk to airplanes again, but some were still very bitter. The vast majority were (and are) very good people and very good controllers, and I have personal relationships with a few of them.

I attribute their actions to a lack of contact with average people. I am a second-generation controller, and my dad worked at one of the en-route centers. Centers typically have a contingent of around three hundred controllers. When I was growing up, my dad and mom were in controller bowling leagues, attended controller parties, and associated with other controller's families.

The way I see it, the poststrike controllers are, as a whole, above average in intelligence and typically spent four years in the military immediately after high school before going to work for the FAA. The vast majority never went to college and worked in a very narrowly defined, complex occupation. The FAA was an environment dominated by a military mentality. Birds of a feather flock together, and it was natural for this group of people to gravitate towards one another. They all came from the military and performed duties that were very difficult to explain to the average accountant over a can of Schlitz at a backyard Fourth of July barbecue. The PATCO controllers had everything in common with one another: wives, kids, prior military experience, and a complicated-to-explain occupation. The downside was a set of dominating beliefs: "no one else can do what we do" and "they can't fire us all." Hint: John F. Kennedy, the most powerful man in the world, was dead only a few hours before he was replaced. PATCO and the strike were doomed before the strike started. They walked, Reagan fired them, and the rest is history.

Ironically, the strike couldn't have happened at a better time, statistically speaking. It came during a recession in the US economy. And when it happened, the FAA was prepared for it. Years before, PATCO had organized a national sick-out to show the FAA it had power. The sick-out went as planned but backfired very badly. The sick-out clearly illustrated to the FAA that it was vulnerable. So the FAA began to staff management at record levels—supervisors, assistant managers, and staff at regional offices and headquarters. Why? Management were not PATCO. However, realistically, there was no way management could staff the controller ranks in the event of a strike. So where would the other ten or eleven thousand controllers come from? Easy. The military.

The FAA, with the cooperation of the Department of Defense, developed a plan to use military controllers as a stopgap measure in the event of a controller strike. In August 1981, those measures were put into effect. The FAA was more than prepared for a foolish attempt to bring down the nation's most effective and efficient mode of commerce. Ironically, PATCO had committed suicide with the sick-out. I know. My dad was working at a center at the time and had an appointment to have his wisdom teeth removed, arranged and approved months before, and he caught hell for taking sick leave. A PATCO member, he left the union shortly thereafter because PATCO refused to stick up for him and instead linked him to the cause.

With the economy in recession, air travel was down, making "spooling up" to work at Los Angeles, Chicago, Dallas / Fort Worth, and Atlanta easier, but definitely not easy. Military air traffic control is a lot easier than civilian air traffic control. Military controllers who have never worked traffic in the FAA will argue this point, but ignore them; they don't know what they are talking about. Any former military controller who went to work for the FAA at any of the busiest airports in the United States will set them straight. Why? Military controllers, with very few exceptions, work military airplanes that have military pilots. Military pilots go through extensive training, are very well-qualified to fly in all sorts of weather, and fly airplanes that are, fundamentally, comparable in speed and mix very well. Believe it or not, F-16s and C-141s are relatively compatible. Civilian FAA controllers, on the other hand, work with a very wide variety of aircraft, including some that cannot exceed 100 knots and others that can easily maintain 250 knots at very low altitudes. The qualifications of the pilots vary just as greatly, making the environment much more complex than the military environment. Military controllers who argue the point do so because they have not experienced the difference. I know because I was one of them who thought the transition would be a simple one.

With the recession, air traffic was reduced, making the transition for military controllers easier. Even so, Reagan initially reduced air traffic by as much as 50 percent to ensure safety during the training and spooling-up process. Controllers who came in after the strike had discipline from the military, enthusiasm for the job, and incentive in the form of an enormous pay raise. GS-14 pay (in 1981 about $55,000) was a hell of a lot more than E-5 pay (about $12,000). The military mentality brought with it another aspect that was crucial: very high standards. Washout rates at the busiest airports were in the neighborhood of 50 percent and sometimes higher. This was a double-edged sword. On one hand, the quality of the average controller was very high; on the other hand, such a high washout rate, especially at the airports in areas with a high cost of living, made staffing extremely difficult. The money was appealing, but the level of traffic and the high cost of living were prohibitive to many. It just wasn't worth it.

The PATCO controllers had been fired. They had violated the law by going out on strike, and Reagan had fired them. This is a very important distinction because many of them were adamant about returning to the controller ranks as though nothing had happened—no harm, no foul, and therefore, no penalty. Many PATCO rehires expressed to me personally that they saw their situation as a "reinstatement" and not a rehire. The difference is, a reinstatement would bring along with it a return of benefits and privileges that were previously enjoyed, as opposed to being forfeited. The three main issues were sick leave, annual leave, and probably most importantly, seniority.

The average PATCO controller lost a lot—a whole lot—of sick and annual leave. It was not unusual to have hundreds of hours of sick leave and a few weeks to a month or more of annual (vacation) leave. These were all forfeited when the PATCO controllers were fired. The big issue, however, was seniority. Seniority dictated a controller's days off, the pecking order for summer vacation, and even which shifts a controller would work. Controllers submit a request for two weeks of summer vacation just like everyone else, and seniority determines who gets the first, second, and third pick and so on. Days off are the same. The rehired PATCO controllers lost sixteen years of seniority, making them junior to the vast majority of the poststrike workforce. So the PATCO controllers walked back in the door well out of their prime at the bottom of the pay scale, with no leave on the books and no seniority. Many of them were given crappy days off, such as Wednesday and Thursday.

From the very start, the PATCO controllers wanted to change all that and viewed the Clinton administration rehire as remedying a mistake and making them whole again. Their logic dictated that annual and sick leave they had on the books when fired, should be reinstated and their seniority adjusted, which obviously pissed off the poststrike workforce. The poststrike workforce had earned their seniority fair and square and, to my knowledge, held no animosity toward the PATCO rehires until issues such as this emerged. Additionally, many of the PATCO union officials wasted no time assessing the NATCA situation and decided it desperately needed to be rescued by the only people qualified to do so: PATCO rehires.

I was out of the FAA and teaching at the academy when the PATCO rehire effort was at its peak, but my friends (many at major airports) told me about the PATCO antics in the field. Even after sixteen years, they were still controllers, and a select few asserted themselves in a controlleresque manner, believing that they had been given an opportunity to redeem their dignity now that the big misunderstanding was finally cleared up. The PATCO controllers could finally return to business as usual, which was to turn management inside out, except for one itty-bitty problem. The PATCO rehires honestly believed that they were senior and knew more than the NATCA controllers did about running a union and dealing with management, even though *everything* had changed in sixteen years, including attitudes, personnel, and philosophies. But those changes didn't seem to register with the former PATCO controllers. You can't blame the PATCO controllers, though; arrogance is part of the identity of a controller, and controllers are not known for being humble.

Working with the PATCO rehires at the academy was equally enjoyable and frustrating. Many walked up to me after class, shook my hand, and voiced their appreciation for my efforts—an event that rarely, if ever, happened in the field. It was very inspirational. Studies indicate that people would rather be verbally acknowledged for their performance than receive monetary compensation. I don't know how accurate that study is—I kind of like money myself—but their gesture was appreciated.

On the other hand, some rehires just didn't care. Many, during training at the academy, didn't study the airspace, frequencies, or procedures, so consequently, we (the instructors) wrote critiques that would be embarrassing to most people, but not these guys. In the radar simulation labs, they ran aircraft one and a half miles apart, when three miles was the minimum separation, and laughed about it, shouting, "Too close for missiles—switching to guns." No wonder they had been fired. Sixteen years later, and they were still didn't realize how fortunate they were. I was told a fair number of them washed out at the facilities to which they returned, but most, certified and contributed to the operation with enthusiasm.

After the strike, PATCO had collapsed. With no employed dues-paying members and millions in fines, the plug was pulled and life support terminated. Time went by, and even the die-hard PATCO members finally succumbed to the inevitable admission that their actions had had life-altering effects they would have to live with, and it was time to get on with the immediate business of pursuing a new career.

It was only a matter of time before a new union emerged. In the mid-1980s the National Air Traffic Controllers Association was born. The power struggle during the first days was amusing because the new controller workforce was made up of about 90 percent prior military controllers. We were accustomed to taking orders and to having very little, if any, input in the decision-making process. The vast majority of us were junior-level military controllers who actually talked to airplanes and not senior enlisted members who worked in the office, interfacing with senior officers such as squadron commanders and operations officers. The idea that we could negotiate working conditions, equipment, overtime, hours, shifts, days off, and even proper attire was completely foreign to us. In the uniformed services, you're told what to wear, when to work, where to work, and what equipment to use without discussion. I found it humorous to watch the jockeying, not just locally but nationally, to climb the food chain and assume control.

Power corrupts, and absolute power corrupts absolutely, which is what makes the labor–management relationship work. No single entity has complete power. I was never directly involved in the power struggle for two reasons. One, when NATCA was born, I was in training as an FAA employee at Oxnard tower, in California. My attention was focused on successfully completing the training syllabus. Two, I was at a small airport, not LAX, Chicago, or Atlanta. We made our work schedule and fulfilled the duties of training, quality assurance, and plans and procedures specialist all while working traffic every day. Large facilities had staff specialists responsible for all these duties, who merely maintained currency (generally eight hours on each position per month) without necessarily plugging in and talking to airplanes every day. Heck, we didn't even have a supervisor at our little facility and were directly responsible for running the shifts ourselves. There was no management between the controller workforce and the facility manager, and we liked it that way.

There are one hundred people who each believe they are the most qualified person in the world to run the United States: the US Senate, made up of one hundred people who are so full of themselves that they would assuredly go broke if they had to pay to feed their egos. Like the US Senate, the major air traffic facilities had egos coming out the wazoo, and many of those controllers believed they were the only person in the air traffic controller workforce who could salvage the sinking hulk of the philosophy behind PATCO, right the ship, and sail it into port for repairs.

In the navy, the first crew members of a ship are referred to as "plank owners." In the old days, when ships were made of wood and men of steel, as my dad would say, sailors on that inaugural crew would carve their names into the quarterdeck planks and be rewarded with those planks when they left the ship.

I am a NATCA plank owner, a member from the very beginning. When NATCA was formed, it was a really dicey proposition, and there was a lot of debate as to whether it would live to see its first birthday. NATCA was formed with the support of the AFL-CIO and consequently accepted a large loan to get things up and running. We (potential members) were told that if NATCA did not survive, we would be responsible for repayment of the loan. I was a GS-11 living in Ventura, California, at the time, in the second-most expensive county in the entire United States, and renting a room in a four-bedroom house. I couldn't afford to pay attention much less pay toward a defunct union loan, so the initial investment for us, as NATCA plank owners, was a real leap of faith.

As with most unions, NATCA is more of a lobbying effort than anything else. It lobbies congressional representatives and senators who are sympathetic to its cause, hoping for support when needed. Since controllers can't strike, NATCA really has no teeth—a pit bull named Chardonnay. The union's only ace in the hole is the "safety" card, which is effective only when played to the press, which is a double-edged sword. When the controller workforce wants something very badly but has very little chance of getting it, "it's a safety issue!" is screamed. Playing the safety card gets immediate attention. Playing the safety card too often paints NATCA as a little boy crying wolf.

Although I was a member from the very beginning, I'm not a NATCA maniac by any stretch of the imagination. I do know controllers who have NATCA tattoos. Phew! Typically, hard-core union folks are difficult to come by west of the Mississippi, and the NATCA union was no exception. There were, however, a few West Coast controllers who did make a run at the top spot. Unfortunately for them, history is on the side of unions and facilities in the Rust Belt. Chicago and the Northeast generated the greatest interest, which translated into votes, and consequently, controllers from those areas—not always, but for the most part—filled the top positions.

NATCA achieved its goal by being awarded a charter and building a contingency, but as expected, it struggled in the early years to find direction. Then came Bill Clinton, and everything changed. During his first four years in office, NATCA planted seeds that came to fruition in Clinton's second term.

By the mid-1990s, NATCA had stretched its legs and gained footing. The FAA paid many—and in some cases, all—costs associated with conducting union business, including time off. The FAA allotted space within each facility for NATCA offices, including telephones and computer lines. But NATCA did have expenses, and to pay them, 1 percent of each member's salary was deducted as dues, and dues were increased to 1.5 percent a few years later. None of us knew the first thing about union representation, so we really didn't know how the system worked. Being controllers accustomed to immediate gratification, many members withdrew their membership when things occurred that they didn't like. Because our union dues were automatically deducted, this whimsical, reactionary attitude caused a great deal of hardship on not only NATCA but also the FAA. I'm sure NATCA was having trouble maintaining accurate books because of fluctuating dues, and the FAA human resources branch was pulling its hair out making changes to payroll deductions every month.

NATCA, assuredly with the FAA's blessing, resolved the issue by allowing controllers to join NATCA at any time but allowing them to resign only in a particular month—February, if I remember correctly. It seemed unfair at the time, but in retrospect, it made perfect sense. For the union to adequately represent the controllers, a firm knowledge of funding was essential. Lobbyists aren't cheap. NATCA grew, and the poststrike situation settled into a comfortable routine, which is another way of saying, "Let the games begin!" And they did.

The game was amazing to watch, and I had a front-row seat. Initially, each facility had a great deal of leeway in deciding its fate. Among the most important aspects was our freedom to decide seniority: a game of Air Traffic Control Survivor. Bargaining unit members ("BUMs"—seriously, we called each other BUMs) banded together in controller gangs and tailored seniority scenarios that benefited each gang the most—screw everyone else.

"Okay, if we use FAA time, military time, and the first letter in our last name to decide seniority, the five of us will be the most senior."

"Sounds good to us. Let's submit it to vote."

Laugh if you want, but conversations like this did happen.

Remember—the air traffic facility had to be staffed twenty-four hours a day, seven days a week, so a controller low on the seniority list could end up with Tuesday and Wednesday as his or her days off. For the most part, we were young and many of us still single, making days off in the middle of the week a tough pill to swallow. It was hard to get a date on Wednesday night or tell your main squeeze she'd need only one ticket for the Aerosmith concert because you had to talk to airplanes Saturday night. The seniority issue was a fundamental reason controllers left NATCA. Most regular working people have weekends and holidays off and take them for granted, but in the controller workforce, very few were that fortunate, and days off were serious business.

Management wised up quickly and played the game too. I remember our NATCA representative at Tucson TRACON coming up on the end of his tour, due to rotate back to the controller ranks in a few months. About the same time, it was made public that a supervisor position would be advertised, and the scuttlebutt was that our union representative was the odds-on favorite. He had a close relationship with the facility manager, routinely showing up in the early evening on the manager's front porch with pizza and beer. I laughed at the absurdity of the idea, but everyone else saw the obvious.

Coming from the navy, my learning curve was steep enough, but just when I thought I had things figured out, everything changed. As it turned out, the FAA management career ladder quite often had a rung on it named "NATCA facility representative." I guess management figured they might as well take advantage of their investment by moving the enemy into their ranks. After all, management paid for all the training, office space, and union representative time, so why not show a positive cost/benefit? But if you think about it, a positive cost/benefit is contrary to the federal government philosophy and violates every rule of the federal bureaucratic system. I always wondered how NATCA officials viewed the actions of former NATCA representatives who accepted management positions.

NATCA continued to assert its limited authority, taking advantage of every chink in the FAA's armor, of which there were many, slowly and steadily learning which situations could be exploited and which would become bargaining chips. The bargaining-chip concept is as old as the system of union and management itself and forms the basis for change in the workforce. Unions and management will not admit it, but they regularly use grievances as bargaining chips, which is probably why it's called "collective bargaining." Like kids on the playground trading baseball cards, NATCA and FAA management at all levels sat down and argued over which complaints had merit and which didn't: I'll trade you an EEO complaint for an insubordination charge. It's a mutually beneficial system as long as your facility representative comes home with news that your grievance was accepted and resolved to your satisfaction. If not, so sorry. Maybe next time.

However, NATCA does have a tendency to eat its own. On one occasion, a friend of mine was the primary instructor at an en-route facility and was called on the carpet when his trainee was about to be terminated. My buddy explained that the guy tried hard and studied, but regrettably, the ability just wasn't there. He felt as bad about the termination as anyone, but you do the best you can with what you've been given. The situation turned ugly when the NATCA representative, not management, started questioning my friend's capabilities as an instructor and a controller.

"Whoa! Wait a minute! We're on the same side here!" he said.

The NATCA representative didn't let up and continued to badger him until he decided enough was enough and walked out. As a NATCA member, my friend's next question was "Who do I file a complaint with? My NATCA representative?"

It turned out the trainee had dyslexia and knew it but had decided not to share this little tidbit of information with anyone else. He was transferred to another facility and certified there. Seriously, a dyslexic controller. Simply amazing.

Being the clever opportunists they are, controllers put their deductive reasoning skills to work and devised a system to augment their retirement. Controllers who worked at small airports that happened to be quite close to very large, very busy airports quickly figured out how to parlay a few years of duty at that large, busy airport into a hefty raise in their retirement check.

Here's how it works. Controller retirement is based on the controller's "high three," or the average of the three highest-salary years during a controller's career. Typically, these years are the last three years of a controller's career, but not necessarily, not if you're creative and know the rules of personnel management. Controllers at a lower-level, less-busy airport—say Rockford, Illinois, which is located very close to O'Hare TRACON, a much busier and therefore more highly paid facility—can use this association for retirement. How? Allow me to explain.

O'Hare always needs controllers, and Rockford controllers figured out that they could go to O'Hare, train for a while (say two years or so), wash out, and go back to Rockford with their base pay now as much as 50 percent higher. How does this happen? While at O'Hare, they get a big pay raise just for walking through the door every day. Although they are not certified, technically, they are O'Hare controllers and therefore eligible for a pay raise. Their salary is not the same as a fully certified O'Hare approach controller, but it's nothing to sneeze at either. After a few years, they wash out, go back to Rockford with a healthy pay raise, and let the next Rockford controller take their place. For a few years of BS, you too can work a low, slow tower and make a lot more money doing it. The best part is that their high three is based on the time at O'Hare.

I'm not picking on the Rockford controllers or trying to make them look like frauds. At the time, this practice was popular throughout the FAA. Besides, how do you prove it? Some people have what it takes to work O'Hare; some don't. Maybe it's just a coincidence that Rockford controllers washed and returned with a fat pay raise. Maybe. Maybe not. This scenario came from a high-ranking NATCA representative over lunch in DC. I asked about the way this practice is viewed. He just stared at me like a dog watching television. Yes, it is possible to ask a stupid question.

On one hand, these people were screwing O'Hare controllers royally. O'Hare was consistently understaffed, and these people were only making matters worse, both by taking up valuable controller slots and by forcing the O'Hare boys and girls to waste their time training controllers who had no intention of certifying. Did I say that? I meant training controllers who did not have the ability to certify. On the other hand, the washouts were NATCA members, and 1.5 percent of Rockford salary was a lot less than 1.5 percent of Rockford plus O'Hare salary. Quid pro quo? No itchy backs here; they've all been scratched.

NATCA versus Management

People on both sides of the table will argue the other is corrupt, self-absorbed, and power-hungry, but the way I see it, the process is the best we have in a free society and will probably continue this way until unions disappear. That's right—unions, not management. But they'll be back soon enough. Statistics show unions, across the board, are struggling and losing members in record numbers.

The world as a whole has finally realized that communism doesn't work for one reason: human nature. I took a philosophy class in college and picked Karl Marx as my term-paper philosopher. Being a born-and-bred red-blooded capitalist, I wanted to know what countries that adopted communism as a socioeconomic lifestyle saw in it. After reading books and biographies that I otherwise never would have read about Marx and Marxism (being the humble little revolutionary he was, Karl Marx did not like the term Marxism, by the way), I came to the conclusion, on my own (that's what college does for you), that communism (a.k.a. Marxism) fails because of human nature.

Communism is based on everyone having the same thing. Everybody has a shitty house, a shitty car, and so on. Human nature, however, dictates that someone always believes he or she can do better and is therefore the fatal flaw in Karl's philosophy. This is the reason the free world has adopted a capitalistic, to one degree or another, lifestyle. Even China, which was widely regarded as the most truly communist country in the world, is rapidly becoming capitalist. Don't believe me? China retook Hong Kong years ago but opted to leave well enough alone. I've been to Hong Kong, and it is the most capitalist place I've ever seen. A space between two buildings is filled with plywood and cardboard in a makeshift kiosk.

Currently, the European Union (EU), "union" being the operative word, is financially in the toilet. Unions have demanded—and received—concessions that are prohibitive to financial stability. Many in the EU can "retire" at age fifty, drawing a government check each month. Who pays for it? Young people who work. The problem is, unemployment rates are through the roof, severely limiting the tax base, which pays for retirees. It is a vicious circle.

Virtually all of Europe takes the entire month of August off. Why? Union contracts. Even senior level VP's have a contract with their companies. I'm not talking about "golden paachute" contracts, I'm talking about working hours, days off, etc.; issues covered under hourly employee union contract. In the states, supervisors, directors, and the like, are not hourly employees, therefore not covered under union contracts. Are there management covered under union contracts in the states? Maybe. But, I don't know of any. Can you imagine how Apollo 13 may have turned out if the ground support people were covered by union contracts limiting hours worked and working environment conditions?

The United States is very limited when it comes to unions, which is why there is only one flag on the moon. The United States will remain capitalist, which is the reason management will outlast unions. Unions do have a place—conditions in the early 1900s clearly illustrated this—but they are self-destructing today. Or maybe they are just running out of gas.

In the world of air traffic control, a well-educated, much more diverse, nonspecialized controller workforce capable of moving—and more importantly, willing to move—on to something else instead of fighting management has emerged. I can clearly see the controller workforce destined to inherit NATCA moving to greener, less confrontational pastures rather than standing and fighting. Their decisions, like those of NATCA plank owners, are rooted in the cost/benefit of their actions. The cost of fighting FAA management was worth it to us; we had everything to gain and nothing to lose. However, the next generation of NATCA controllers have options such as other career prospects and are willing to exercise those options. We, by and large, had a high school education and four to six years of experience talking to airplanes in the military, and that was it. We had one option: work for the FAA. The new kids have college degrees in computer science, business, finance, and so on, which gives them many options.

I was told by a facility rep that NATCA is experiencing a slowdown in membership. I didn't research this, so the information should be taken with a grain of salt. However, the point is, the new controller workforce is skeptical of the value of NATCA. Unlike the private sector, FAA air traffic control is not a closed shop. Each controller is free to decide whether he or she wants to pay dues or not. Controller salaries as of 2016 range from approximately $85,000 at small facilities to $170,000 at Chicago, New York, and Atlanta TRACONS. That's *base* pay. Add 25 percent for Sunday pay, 15 percent (if I remember correctly) for evening differential, time and a half for overtime, and double time for holidays, and $170,000 can easily turn into more than $200,000 annually. One and a half percent of $200,000, multiplied by three hundred controllers, at only one facility, is a lot of money going into NATCA's coffers. Young controllers with math skills are running the numbers, comparing the benefits, and finding a cost/benefit ratio that they may find unacceptable. The key here is that NATCA must represent *all* controllers, whether they are dues paying BUMs or not. Most controllers, through their career, never file a complaint with their rep. Why pay dues for representation you may never need? NATCA does, however, negotiate issues on a national scale that will benefit the entire controller workforce. Controllers have their own pay scale, completely separate from the rest of the federal government, negotiated by NATCA. That was a real coup.

Controllers can retire, under certain circumstances, at age fifty. Controllers and first-line supervisors *must* retire before age fifty-six. This is a double-edged sword. Many controllers want to stay on after fifty-six, but by law, they can't. Why? The union. The FAA signed off on age fifty retirement because the union—at the time I think it was PATCO—convinced an FAA administrator that the job was so stressful that the ability to retire at fifty was warranted. Fully retire with all benefits most Federal Government employees aren't eligible for at that age. Why won't NATCA go to bat for those who want to continue working past fifty-six? Simple. To do so would be admitting, by default, that the job isn't that stressful, which would take away a bargaining chip or two from NATCA.

Will unions go away forever? Anything is possible, but I don't see it happening, not totally and not forever. Today, we are reaping the benefits of sacrifices made during World War II, and the average worker is also reaping the benefits of unionization in our past. Quite simply, the pendulum is swinging the way of management right now, but it will return to the center and maybe even favor unions once again. For now, controllers have their own pay scale, health care, matching retirement contributions, and a great retirement plan. If a young, college-educated controller at one of the busiest facilities, moving to the top end of the pay band over their career, invests the maximum amount allowable, that controller could comfortably retire (I know Controllers who are grossing over $100,000.00 in retirement) at fifty and start a second career. He or she just has to be prepared to work weekends, holidays, and overtime and fight back panic attacks.

The plank owners of NATCA are getting old, and the second string is waiting on the bench. The NATCA bench will surely be the deciding factor in the union's future, and it will be composed of a large number of college graduates with skill sets well beyond the skills of the poststrike NATCA founders and BUMs; these incoming controllers are much more a reflection of the future of FAA management than the past or present controller workforce. Many NATCA maniacs see this outlook as blasphemy, but they are blinded by idealism. God bless their idealistic little hearts. Whether you love or hate unions, NATCA did make a difference.

10

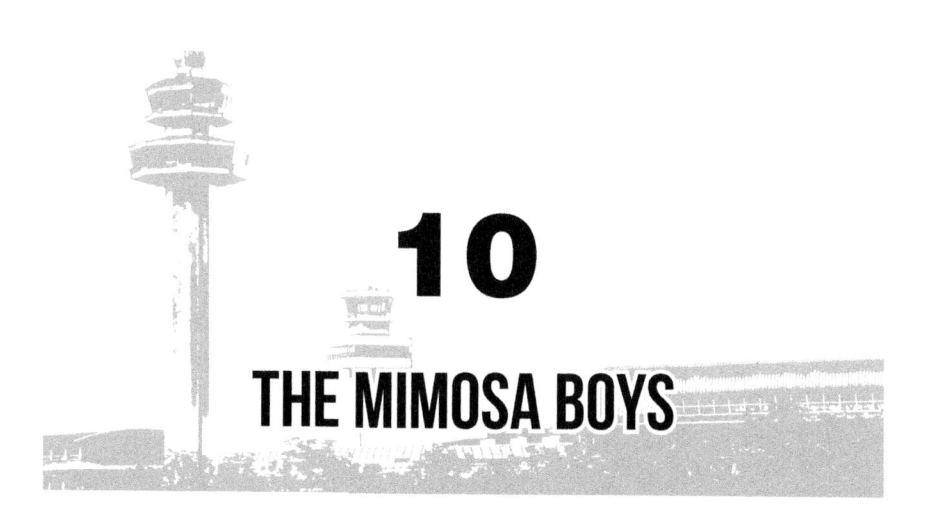

THE MIMOSA BOYS

During my time in Washington headquarters, I worked on several radar systems, learning more about the technical side than I ever wanted to know. Controllers work closely with the airways facilities technicians (maintenance people) but rarely get involved in the technical aspects of the equipment. The vast majority of controllers just don't care how things work, as long as the equipment does work. However, there are exceptions to every rule, and this one is no different. Some controllers choose to pursue careers in the software programming of the FAA air traffic control automation system, which displays aircraft call signs, altitudes, airspeed, and so on to a radar screen, but they are definitely a minority. Most controllers are content to go to work, talk to airplanes, and go home, leaving staff, management, and technical issues to others. Until I left the FAA, I was no different. However, after walking the halls of FAA headquarters, my interests changed.

I began my FAA headquarters experience supporting Randy Bowen, a fantastic guy and air traffic controller who was in charge of ensuring that air traffic requirements for the airport surveillance radar-11 (ASR-11) were met. The ASR-11 is a big antenna that sits atop a tower and turns in circles. The ASR-11 was designed and intended for use at small- to medium-density airports such as Stockton, California, and Beaumont, Texas. Another radar system, the ASR-9, had been installed at airports such LAX, Dallas / Fort Worth, Atlanta, and New York. What's the difference? The processor.

Okay, Radar 101. Very simply, a radar emits a pulse of electronic energy hundreds, thousands, even millions of times a second. The pulse goes out, hits something, and bounces back, creating a "return." The radar "time-stamps" each emitted pulse and each return (i.e., it makes an internal note of the time each is transmitted and the time return is received). The time difference between the two is calculated, and with a predetermined rate of travel—the speed at which the pulse traveled—the distance of the object from the antenna can be calculated. If a train travels at sixty miles per hour for one hour, it traveled sixty miles. It is the same with radar, only a lot faster.

All radar "see" too much. Electronic pulses routinely hit birds, trees, cars, and even clouds (or, more accurately, the moisture that constitutes a cloud), which the radar perceives to be targets. Targets such as these are of no concern to air traffic controllers, so the radar processor, a computer, must filter out these returns. Herein lies the fundamental difference between the ASR-11 and the ASR-9. Remember—this is Radar 101, not Radar 501. There are many, many particulars that make these systems different, but the main difference is the ability of the computer that processes the radar returns. As expensive as the antenna and all its moving parts may be, the processor is a critical element and very costly, which brings us to the foundation of the ASR-11 issue. Performance of the ASR-11 is dictated in the requirements document, which is where Randy Bowen and the air traffic requirements team, of which I was a member, come in.

Randy held a master's degree in psychology, and before going to work for the FAA, he was some sort of counselor or psychologist. Randy fit the part. A fairly large guy and fairly fit, he was somewhat imposing, until he opened his mouth. Randy had a voice and demeanor as calming as a walk on the beach at sunset. Sitting in his office, legs crossed, he would ponder a question with a half smile while straightening the crease in his pants, looking the part of a professor. Randy was born and raised in the Northeast and had chosen headquarters as his career after what appeared to me limited time in the field. He came across as someone who could do the job but didn't have a real passion for it. I had previously viewed controllers such as Randy less than admirably, but after my post-FAA experiences I began to realize that water seeks its own level and some controllers were just better-suited to duties outside the radar room or tower. Randy was one of those people, and the more I got to know him, the more I appreciated his dedication to the job, the FAA, and most importantly, his obligation to the controllers in the field.

The definition of an Irishman is a man who can tell another to go to hell such that he looks forward to the trip. I don't know if Randy was Irish, but more than once, I watched him explain in detail the shortcomings of the ASR-11 in a manner that can only be described as poetic. His writings were equally impressive—technically romantic. Randy could make the French Foreign Legion sound like a hiking club in search of the perfect mountain trail. He was a natural fit for the terminal (tower and TRACON) requirements manager position.

The ASR-11 had fatal flaws everywhere we looked, and Randy found them all. To his benefit, he did have a team of radar engineers supporting him who were as intelligent as they were uncontrollable—my kind of guys.

Carl Ralston was one of the radar engineers. One morning, Carl came into the office a little late and obviously hungover. We chatted about the previous night's activities, and I deduced that those activities were the reason he was late. To the contrary, Carl explained, the apartment complex in which he lived had a huge hot-water boiler. It was so big that it never ran out of hot water. Carl would routinely, after a night out in DC, crawl in the tub, turn on the hot water, and go to sleep. A hot shower, in the tub. All night. Engineers... This morning, he had just overslept.

On one trip to Denver, we were all in business class (we traveled a lot and had the frequent flier miles to prove it) when shortly after the "Fasten Seat Belt" sign was turned off, the flight attendant made her first of many trips down the aisle. Carl leaned all the way out of his seat, blocking the aisle, and loudly moaned, "Mee-mo-saaa." The flight attendant stared for a moment too long, and the other four of us joined the chorus. Mimosas with a side of tequila for everyone! After all, it was 9:00 a.m., we were taking cabs from the airport to our hotel, it was a travel day (no work), and our employers had known what they were getting when they hired us, so it wasn't as though we were going to embarrass them.

LIFE WITH A VIEW

It was a great team. Most of us were contractors, but there were a few FAAers sprinkled among us. Randy was equal parts hard work and play: take care of business and then hit the town. The Raytheon engineers had a love/hate relationship with him; they knew that Randy was doing his job by holding their feet to the fire, but they also knew they had to get the ASR-11 commissioned as soon as possible. The Raytheon engineers tried tricks to make the ASR-11 meet FAA air traffic requirements that were ingenious but didn't fool our crack team of mimosa drinkers or Randy.

Now for Radar 201: The ASR-11 scans a portion of the sky (one-fourth), accumulating a lot of information, and processes all that information at once. It gathers so much information that the processors couldn't weed out the birds from the airplanes and display the results on the air traffic controller's scope within the required amount of time (around one second). This requirement was a lot to ask, but the FAA bought the system because Raytheon claimed the ASR-11 could meet FAA air traffic requirements. Remember that the fundamental difference between a high-density radar such as the ASR-9 (a Grumman system and a damned good radar) and the ASR-11 is the latter's ability to filter out unwanted information. So to make the ASR-11 meet requirements, Raytheon programmed it to dump any information over the maximum it could process and display within the required time frame. Simple, huh? But what if some of that dumped information contained an aircraft target? Oops. American Airlines flight 243 was there one sweep and not the next. Amazingly, Raytheon didn't care and refused to acknowledge our findings when confronted. When Randy didn't let up, threatening to take the trickery upstairs to the administrator's office, the Raytheon engineers remarkably found an error in their math and admitted Randy might, just might, be right.

It didn't stop there. There was a minimum speed built into the processor's algorithm. In other words, if the radar sees a target moving at less than sixty miles per hour, it can ignore it, reducing the amount of work the processor has to do, making it much more likely that the processed information will reach the controller's scope within the one-second time frame and meet requirements. Raytheon made some adjustments in this area too, and presto, the ASR-11 functioned perfectly! The problem was, the mimosa boys smelled a rat and found one.

The Raytheon engineers had changed the minimum speed requirement, reducing the amount of information to be processed, allowing the system to meet requirements. Raytheon protested until we illustrated the potentially catastrophic results of their decision.

What aircraft go slow? Landing Cessnas and helicopters. What if the new and improved ASR-11 dumped a Cessna or a helicopter target during bad weather and the air traffic controller couldn't see it? "Midair" is one word that comes to mind, but there are others. Even worse for Raytheon, if the NTSB found the unauthorized alteration, Raytheon, not the FAA, would be left holding the bag, and former Raytheon engineers, Copernicus and Pythagoras, would be explaining the thought process behind those changes. Bad juju, baby.

I left the program knowing that as long as Randy was at the helm, the ASR-11 ship would not leave dry dock before it was seaworthy. Two years later, as I walked out of the FAA building in DC, I saw one of the mimosa boys. When asked how the program was going, he responded, "Puttin' lipstick on a turd."

During my days with the ASR-11 program, I experienced my first "unfunded" congressional mandate. An unfunded congressional mandate is a job or task issued by Congress with no funding attached. Years ago, federal government agencies pitched a fit about these tasking orders and finally got a reprieve, sort of. Congress had a bad habit of writing a letter to agency administrators, simply instructing them to implement a policy, procedure, or program because it was a good idea. Many of these were indeed good ideas and would have had a positive effect; however, changes affect agencies in many ways, all of which are financial. Change for the sake of change sucks, but change for a very good reason cannot be successfully argued, unless the change has no funding attached. After a great deal of fussing and fighting, Congress finally agreed to stem the flow of unfunded mandates.

One morning, late in the year, as the ASR-11 requirements team sat in our office, busy little bureaucrats that we were, a letter floated through the door. It was an unfunded mandate from Congress, and it instructed the FAA administrator, Jane Garvey, to rehab, transport, install, and operate an ASR-9 radar from Boston to the Palm Springs airport before winter activities began.

Here's what happened. There are two ways to sequence aircraft into an airport: radar and nonradar. We know about radar. However, nonradar, "manual control," is based on time and distance. Remember driver's education class? The proper distance between your car and the car ahead depends on speed—one car length for each ten miles per hour of speed, so fifty miles an hour calls for five car lengths. It is the same with nonradar. With nonradar, depending on the conditions, aircraft are sequenced ten minutes—fifteen or more miles—in-trail of each other.

Aircraft are typically issued a holding point, a navigational aid, which they circle at a designated altitude. Aircraft in holding are stacked over the holding point, one thousand feet apart: at three thousand, four thousand, five thousand feet, and so on. One aircraft is cleared for an approach into an airport, and no other aircraft can be cleared for approach until the first aircraft reports to air traffic control that it has safely landed. This is *very* important! Reporting to air traffic control can be as easy as keying the mike in the cockpit and saying, "Approach, Hawker 23 Bravo is on deck terminating IFR services."

However, if the airport is on a mountain or is surrounded by mountains, making radio contact impossible, what does the landing pilot do? They find a telephone and call the TRACON or center. Seriously. Air traffic control *cannot* assume the aircraft landed safely and therefore cannot clear the next aircraft for an approach. Air traffic control must assume the worst if it does not hear from a pilot; perhaps the pilot did not see the runway due to bad weather, for example, and executed a missed approach. Typically, the missed approach procedure takes the pilot back to the original starting point, at the original altitude. It is a very organized and rudimentary operation unless the controller has a pant-load of aircraft. Busy radar sectors are a walk in the park compared to busy nonradar sectors. In the latter the delays are enormous. It can easily take an aircraft fifteen to twenty minutes to fly an approach, land, and notify air traffic control that it has landed safely before the next aircraft can begin the same approach. In other words, with radar, the arrival rate at LAX is about eighty an hour. With nonradar, maybe twenty. What does this have to do with Congress?

The Palm Springs congresswoman represents the Palm Springs, California, area, and the wealthy flock to Palm Springs during January, February, and March. Weather during these months is the best and worst. Good days are warm, in the seventies, and sunny. However, Palm Springs has its worst weather during these months also—cloudy with showers. Wealthy folks in their corporate Gulfstream and Hawker jets flying in to watch golf and tennis tournaments need instrument approaches to get below the cloud deck and land safely.

However, at the time the FAA received this unfunded mandate, the Palm Springs airport radar was out of service. Nobody had really cared before now because the only time it was needed was during the winter months and sparingly then. Even when the weather was bad, it wasn't bad for long. The airport just wasn't busy enough for the FAA to move the ASR-11 radar installation up on the priority list or focus attention and money on a temporary replacement radar. The Palm Springs locals did make a little bit of a stink about their treatment, but no one listened—and for good reason. Airplanes were being delayed during bad weather in the winter months, but they were mostly corporate aircraft, and their voices were not heard, at least not until they gathered together, harmonized, and threw money at the problem.

The following is a summary of meetings I attended and information that was given at those meetings. It appears a few of the wealthiest were sitting in their Gulfstream jets in holding, waiting for a nonradar approach clearance, sipping $200 champagne, and decided that if they pooled their resources and made a large donation to the congresswoman's reelection coffers, maybe she could get a radar into Palm Springs. During nonradar operations, the arrival rate was around four aircraft an hour, about fifteen minutes between aircraft. With radar, there would be three or four minutes between aircraft. The wealthy jet owners made their wishes known and presto! In the finest tradition of Washington politics, plans for a replacement radar soon magically appeared.

Palm Springs was scheduled to get an ASR-11, but not for a few years. The marketing boys at Northrop-Grumman heard about Palm

Springs' plight and came to the rescue. Grumman had recently acquired two ASR-9s from a South American country, which were stored in a Boston warehouse. Airplanes do not make money when they sit on the ground, and a radar doesn't make money if it's in boxes in a Boston warehouse. As I understand it, Grumman offered an ASR-9 for a cool $4 million. The congresswoman probably went to her buddies in the House and convinced them to pilfer a little here and a little there from assorted programs to come up with the cash. No problem, right? Nope, big problem.

Four million merely paid for the radar—a radar that had been sitting in a South American jungle for years, requiring a complete rehab; a radar that required transport from Boston to Palm Springs; a radar that had no secondary or computer processor and needed both; a radar that had no home because the Palm Springs tower supporting the old radar had been condemned. How much would all this cost? Another four million, which is were the unfunded congressional mandate comes in.

Congress provided the radar for Palm Springs but neglected to provide the funding for any of the logistics. So where would the money come from? The FAA was getting the radar, so the FAA should cough up the cash. Right? Makes perfect sense to a bureaucrat.

The mandate that we, the ASR-11 team, received that day had an attachment instructing all program managers to trim their budgets and contribute to the Palm Springs cause. Our budgets had already been trimmed to support another overbudget program. Money for the Palm Springs radar had to come from somewhere, so it would come from all the other "overfunded" programs, like the ASR-11 program.

Our ASR-11 team, with Randy in the lead, attended a meeting with all other program managers to discuss the issue. As it progressed, I realized that Congress intended to pillage not only program funding but also our physical assets. Someone had to rehab the replacement radar, transport it 2,500 miles, dig up the computer processor, install and operate it. Guess who got the nod? Engineers scheduled to perform tasks associated with our program and others. And it got worse.

In addition to the requirement that programs give up funding that none of the programs could afford to lose, redirect assets, and put program installations and progress on hold, the Palm Springs ASR-9 installation had to be done in less time than a radar installation and certification had ever been accomplished. It was late in the year, and Congress's efforts would be for nothing if radar services were not available for the peak season in Palm Springs. We did manage to finance, transport, install, certify, and operate the radar according to the time schedule but not without consequences. Have you ever wondered why the federal government can't do anything on time and within budget? Now you know.

The pillaged programs had schedule changes, causing them to "slide right" on the schedule, or be delayed. So the schedule slides a little. No big deal, right? Most of the affected programs were national. Program managers had engineers, technicians, and manufacturers scheduled for deliveries and installations a year or more in advance. Air traffic managers, airport managers, and airways facilities managers had plans and procedures in place to meet that schedule. All were affected, costing tens and hundreds of thousands of dollars.

For instance, say a new air traffic control technology is set to be integrated into a facility. Technicians and air traffic controllers must be trained to operate and maintain the equipment. Believe it or not, training has a shelf life. Controllers and technicians receive training according to the implementation schedule. Training conducted too far in advance is forgotten, and in the aviation industry, retraining is essential to ensure competency. We read about the results of poor training on the front page of newspapers and in NTSB reports. But training is only one part of a program and a relatively inexpensive part—relatively. To implement and integrate many of these programs, many projects (parts of a program) need to occur in a specific sequence.

Trenches need to be dug for electrical and communication cables. Local contractors are hired to dig these trenches on a specific day or week. When money dries up, as in this case, that contract is broken. Just reschedule the backhoe—no problem, right? But what if the backhoe operator is self-employed and turned down other work for this job? What does he do? Just go find other work? Probably not. I grew up in the South, where construction happened year-round. In the North, however, there are two seasons: winter and construction season. Self-employed backhoe operators in Wisconsin have to "make hay while the sun shines." Downtime affects their bottom line, and a canceled contract can very well result in downtime. If backhoes aren't digging, backhoe operators aren't making money. Just like everyone else, backhoe operators in Wisconsin need money to pay the mortgage, put food on the table, put shoes on the kids' feet, and maybe have a little left over for a six-pack or two of Pabst and a few brats with the boys while watching the Pack come back. This is a fact of life that should, but assuredly didn't, cross Congress's mind when they were working their political magic.

The backhoe operator is a simplistic example. Imagine a company like Lockheed that is contracted to perform hundreds of thousands of dollars' worth of work but can't because the trenches haven't been dug. The next time you read about a federal program millions overbudget and years behind schedule, start looking at your local elected official before blaming federal program managers.

Are there incompetent program managers? Hell yes! Not all overbudget and late programs are the result of irresponsible politicians. Some are directly attributable to mismanagement and incompetence. Once again, the federal government does not pay that well but compensates with a high level of job security. Consequently, a certain percentage of program managers are pathetically underqualified, and it shows. You get what you pay for. But, there was Randy Bowen, Carl, and a few others that gave me hope.

Congress's folly caused a serious reduction in funding to many programs and a slide in schedules. An audit of the expense attached to the sliding schedules clearly would have revealed wasted money. However, who would order such an audit? Congress didn't want an audit for obvious reasons. The direct beneficiary was a Republican, so exposure of influence utilized in this manner could only benefit Democratic opponents, right? Nope. The money probably came from a committee—a group of people, not just one individual. Some of those members were Democrats. How can this be? Democrats and Republicans make deals in Congress all the time in which obligatory "chits" are issued, chits redeemable on demand. A chit-holding Democrat submits a pork proposal contrary to a Republican's philosophy, and it is approved. Have you ever wondered why a politician breaks a campaign promise? Now you know.

So why didn't the Palm Springs congresswoman go back to her political buddies for the extra four million? Too many chits would make her a Democrat. There is a point of diminishing returns. Paying for the up-front cost of the radar, she could safely escape the "unfunded congressional mandate" criticism that would have attached to the first four million. But going back to the well for the other four million would leave her very vulnerable. As with air traffic management and NATCA at the grievance table, quid pro quos work only when doled out sparingly.

The end result: Palm Springs got an ASR-9 and a two-ton dual-axle truck with a forty-foot gooseneck when it only needed a '69 Ford half-ton with a three on the tree. And again, the eight million spent was only part of the problem. Numerous program schedules took hits that will never be measured for two reasons: no one wants to know the truth, and there is no money to perform the audit, ironically. The waste does not end there. The ASR-9 in Palm Springs doesn't operate, power, or maintain itself. The estimated annual cost of an ASR-9 is in the neighborhood of $1 million—technicians, replacement parts, electricity, and so on.

The congresswoman is not alone. I use her and the Palm Springs issue as an example because the low-hanging fruit is easiest to pick. Sadly, there is a lot of low-hanging fruit out there, which makes me wonder where the ace, crackerjack reporters are. Hanging out in a "safe zone" bar in Baghdad, sucking up equal amounts of per diem and scotch, I'm sure. This is not terribly difficult stuff to figure out. But then again, most reporters are arts majors, which explains a lot. There are many other examples on both sides of the political aisle. It's hard to blame politicians, though; it's their job to represent their constituents, and what better way to represent them than bringing home the bacon—even if, as with this case, the bacon is actually prosciutto-wrapped veal roast with a black truffle sauce.

As irritating as this event is, it's the backhoe operator in Wisconsin that really bugs me.

In 2004, cancer took Randy Bowen from us. He was one of the good guys. This chapter is dedicated to him, his lovely wife Sue, their two sons, and the controller workforce who will now know why the ASR-11 works properly. Contrary to popular controller opinion, there are people in headquarters and the regional offices—and staffers everywhere—who do very important jobs very well. They don't get enough credit.

Thanks also to Bruce Kinsler, who got me the job supporting Randy. It was a learning experience that I do appreciate.

11
DC

In his book *Faith of My Fathers*, Senator John McCain describes an incident at the end of his grandfather Admiral Sid "Slew" McCain's career that had a profound effect on his life. Immediately prior to the invasion of Okinawa during World War II, Admiral McCain was commanding officer of Task Force 38, constituting the majority of the Third Fleet, and reported to his very good friend, Admiral "Bull" Halsey, commanding officer of the Third Fleet. Search aircraft reported a typhoon on the horizon, and the weather guessers suggested staying put, but Halsey decided to attempt to maneuver around the storm, essentially sailing the fleet into the heart of it. Realizing his mistake, Bull Halsey issued tactical command for safe navigation of Task Force 38 to Admiral McCain, who in turn, considered the situation for, according to historical reports, about twenty minutes.

A subsequent court of inquiry deemed that the loss of 142 aircraft, the deaths of six drowned sailors, and the damage to four aircraft carriers were a direct result of Halsey's poor decision and McCain's delayed decision. Fearing a catastrophic loss of morale from the relief of both Halsey and McCain, Secretary of Defense Forestall opted to retain Halsey and relieve McCain. Admiral McCain remained commander of his task force through the Okinawa invasion, which proved to be the end of World War II, and was present during the signing of the Japanese surrender but only by direct order of Halsey. According to Senator John McCain, his grandfather never spoke of the incident to anyone, suffering a fatal heart attack a few days after the Japanese surrender and one day after returning stateside.

In the mid-1960s, a young army helicopter pilot returned from the war in Southeast Asia, having been shot down a number of times but, fortunately, shot up only once. While in rehabilitation, he decided being a lawyer, even with all its downsides, would be safer than flying helicopters in combat. After law school and years of exemplary legal performance, first in the army and then as a civilian for the Department of the Defense, he was given the responsibility of assessing a high-ranking private-sector executive's security clearance. Essentially, this young, well-decorated lawyer would single-handedly decide whether defense industry executives could represent their company regarding a government contract worth millions of dollars, for which a secret security clearance was required.

In the end, the young lawyer ruled against awarding a security clearance to a particular Vice Pesident and discussed his reasons with senior management, who in turn agreed to support him and his findings. As with Admiral McCain's situation, this issue was of immediate concern to high-level individuals—in this case, cabinet-level brass—and the implications were obvious. Time passed, with the silence from the lawyer's colleagues becoming more ominous and obvious each day, until he was called into his boss's office and told he was being reassigned. As with Admiral McCain, the lawyer knew the obligations of his position, executed them dutifully, and had been prepared for the consequences of his decisions, but not for his abandonment.

I open with these stories to illustrate the level of brutality that still exists in Washington, DC. The common thread connecting the two events is obvious, and this chapter will describe a personal experience with the politics driving our government. Make no mistake—I do not consider myself of the same caliber as the previous two fine men. I have never seen combat, and I have encountered life-and-death situations only on a few occasions, mostly due to a combination of living in foreign countries while drinking too much alcohol and exercising too little good judgment, but, on occasion, through the inevitable results that come with aviation. These distinguished gentlemen stared death in the face on a daily basis, making decisions and living with the consequences. On a lesser level, I was not the first sacrificial lamb and will not be the last, but knowing that didn't make my situation any easier to handle.

Safe Flight 21 (SF21) was an FAA program intended to perform research and development of emerging technology and assess the benefits of integrating that technology into the National Airspace System. From the very first day that I heard about SF21 and its mission, I knew that being a member of a team working on reinventing aviation and taking it into the twenty-first century was everything I wanted. I imagined sitting on my front porch, grandkids by my side, explaining that I was a member of a team that had made a difference. When offered an opportunity to join the team, I gave Randy Bowen my resignation, immediately accepted the new position, and felt as though I had just stepped into heaven. What I didn't know was that a year and a half later, I would become another DC scapegoat. Heaven is overrated.

I'll refer to the SF21 program manager as "Neidermeyer," after Doug Neidermeyer in the classic comedy *Animal House*, for two reasons. First, it fits. In the movie, Neidermeyer was an anal-retentive ROTC commander who would make a four-star marine general look like a Boy Scout leader. Second, it's the nicest name I could come up with.

Neidermeyer and I had a love/hate relationship. He loved to hate me, and I hated him back. In the movie *Animal House*, Neidermeyer beat up on defenseless Delta House pledges while sucking up to Dean Wormer. Their association stopped just short of homosexual and formed the wall that Delta House routinely targeted for throwing eggs and spray-painting. The Neidermeyer in my world was an air force flight school washout who couldn't keep his lunch down during low G turns. He spent the rest of his active-duty obligation wandering the halls of the Pentagon, satisfying generals' cravings when their wives didn't, and honing skills needed to advance through the ranks of mediocrity in the federal government by protecting F-16 program money so that flight school graduates could fly the same airplanes he had been denied. Life can be so ironic.

Neidermeyer and I never got along, and I don't know why. I was told I said something somewhere along the line that pissed him off. I've been known to do that, although I don't know exactly what I said, and I guess it doesn't matter now. Sometimes people don't like you just because you part your hair on the wrong side.

He was around five-ten and balding, with Coke-bottle glasses and a hint of a lisp. I figured the lisp had been a lot worse in the past, but while practicing his acceptance speeches for awards others would earn for him, he had de-lisped most of his lisp. Being a nonpilot, Neidermeyer had quickly deduced that his air force career would be limited to supply officer, so he had bailed after his mandatory service, taking the next logical step and becoming an FAA bureaucrat. Bureaucrat being a gracious term.

Determined to achieve his rightful place in mediocrity, he became known as the fair-haired boy in the emerging technology branch of FAA headquarters. He was a hard worker, diligent, and always mindful of the details, but whether it was intentional or not, he had a pervasive condescending attitude that stifled his acceptance among the troops. At first, I thought his attitude was aimed exclusively at me. I do have a way of pissing people off with minimal effort; however, more often than not, I had to be obnoxious to get people to wish me ill. After a while, it became obvious that I was not nearly as condescending and not in Neidermeyer's league. He was much more subtle, and his loathsomeness was as dry and nonchalant as British gin.

My first day in the SF21 program began with a plane ride from Washington, DC, to Memphis. The program was based in a "shared responsibility" relationship between the FAA, users (airlines), and corporations that would develop the technology and eventually market and sell it. SF21 was based on the idea that all three stakeholders had mutually beneficial investments. The FAA would show increased safety and reduced delays; the airlines would see reduced delays and a more efficient, cost-effective operation, and the avionics manufacturers would have a product to sell.

With conventional radar, the target update rate was every six seconds, which is the length of time it takes a radar antenna to rotate in a complete circle. This system also had an error rate of a quarter of a mile, sometimes more. The technology we were evaluating determined aircraft position and altitude once every second with an error rate believed to be as little as nine feet.

Fred Smith, founder of FedEx (based in Memphis), recognized the potential benefits of such accurate information if he could access it. He foresaw an opportunity to better utilize ramp personnel by securing a more exact idea of when aircraft would arrive on the runway and, therefore, at their respective spot on the ramp. The information could reduce the idle time of ramp teams who unload, sort, transfer, and reload aircraft from fifteen or twenty minutes to less than five. FedEx did the math, and the savings were in the millions. As I understand it, Fred convinced the local congressman to secure funding for research at the Memphis airport, and the SF21 team was off and running.

We arrived in Memphis, mustered together, and Neidermeyer introduced me to the other SF21 members. Aside from me, Larry the Lizard was the newest addition to the team. Do not misconstrue the nickname—it is not intended to slight his character because he was a decent person, and I admired him. Short and chunky like an Arizona Gila monster, the Lizard was a decorated army Gulf War veteran who had served with a parachute company and seen war and all its realities. Like a Gila monster locking onto prey with a death grip, the Lizard would accept tasks and pursue a successful conclusion without hesitation. I knew immediately that he would be as loyal as a Labrador retriever, but he had been around enough to see things as they were, making it difficult for him to follow Niedermeyer's orders "just because." Born, raised, and formally educated in Memphis, he was a fellow redneck, and I was comfortable with him from the beginning. The Lizard would prove to be someone I could go to for unfiltered information, no matter what the topic. He had a unique ability to give me the information, quite often derogatory toward Neidermeyer, without violating the perception of loyalty and fidelity. A diplomatic redneck—revolutionary.

The Lizard was Niedermeyer's right-hand man, always closing the loop, digging up stuff that was hard to find, and recognizing compromising situations that might put a haze on Neidermeyer's halo.

He'd come to the position through the "old girl" network. The Lizard's wife and Niedermeyer's wife were best friends who, as I understand it, had met while attending college in Memphis. Before taking this position, the Lizard had been working a post-army job, and Mrs. Niedermeyer wanted to be close to her sorority sister. Niedermeyer liked getting the occasional hummer from Mrs. Niedermeyer, so he created a position and promptly filled it with the most qualified candidate in the entire United States: the Lizard. For Niedermeyer, the loyalty required of such a position could not be underestimated, so considering the discipline associated with Lizard's army officer background and the fact that Mrs. Niedermeyer would be happy, it was a match made in heaven—or Memphis as it were.

The next morning, we attended mandatory meetings, shaking hands and looking interested and pleased at progress, and then headed for our hotel in downtown Memphis and our real purpose for the visit: blues, barbecue, and beer. As if his heavy southern accent didn't remind us enough, the Lizard felt obligated to prove his Memphis roots and insisted that he would take us to the best barbecue joint in the area, a half block from Beale Street, for dinner: The Rendezvous. After enjoying the prerequisite happy-hour cocktails in the hotel bar, we headed toward our first stop, a beer bar famous for some ungodly number of brews on tap from countries not exactly famous for their beer.

There were five of us: Niedermeyer, the Lizard, Bobby from Boston, the Catfish (whom nobody liked), and me. Bobby was a Naval Academy graduate, or a "ringknocker," a term that is sometimes negative in nature. While in the navy, I had worked for a living, so I wasn't allowed in "officer's country" and did not associate with them, except for the marine "black sheep" pilots in the Philippines—another story for a less family-oriented book. As it was explained to me, the term "ringknocker" comes from Naval Academy graduates' habit of rapping their rings on a conference table, in a not so indiscreet manner, whenever a nonacademy officer suggests a course of action contrary to their own. Bobby screwed things up the first time I met him by admitting that he was a ringknocker. It was like a controller, me, admitting my asshole nature on initial contact. There was a time when my favorite ex-wife, Roseanne, in a fit of frustration, asserted the obvious, deeming me to be an asshole. "Yes, I am, but I am a perfect asshole," I would reply while looking at her with one eye through an "o" formed by my index finger touching my thumb. How do you respond to that? Roseanne turned and walked away, muttering, "I don't know why I said 'I do.'"

With Bobby, I was speechless, and for a man who talks for a living, that was a profound defeat. Bobby was born and raised in Irish Catholic Boston, and his accent ground on me like a Texas accent on a Bostonian. However, anyone who could disarm a controller immediately upon introduction was okay with me. Although he was a ringknocker, I liked Bobby. He was a straightforward, no-bullshit guy, and he cursed like a sailor. Most people used "hell" and "damn" on occasion, but Bobby threw around "shit" and "fuck" in the office with reckless abandon. The enlisted ranks referred to the Bobbys of the world as "shit sponges." No matter what shit came through the door, shit sponges would catch it. Believe me, I know. On far too many occasions, I've been the designated shit sponge. I'm convinced that if it weren't for the relaxed Naval Academy standards during the lean years of the late 1970s, Bobby would have been an enlisted. It's not that Bobby wasn't smart; he just was not the epitome of academy material.

My initial assessment of the Catfish would prove to be accurate. Even in this day and age of upward mobility, I still run across the occasional example of "white guy" EEO. The name Catfish came from an enormous pillow in the shape of a catfish hanging from the ceiling of his office. He hailed from south Florida and was right proud of his catfish heritage. Catfish had been a helicopter pilot, serving his country in Vietnam, and for that, he had earned an appropriate degree of respect. However, I failed to understand the reasons for his presence on this trip or in the program. He constantly had an argumentative position. It is said that if twenty-three countries can agree on any one thing, the French will disagree on principle alone. Maybe the Catfish liked frog legs as well.

At the beer bar, the five of us ordered a couple of rounds of "sampler platters"—numerous glasses, slightly larger than shot glasses, of worldly beers. We sat sipping and comparing as if we really knew the difference between a pilsner and an ale. Neidermeyer, of course, took the lead and ordered a pitcher of dark beer and a pitcher of light beer. He and I sat next to each other, discussing our experiences in aviation, while Bobby, the Lizard, and the Catfish played a game of cutthroat at the pool table.

None of us had eaten any lunch to speak of, and the hotel's complimentary happy-hour cocktails were beginning to kick in when our conversation turned to my career. I briefly explained my retirement from the FAA and covered my ATC accomplishments. Neidermeyer described his college years and his time in air force flight school. Understandably, he left out many of the details of his unsuccessful attendance but did emphasize his disappointment with the manner in which management had handled his release. Nothing happens in a vacuum, especially termination of training at a military institution. It is the most publicly, private event I have ever witnessed. As with the dressing-down I received from my sergeant in ATC school, the air force chooses to release training failures out of the public view, the "public" in this case being Niedermeyer's classmates.

On that fateful day, management called Neidermeyer, along with his instructor, into the commander's office and delivered the news. They explained that the decision was not appealable and ordered him to remain there until the other students had returned from their sorties, showered, and departed; then he could go empty his locker. It was their way of hiding an elephant, but it prohibited Neidermeyer from saying goodbye in his flight suit, which was the way he wanted to be remembered.

My dad once told me that being prepared and pursuing a goal to the best of my ability would mean never failing. His point was simple: if you do whatever it takes to prepare, position yourself as best as possible to achieve a goal, and then work as hard as needed, you will never fail. You may not be successful, but you will not have failed. Failure comes when you were not prepared or did not put forth your best effort to achieve a goal. We can't all be Olympic athletes, business moguls, or even fighter pilots, but if we put forth our best effort during the attempt, we never fail either. Neidermeyer would prove to be a prick, but in this case at least, I believe that he simply did not achieve his goal.

Deciding dinner was in order, Neidermeyer relinquished his leadership position to the Lizard. Larry navigated the most direct route, through backstreets and even the lobbies of famous hotels. I didn't know lizards liked baby back ribs with a dry rub, but we strapped on the feed bag and consumed a meal that was everything he had said it would be and more. With the business of the day concluded, full bellies, and the next day's schedule including nothing more than a morning flight back to DC, we ordered a few more rounds of cold beer and agreed that some blues bar on Beale Street had a table reserved for us. Being within walking distance of home made our evening more enjoyable and, to some degree, relaxed our usual self-imposed limits on alcohol. I made a mental note of my consumption, but it was becoming apparent that the Lizard and Catfish were not handling the effects as well as the other three of us.

As we progressed to a blues bar, we were rapidly approaching the peak of our evening. The ribs had fought a courageous battle to minimize the effects of the alcohol, but the Lizard and Catfish were succumbing to overload. Struggling to maintain, the Catfish retreated to himself, content to observe the crowd, while the Lizard chose a completely different tack, hooting at a fine southern beauty occasionally, although not in an offensive manner. I split my time between Neidermeyer, continuing our previous amicable conversation, and Boston Bobby, trying to find common ground in our navy experiences, a nearly impossible task. As discussed, there are black shoes and brown shoes in the navy. Their environments and lifestyles are as different as Boston Bobby and I were. I was a brown-shoe Airedale. Bobby was a black shoe. I was from Texas; Bobby was from Boston. I was enlisted; Bobby was a ringknocker. However, we did have one thing in common: we were navy, and Neidermeyer was air force. So we made fun of Neidermeyer and how cute he must have looked in his powder-blue Michael Jackson uniform.

The evening progressed as most evenings in a bar do. We all had a shade too much, Bobby and I got tired of making fun of Neidermeyer, and at one o'clock in the morning, we decided it was time to head home. Neidermeyer, Bobby, and I were as good as expected, and the Catfish was shaky yet holding his own, but the Lizard was in trouble. We headed out the door, the three more sober of us in the lead. Catfish, refusing to give up a drink that had been "paid for in full," insisted on a "go" cup before following us, and the Lizard pulled up the rear as best he could.

LIFE WITH A VIEW

    Home was four city blocks away when years of air traffic controller experience, enlisted navy experience, and piss-ass drunk Philippines experience kicked in. I took a quick inventory of my resources—wallet, hotel key, and cell phone, all present and accounted for—and continued to inventory my companions. Neidermeyer and Boston Bobby were five paces ahead of me (so much for flight integrity), the Catfish was three paces behind me, and the Lizard, our trailing wingman, was using a brick wall for navigation. Bad juju.

    I shouted at Neidermeyer to wait, drawing the attention of two of Memphis's finest who were passing in a cruiser, and proceeded to tell Catfish to dump the "go" cup. He refused until I pointed out the cruiser and the stares coming from it. Drinking in public wasn't illegal on Beale Street, but being drunk in public was—southern humor. Downing the entire cup in one fruitful swallow, the Catfish slammed the empty remains into a trash bin, assumed a contented grin, and surged forward to join our illustrious leaders. One problem down, one to go.

    Shouting over my shoulder for Neidermeyer to wait once again, I strode toward a now struggling Lizard. As I had with my enlisted brethren so many times before, I grabbed the Lizard, my first officer, by one arm, wrapped his other arm around my shoulder, and turned toward home. By this time, Neidermeyer and Boston Bobby were ten paces or more in front of us, having delayed long enough to observe the salvation of the Lizard, and Catfish was close on their heels.

    A struggling Lizard patted me on the chest and slurred, "You're a good guy. I like you." He was oblivious to the ominous scene developing in front of me. I knew I could find my way home and get the Lizard to his hotel room, but refusing to acknowledge the facts I faced, I once more hoped for a show of solidarity and shouted to Neidermeyer, Boston Bobby, and Catfish. Neidermeyer turned, saw the Lizard hanging on my shoulder, looked at Bobby, shrugged his shoulders, and resumed his pace.

    With that look, I realized Neidermeyer had made a decision on that fateful day when he stared out the windows of the training wing commander's office, waiting for his classmates to leave: that he would never be left behind again, no matter what. As for Boston Bobby, he was an admitted ringknocker. The Catfish was the Catfish. And I was an enlisted guy, an air traffic controller, raised by a father who believed in a code of conduct and influenced by his brother who had flown helicopters in Vietnam and been shot down and shot up and received medals and commendations just short of congressional because he believed in "never leaving a man behind." I knew then, on that Memphis street at one in the morning, with a decorated combat officer on my shoulder, that Neidermeyer did not and would not adhere to "no man left behind." He had become a solo aircraft on that long-ago day and decidedly had no intention of becoming a member of a flight ever again. The Lizard was so far gone that he would barely remember these circumstances in the morning and certainly not the implications. But I made an indelible mental note that if Neidermeyer ever found himself in a compromising situation, he would not hesitate to offer up one of us to save his skin.

I normally give a person the benefit of the doubt without hesitation, but in this instance, I believe that an intelligent, enthusiastic, hardworking man had not dedicated his best effort to recovering from a very difficult situation. In less than one year, circumstances involving Neidermeyer would confirm, firsthand, this assertion.

We all made our morning flight a little worse for wear, especially the Lizard. He explained the knots on his forehead as the results of stumbling in the bathroom while trying to pee and falling into the bathtub. It was simultaneously comical and sad.

Upon arrival back in DC, I received my first assignment with SF21. I was instructed to find areas in the National Airspace System that would immediately benefit from the new technology and a location in the lower forty-eight states to perform the research and development. The technology we were developing is known as Automatic Dependent Surveillance-Broadcast (ADS-B). Simply put, it was the ability of an aircraft to send an e-mail transmission of information such as position, altitude, call sign, and type of aircraft to air traffic control or other aircraft, once every second. ADS-B relies on global positioning satellites (GPS) to determine the aircraft's location and transmits that information via a data packet, which is essentially e-mail or, more accurately, instant messaging. Following is a breakdown of how it got its name: automatic because the information is automatically transmitted once every second;

dependent because it is dependent on GPS to determine location; surveillance because it produces a target to air traffic control and/or other aircraft equipped with ADS-B; and broadcast because the aircraft broadcasts the information instead of relying on a conventional radar to detect and locate it.

The beauty of ADS-B is its simplicity. The initial ADS-B testing was being performed in Alaska, through a program called Capstone. Evidently, Senator Ted Stevens had lost his wife many years earlier in a plane crash and had a direct interest in any preventive technology. Alaska has the highest accident and mortality rate per capita in the United States, and Senator Stevens wanted the technology tested, developed, and implemented in his state with the hopes of reducing that number—a politician who was truly interested in more than self-promotion. *Thanks Senator*, I thought. *You just single-handedly screwed up everything I had figured out about politicians. And thank you, Senator, for doing a great job.*

In addition to transmitting information to ATC, ADS-B can be received by other aircraft, assuming they are equipped with ADS-B avionics. The ADS-B avionics package came with a small display or TV on which the pilot could see other aircraft, potentially preventing midair collisions. Additionally, a terrain map was available that would issue low-altitude and collision-alert warnings when the aircraft, flying in inclement weather, approached a hard spot such as a mountain. Good technology, great ideas, great place to use the technology, except for one or two little bitty details.

In Alaska, one hundred aircraft were equipped with the ADS-B avionics package at the expense of the federal government—one hundred aircraft in an area twice the size of Texas. If you were going to build and test the next generation of racing bicycle, would you build fifty and dole them out to one bicyclist in all fifty states or give them all to a professional racing team?

It is estimated that only 50 percent of the pilots in Alaska are instrument-rated. That means only half the pilots are certified to fly in the clouds, under direction of ATC, in a state that is famous for bad weather. So what do the other 50 percent do when the weather turns to crap? They stay under the clouds, which is legal as long as the pilot stays a minimum of five hundred feet above the ground over unpopulated areas. What happens when the clouds get so low that a pilot can't stay under them and meet the five-hundred-foot requirement? They fly lower. What if the aircraft has ADS-B on board, broadcasting its position and altitude to ATC, and is less than five hundred feet above the ground, which is a violation of the federal air regulations? Busted! So the pilot turns the equipment off, defeating the purpose of the terrain display technology, inhibiting the warning system, and the pilot pancakes into the side of a mountain. That really happened shortly after installation of all one hundred aircraft was complete. On this particular airplane, everyone walked away from the crash, but the point is that Alaska was the best place to use the technology but the worst place to research and test it. Senator Stevens's heart was in the right place, but unfortunately, he had an uncooperative audience.

SF21 and Capstone had mutual goals but were not a part of one another, which means they had separate budgets. Wasteful duplication of effort? Of course! That is the government way. NASA had similar developments in the works, which NATCA loudly protested and eventually was instrumental in canceling. However, Neidermeyer's objective was a good one: again, I was to find a place in the lower forty-eight states to develop the technology while identifying areas that would immediately benefit from its use.

My research led me to Prescott, Arizona. Prescott, located approximately seventy miles north of Phoenix, is in a bowl, surrounded by mountains. It is also the West Coast home of Embry-Riddle Aeronautical University, a well-respected, private school for all types of aviation specialties, especially pilot training. Embry-Riddle had seventy aircraft—fifty single Cessnas and twenty twin-engine trainers that were flown two and sometimes three times a day. The vast majority of the flights were to and from training areas less than forty miles from the airport, resulting in extremely congested airspace and, of course, a large number of near midair collisions. My research revealed that one midair collision had occurred nearly ten years earlier. But the real icing on the cake was a lack of radar coverage.

Here, we had a remotely located airport that had more air traffic operations per year than La Guardia; seventy locally based aircraft, flying two to three times a day; no radar coverage; a list of near midair collisions as long as my arm; and a prestigious university with which to partner. Life was good. I contacted the university's chief pilot, a retired navy captain, described my assignment, and asked for his help. He gave me a stack of letters signed by everyone from the tower chief to Senator John McCain indicating a need for radar at the airport. However, the one critical factor that would get the FAA bureaucrats' attention and support was the reports on near midair collision that were kept in-house.

On occasion, a pilot would file a near-midair report with the NTSB, but the treasure trove I needed was secretly filed away with the university. These reports were a double-edged sword. They depicted how unsafe routine flight was in the Prescott area while driving home the need for radar coverage. However, if these statistics got out, Mom and Pop Johnson in Omaha, Nebraska, would never let aspiring pilot Johnny Johnson go to Embry-Riddle. So the chief pilot really stepped out on a limb when he faxed me a copy of the reports, with one condition; the reports stayed in-house. Confidential. With this information, I could illustrate an area that would immediately benefit from the technology and identify the perfect place to research and develop it. Having a letter from a senior senator like John McCain, combined with the fact that he was the chairman of the Senate Transportation Committee, didn't hurt.

I continued to look around and found areas with a hole in radar coverage that constituted an "area of benefit" needing a quick, inexpensive fix, one of which was Vero Beach, Florida. Vero Beach is a primary training area for, ironically, the main Embry-Riddle campus in Daytona Beach. The midair incident rate was a bit higher than at Prescott, and pilots had been begging the FAA for years to install a radar and provide services.

I finished the analysis and conducted a briefing of my findings. Neidermeyer was happy with the results, but in his usual condescending manner, he gave me a noninspirational "attaboy," delivered with his now familiar hint of a lisp. He had the ability to compliment you and still leave you feeling like you had just run over the family cat—not bad enough to kill it, but leaving it maimed, so that the kids would be reminded of you every time they saw the wretched animal. The guy was amazing.

DC

The chief pilot from Embry-Riddle requested a copy of the analysis, so after the festivities were concluded, I asked Neidermeyer for permission to release it. I explained that the chief pilot had really put his dick on the block for us by delivering the near midair statistics, and giving him a copy would be a favor returned. Neidermeyer considered it for a minute, eyeing me as if I were Nazi SS trying to convince him to walk into a banquet hall with steel doors that bolted from the outside. He finally agreed, and I transmitted the analysis via e-mail that afternoon.

Two days later, the chief pilot called me, enthusiastic as hell and wanting to know how to get "on the list" for ADS-B. I explained that SF21 did not have the money and that he would have to be patient while the request worked its way through the chain. He insisted that had already been done, citing Senator McCain's letter as evidence. I reiterated that the program could not fund his request, although Neidermeyer would have jumped at the opportunity, and his best option was to be patient. We said our goodbyes hoping for the best but fully expecting the status quo.

A year went by, and the wrath of Neidermeyer eased a smidge. I saw him from time to time hustling and bustling around like someone who was important, which gave him the perfect excuse to ignore people. He would peer at you with bulging eyes through his thick glasses and say, "Oh! Sorry. I was so deep in thought that I didn't even notice you there." With the Lizard following close behind, he'd scurry off, lisping orders, destined for another meeting.

With my analysis complete, I was assigned to support the terminal applications manager in a number of ways. Some tasks had real potential, but most, sadly, were just FMWPs: federal make-work programs (a Tippy-ism). Things rolled on as usual. I had collateral duties with one or two other programs that got me out to the West Coast occasionally and provided an opportunity to see old friends. But the FMWP programs were taking their toll on me. I was a controller. We don't do FMWP. Everything has a reason, a purpose. I was having conversations with engineers on a regular basis, discussing research and development projects that had no hope whatsoever of becoming successful programs. Worse, I was trying to go to graduate school for an MBA, and trips to

Long Beach, California, every other week for the past six months were nixing my plans. The bullshit factor became exponential, along with the frustration factor. My controller instincts kicked in, and in rebellion, I developed a "closed door" policy that irritated Jimmy the Greek, the owner of the contracting company for whom I worked. In my office, there were four of us—me, Flounder, Chris, and the Yeti—across the street from the FAA building. I was the oldest and the only one with any real antagonistic skills, taught by David Dodd, Lon Chaney, and Ty Welsh and honed through years of ATC experience, so I incited the others, and they followed me. I was a natural leader.

Flounder had gotten his name from Chris. He looked like Flounder in *Animal House*—overweight and boisterous—and knew it all. If asked a question about anything, Flounder would give a somewhat believable answer. Imagine my surprise when I found out that I was not the only know-it-all in the world. We called him Flounder but never to his face until Jimmy the Greek marched in one day and let the cat out of the bag. Apparently unaware that Flounder didn't know about the nickname, the Greek just blurted it out to Flounder's surprise. The Greek stared at the quizzical look on Flounder's face and then surveyed the room, finding Chris and the Yeti buried in their work yet shaking uncontrollably from laughter. I looked him straight in the eye with a half grin. The Greek finally deduced that he had just made a complete ass of himself and been the butt of our joke. I liked Flounder—he was a lot like me but fatter and knew the few things that I didn't. He had a habit of taking his shoes and socks off and putting his feet on his desk, which drove Chris nuts.

Chris and Bernie, the Yeti, were good guys. Chris was a young, very intelligent engineer, although the Greek found him to be less than enthusiastic and felt it his duty to regularly inspire Chris to be all that the Greek wanted him to be. Jimmy's occasional sermons had the same effect as Flounder's bare feet, but Chris took it in stride, knowing that the Greek intended well. I liked Chris because he worked hard when he had to, and when things were slow, he skipped out with me and Bernie for three-hour lunches at an Irish bar next to Chinatown.

Bernie was another good guy, and at six foot six, he was easy to pick a nickname for—the Yeti. Dark curly hair and an ever-changing facial environment confirmed my choice. He maintained a mustache, but for the rest of his face, every week was different—a beard one week, a goatee the next. The Yeti was one of those guys who could sneeze hard and have a full beard. He was covered in hair, and his back looked like a carpet sample. The Yeti wore a coat in the winter, but I never understood why. Bernie was very intelligent, kind, considerate, hardworking and had the ability to shame Chris into bailing out of the office with us for a trip to Chinatown for "just one beer." Our foursome was a good one, and these men would help me through what would be a very tough time.

Nearly a year had passed since my Prescott presentation with no word of progress. We were required to spend one day each quarter giving a presentation illustrating progress on our programs. The idea was to give Neidermeyer, Boston Bobby, and other FAA management a warm fuzzy feeling, knowing their money was being spent wisely. I couldn't make a particular meeting due to other very important meetings I had to attend. So I gave my presentation to the Lizard, coached him on the high points, and sent him off to impress Neidermeyer.

Early that afternoon, the Lizard came into my office, excited as a schoolgirl who had just gotten her first kiss. Apparently, the seed I had planted with the Embry-Riddle chief pilot had come to fruition. Neidermeyer had made it public at the quarterly meeting that a request from Senator McCain's office, with my analysis attached to it, had arrived on his desk. The request was to look at the expense, time frame, and benefits of ADS-B at Prescott. Neidermeyer was ecstatic. The Lizard told me I had been placed on Neidermeyer's Christmas card list. Yipp-fucking-ee.

The request was unfunded, so SF21 would have to come up with the money, but it was an enormous step in the right direction, and Neidermeyer could envision his windowed office with a view of middle management already. I must say that I was happy, and for one night, I actually believed that things could work out for the best.

Then came the enema. Early the next morning, as I was walking across the street to our office, I saw the Greek getting out of his car. I had not seen him since receiving the good news, and I was confused by his frown and insistence that I follow him directly to his office for a conversation. There he explained that two developments, independent of each other yet simultaneous, had occurred the same day—yesterday. It was the perfect bureaucratic storm. I was aware of one, the request from McCain's office. The other would have a completely opposite result. As usual, no one was about to stand up and face the music, so the following information came piecemeal and, for the most part, through third parties.

Apparently, after I sent the analysis to the chief pilot at Embry-Riddle, insisting he keep it in-house as I had his near midair documentation, it had grown arms and legs, stolen an airplane, and flown itself to the Embry-Riddle main campus in Daytona Beach. He insists it didn't leave his office, and I have no proof otherwise, but it did wind up 2,500 miles away. Stranger things have happened—Neidermeyer's commission in the armed services, for example. From Daytona, someone took it to the air traffic division in the Atlanta regional office, where someone in the air traffic branch liked the idea and took it to a congressperson (I never did find out who), which constituted lobbying or something like it. I do not know the laws and really don't care, but the event pissed off the congressperson, who, as the story goes, called the FAA administrator, Jane Garvey, on the carpet.

Jane had her tits put in the ringer and was highly pissed after receiving a Congressional mamography. She marched back to headquarters and called the head of Neidermeyer's division on the carpet, kicking the turd downhill. The manager had assumed the position only two weeks earlier and did not like being blamed for something that had happened on someone else's watch. With the transfer of the brown baton from Jane to the manager complete, the brand-new pissed-off manager called Neidermeyer on the carpet. According to my sources, the new manager all but accused Neidermeyer of being directly involved with the lobbying effort. The central focus was on how my analysis had gotten into the wrong hands.

I had been verbally authorized by Neidermeyer to release it to federal government officials *and* the chief pilot, but without a "get out of jail free" e-mail stating as much, I was now being served up as the catch of the day. The Greek finished explaining the scenario to me, and I stood there dumbfounded. "Is Neidermeyer going to fire me?" I asked.

"He said to fire you, yes," the Greek replied.

"Well, shit, fire me!" Immediately, I knew my time with the program was over, no matter what happened with Prescott. Neidermeyer was never going to reward my silence with a choice position—that was not his style—so it was time to go.

"No, no, no! I'm meeting with him in a few minutes, and I'll talk him into keeping you."

I shouted, "He can't fire me—you know that. It's against the law! Only you can fire me, and you're not going to because you don't have grounds. But what he will do is give me some crappy job that nobody else wants, putting me in the corner and covering me with shit until I get up and walk away or mushrooms start growing!"

The Greek stared at me, knowing that I understood my days with the program were over. He proudly admitted to being a liberal Democrat who believed in workers' rights and going to bat for the little guy. However, the competition among contractors in DC was intense, and he could not, or would not, allow one employee to derail his business plan. The Greek walked over to me, put his hand on my shoulder, closed the door, led me to a chair, and just looked at me. With a heavy sigh, he calmly restated his previous intention. I could see in his eyes a recently purchased million-dollar house and a lucrative navy contract about to be awarded to his company that would put him in the big leagues; that was what dominated his thoughts. And with that, Neidermeyer had become a bureaucrat, and the Greek had become a limousine liberal.

In *The Art of War*, Sun Tzu states, "Never press a desperate man." A single desperate man can do more damage than an entire army. The Greek was concerned that the controller in me would take over and would not be content until the body count was high enough. I had attended a number of meetings in which Neidermeyer had stated, moronically, that certain analysis results could be the death of the program if they were made public. Jimmy also knew that I was very familiar with tactics used to ensure his company would maintain the source code for potentially profitable technology—technology that was paid for with taxpayer funds, making it public domain, not his alone. Every company does it, but that doesn't make it right. He also knew he had screwed up royally by admitting that Neidermeyer had instructed him to fire me. He searched desperately for words to express his dissatisfaction with the entire event, all the while knowing they didn't exist.

The Lizard came by my desk later in the day and expressed his sympathy. I could tell he felt as bad about the incident as the Greek, and that meant a lot. An environment in which teammates are left to fend for themselves was as foreign to him as it was to me. He did the only thing he could: shrugged his shoulders, apologized for something he hadn't done, and left. I still don't think he realizes what happened that night in Memphis.

I was retained at Safe Flight 21 and, as expected, given a crappy job that the Lizard had been monkeying with for some time. A driving force in ADS-B was the prevention of runway incursions, or the prevention of pilots straying onto active runways and being hit by landing aircraft. Most people don't realize it, but the view from the cockpit of a small plane at a big airport is a sea of concrete. Runways and taxiways are marked, but it is very easy to get lost and cross an active runway unknowingly. My job was to build the blueprint of a database for the digital airport maps that ADS-B would use to display airport layouts. They are similar to GPS navigational maps but with much more detail and accuracy.

I worked for a retired navy pilot and a nice guy who was just trying to put enough money in the bank to build his dream house on some previously purchased property in Florida. Gritting my teeth, I bided my time, and the database blueprint progressed steadily. By now, most people knew of Neidermeyer's exercise in bureaucracy, and when the shock wore off, it was business as usual—every man for himself.

I let the shit pile up until I could not take it anymore and submitted my resignation. The Greek accepted it without argument but did ask me to stay on for a month instead of just two weeks. He told me there was a replacement in mind, and he wanted a two-week overlap between the two of us. The fact that he had someone waiting in the wings was not unexpected, but it did sting. I agreed to stay a month; after all, where did I have to go? The month passed quickly, and my replacement never did show up. It later occurred to me that maybe there never was a replacement, but it was just the Greek's way of giving me another paycheck while maintaining a little contact with his former proletariat lifestyle. Try as he might, though, he was a pickle now and could never go back to being a cucumber. He had built a company, in the finest American tradition, from the ground up and was destined to become a Lear Jet liberal.

That last Friday, I left my laptop, my ID card, and anything else that could have been considered company property on my desk, even my company coffee cup, which the previous employee had left, and bailed out early with Chris and the Yeti for our Irish watering hole on the edge of Chinatown. Flounder insisted I check out through the human resources department in accordance with the company manual. My last words to him were "I just checked out."

As I am sure Neidermeyer had done years before, I stared out the window from our table at the light rain falling on Washington, DC, a cold draft Boddingtons beer in hand, and wondered what was next. There had been no goodbyes from my SF21 "teammates," no "we're gonna miss you" going-away ceremony, which was fine with me. It means something only if it comes from the heart, and although there were a lot of fine, hardworking people there, I never felt like a team member and frankly never considered them to be a team. I've seen teams. I've been a member of a few teams. I know what a team looks like. They were not a team, sadly.

A team needs a quarterback—someone to say, "Follow me. This is where we are going, and this is how we are getting there." It is no coincidence that during half-time interviews coaches reiterate, despite being behind, that they intend to stick with the game plan. A game plan is a strategic or long-term course of action. To accomplish the strategic goal, it is essential to have tactical goals that, when combined, equal the strategic goal. Neidermeyer was so focused on looking good that he gave the airlines (users) whatever they wanted, altering the tactical goals, at the expense of the program. The SF21 team was growing more and more frustrated because he changed course every Monday morning in an effort to put a smile on the airlines' faces. His hope was that good words would be said on his behalf, resulting in a promotion. It became obvious that my sacrifice might have been his first but would easily become routine to him. Like minnows in a bucket, with a hand reaching in, the only question was who would be next.

I had learned the meaning of "team" from the sergeant, Robinson, Estes, Scotty, David, Ty, Tony, Pat O'Sullivan, Pops, and others too numerous to name—air traffic controllers who never uttered the statement "I'm not going to let you fail" but who proclaimed it loudly through their actions. In twenty years as a controller, I had seen teams at work, and I knew what to look for and how to recognize them. Teams require leadership, and the beauty of air traffic control is that every team member was also a team leader. We were taught from day one that if you see a problem, you fix it. There was no such thing as "someone else's problem." We were a team, and a problem was the team's problem.

It was not uncommon for someone to shout across the radar room, "He's coming to your frequency, an emergency at five thousand, airport in sight, not yet cleared for the approach. I'll coordinate with tower!"—emphasizing that work that was someone else's responsibility was being handled by a teammate showing leadership. The folks at SF21 were hardworking and honest. However, a team without leadership is merely congregated flotsam on the ocean waiting for a wave to separate it. Neidermeyer was the manager of SF21, but he was a team of one. I left believing that if he didn't change his ways, he would move up the federal government ladder due solely to the hard work and dedication of others, not because he instilled a sense of purpose in their lives. It wasn't that no one believed him—he could be convincing. However, no one believed *in* him.

When I look back and consider those events, I place the blame squarely on my shoulders. I had learned that first night in Memphis that Neidermeyer would do whatever it took to save his hide, and I had subsequently failed. As Dad had told me, if you prepare and then do your best, you will never have failed. I had prepared because I knew what I was dealing with, but I had failed to do my best to protect my ass. As with that nearly tragic monsoon day in Tucson, I didn't consider all the options—the best-case and, more importantly, worst-case scenarios.

In one of the final scenes of *Animal House*, Flounder's brother's car is chopped to pieces by D-Day. Boone puts his arm around Flounder and says very matter-of-factly, "Hey, you fucked up—you trusted us!" And I had messed up in the same way. I had trusted an individual who I knew would leave a teammate behind.

DC

Later, I read Senator McCain's account of his grandfather and reminisced about a helicopter pilot that I know, grounding me in reality. They were a great deal more accomplished than I will ever be and yet were still abandoned by those they trusted implicitly. One spent four years at sea, crying every night for the loss of brave young men in his charge whom he could not save, yet cursing his moral and military obligation to send more to their death the next morning. The other had physical scars to go with the memories of those who never got to occupy an air-conditioned airline seat pointed stateside.

I called that helo pilot, my uncle Bert, shortly after leaving SF21 and asked how he had handled it when he was betrayed. "Drank. A lot," he replied. So I did too. I called back a short time later, just before my third divorce, informing him that his advice sucked and had not worked. With an abbreviated grunt of a laugh, filled with understanding, he said, "Didn't work for me either. Robin, a test of character is not so much how you handle a bad situation, but how you recover from it."

In Senator McCain's book, he tells of how his grandfather just wanted to go home after the Japanese surrender, but Admiral Halsey ordered him to attend the surrender ceremonies. It was an order Admiral McCain surely could have easily ignored but decided to follow, an order for which I'm confident Admiral McCain was grateful.

I'm sure I felt a sigh of relief come from a small, windowless office in the FAA building when I climbed in my truck a few months later and headed south to Atlanta, Pensacola, Houston, and home—Tucson. I visited controller friends along the way, and in Peachtree City, Georgia, I began purging the animosity along with the piss from each San Miguel I drank with Tippy on the balcony of an aircraft hangar, looking at the single runway of the small Georgia airport. It was dark, the runway lights were on, the wind sock was showing minimal signs of life, and I could smell the sweet scent of 110-octane aviation fuel. For the first time in months, I was at ease in the company of Tip, an old friend I believed in and could count on to let me vent. And I did vent. Then we laughed about the fun we'd had in the Philippines, almost wishing we could click our heels and be there again. But they're called fond memories for a reason. Jimmy Buffet sang, "Lines form where the smiles have been," and I believe we look old only when we've smiled enough.

Never more than that night did I miss being a member of a team of leaders, leaders who cared, leaders who never gave me a day off. Leaders like my dad and mom, the sergeant, David, Herman, Juano, Tony, Pops, Pat O'Sullivan and so many more who pushed me to study harder and work harder, constantly quizzing me for the final FAA certification exam *they* believed I'd take. Leaders who would berate you mercilessly for missing something in hopes that you wouldn't forget the next time because missing something got pilots killed. Leaders who would never let you down or let you fail. Leaders who believed that your failing was as much their fault as yours. Leaders who demanded that you pay for the certification celebration because that was an air traffic controller tradition, and you had earned the right to call yourself an air traffic controller. But most of all, I missed leaders who would never, ever, leave you behind, hoping and expecting that someone else would pick you up and make sure you got home safely.

Postscript

A few years later, Neidermeyer once again showed his true colors, abandoning Boston Bobby and the Lizard. The event was as hard on them as it had been on me, but like me, they couldn't say they didn't see it coming. They landed on their feet.

12
TWO TOKENS, TEN DOLLARS

After I'd had my fill of Washington, DC, Roseanne and I decided it was time to go home. The Washington, DC, housing market had gone through the roof, so we had a good deal of equity, making the move even easier. Shortly after we'd settled back in Tucson, Roseanne's phone started ringing, and a former DC employer made her an offer she couldn't refuse, so back to DC she went. I took a job traveling and teaching a training course for the federal government. However, when the war in Iraq started, money dried up, and I found myself gainfully unemployed again. I discussed my next move with Roseanne, which was obviously to return to DC where there was work, but we both knew that was a bad idea. Roseanne suggested I stay in Tucson and fulfill a dream by writing this book. Most aspiring writers never write a book due to lack of time, so I had no excuse.

I spent the next year in Tucson writing a little but found myself routinely frustrated. I didn't have writer's block—I knew exactly what to write—but I had a real problem with motivation. Now in my midforties, I was having the proverbial midlife crisis. All I knew was aviation and air traffic control, but the mere thought of returning to a career field I had once loved was irritating, frustrating, aggravating—pick an adjective. I truly wanted a new career but was prepared for absolutely nothing else. I had a BS degree in business information systems and knew software programming, database management, and system administration. But sitting in front of a computer eight hours a day had all the appeal of a root canal on Monday, a gum scraping Tuesday, the passing of a kidney stone Wednesday—you get the picture. As with most controllers, I'm a "hit the high point and keep going" kind of guy, and computer stuff is way too detail-oriented and boring for me.

Finally, even if this was destined to become my third failed marriage, I decided to return to DC so that Roseanne and I could at least pretend to be married. She bought a one-bedroom condo in a high-rise ten minutes from the District of Columbia, was thrilled with her job, and was enjoying life—well, most of it. All marriages have peaks and valleys, but ours was at the bottom of what was appearing to be at the bottom of an endless swell. I applied for jobs, most of which I did not want, and found myself at the receiving end of the "you're perfect for the job, but there is no funding yet" mantra. All potential employers had become Democrats: "Just wait, you're gonna love this. This is gonna be *great*! Just you wait." All cowboy hat and no cows. The aviation industry was in the toilet. Research and development was my niche, and unfortunately, funding for it had become another casualty of the Iraq war.

They say it's darkest before the dawn, and I believe it. One day, as I joined an old FAA headquarters buddy, Mark "High Speed" Washam, for a round of golf at a public course, I spotted a "Help Wanted" sign in the pro shop. A few days later, I was gainfully employed at the driving range selling driving range tokens. I was earning a little more than minimum wage, but part of my compensation was all the golf I could play and all the range balls I could hit, free. At the time, I didn't realize how good a deal it really was and saw only the downside. I had been an air traffic controller responsible for thousands of lives, an air traffic control instructor, and a system engineer developing air traffic control technology, and now I found myself selling driving range tokens, earning less in one shift than I had previously earned in an hour. "Two tokens, ten dollars."

The driving range job was a real education. It was located across the Potomac River from Washington National Airport and was minutes from the Capitol. I met people I otherwise never would have—former attorney general John Ashcroft, former congressman and presidential candidate Richard Gephardt, *Crossfire* host Bill Press, and a few local

DC news personalities, among others. They were all very nice, and I had cordial conversations with many of them, but the real impressions were left by people who didn't utter a single word, people who couldn't reach the counter to take their tokens, and people who probably never earned a third of my former salary. I do my best writing in the morning, so I offered to work the evening shift, 1:30 p.m. to 10:30 p.m. Monday through Thursday.

I learned a little sign language for two guys who couldn't hear. They were regular customers and appreciated the fact that I learned to sign "can I help you?" and "thank you." Acting like men in their midtwenties, they would check out women who walked in and sign about them right in front of them, knowing no one else could understand their conversation, finishing with a laugh. I found it amusing that the only noise they ever made was a laugh.

Two little guys came in from time to time, and I had to hand the tokens to them because they weren't tall enough to reach the counter. When asked how far they were hitting their five irons, one stated "125 yards" with great pride, and the other would dispute the claim, starting an argument. Right there, in the driving range office full of customers waiting to buy tokens, they'd mix it up over one thing or another as if they'd been married for twenty years. Finally, agreeing to settle it on the range, they'd bump fists and march off, tokens in one hand and five irons in the other.

The closest I came to having kids was Roseanne's two daughters, Melissa and Jackie, who routinely reminded me I wasn't their father until they grew up, had kids of their own, and found themselves needing financial help. When asked for money, I returned the favor and reminded them, "I'm not your father," before coughing up the cash anyway—lovingly, of course. Roseanne once asked me to become more involved in the grandsons' lives. I tried to tell her I'm not much of a role model and wouldn't recommend anyone following in my footsteps, but she wouldn't take no for an answer. Not willing to accept my grandfatherly duties without a fight, I agreed to teach them "the world according to Robin."

"What's that?" she foolishly asked.

"We'll start with the three Fs," I replied.

"What's that?" she once again foolishly asked.

"If it flies, floats, or fucks, rent it."

Shaking her head, she turned and walked away, muttering, "I don't know why I try."

Me either. We'd been married twelve years and together five years before that, and it's not as though I had changed.

However, I have always been a sucker for small children and kept a bucket of balls and spare baskets in my driving range office just for them. It was very inspiring to see dads bring their kids to the driving range. Occasionally, the kids had their own clubs, but more often than not, they were just spectators along for the ride. I'd pour a dozen or so balls from my stash into a spare bucket, pull out one of the few kid's clubs we had, and send them out the door following Dad with their club in one hand and a bucket of balls in the other. Cute.

The driving range office had picture windows on three sides, allowing an unobstructed view of the stalls. One day, I noticed an older black gentleman striking the ball with one of the smoothest swings I have ever seen. As he left the range, I asked where he'd gotten his swing because I wanted to get one too. He laughed, and we talked for a while. As it turned out, he was retired from the State Department, loved golf, and played all over the world with congressmen, senators, heads of state, ambassadors—you name it. It was early in the afternoon, and business was nonexistent, so we had a good, long conversation. It was then that I realized I hadn't shared enough time with my grandmother, Gwen, while she was with us.

One afternoon, I met a Japanese woman who bought several hundred dollars' worth of tokens on the range debit card (a credit card that allowed customers to bypass my little office and go directly to the ball-dispensing machines). She came in on a daily basis, but the day before she bought her card, I had never seen her, so she piqued my interest—professionally, of course.

I watched her hit balls, always two stalls down from my office, for two hours at a time. Tall for a Japanese woman and striking, she finally came in to recharge the card. Politely, I asked her nationality, already knowing the answer, and we struck up a conversation about Japan. I had been to Japan a few times, mostly Tokyo, and loved it. She had grown up in Tokyo, still had a home there, and asked where I had visited. I replied, "Mostly the Shinjuku, Roppongi, and Harajuku districts," areas known for nightclubs, street fairs, and shopping.

Her English was very good, and we talked for a while. I finally asked why she was coming in every day and working so hard at her golf swing.

She answered, "I'm playing in a company tournament in three weeks and need to be better."

Very Japanese. I then realized I hadn't been to Japan in over ten years. Things had obviously changed, and maybe it was time to go visit.

A person I didn't talk to at the driving range was one of the owners, a woman whom I liked and who I found out later wouldn't talk to me because of her inability to understand my reasons for working at a minimum-wage job with so much other experience. I was told she was intimidated. Hmm, I do have a certain effect on women, but I've never had that problem. They've been repulsed, afraid, concerned that they recognized my face on the evening news maybe, but never intimidated. She was cute as a bug, and I liked her but originally just figured she didn't have time to talk, with all the important duties of running a municipal golf course. Sadly, she epitomized what was wrong with the world. Sit down and talk to people. You never know whom you might meet. She never hung out with me or met any of her regular customers. Sad. Her loss.

The driving range added a much-needed dose of humility to my life. Controllers have a tendency to get wrapped up in the "control" part of the job and allow too much of it to control our private lives. It all happens slowly and deliberately until, before we know it, the "control" concept is running the show. I'm now a firm believer that sometimes we need to relinquish control and let the wind take us where it will. Occasionally, unknown destinations can be like stolen kisses, just a little sweeter.

13
ATLANTA

Peachtree City, Georgia, July 2008

My career had taken me all over the world, but I knew it was coming to an end. Roseanne decided we should part ways, and that decision was difficult for me. I had purposely waited five years to propose, hopefully ensuring that we were made for each other and our marriage would last. It didn't.

I took a job as a contractor in Atlanta with the newly formed Air Traffic Organization in the airspace and procedures branch. Within months, I was offered an opportunity to return to the FAA, and I accepted it. I worked as the subject matter expert on ADS-B and supported the Memphis district with the nuts and bolts of air traffic control. Both jobs kept me on the road constantly, which, being single and living in a one-bedroom apartment, I was okay with. I spent the next few years conducting business as usual and traveling three weeks out of the month.

In 2011, I took a one-year detail back to Washington, DC, in the international branch. It was a great job during which I traveled to Ottawa, Canada, and Mexico City on official business. David Dodd was in DC at the time, working as the terminal procedures manager, and we supported the Peruvian air traffic control manager in designing a thumbnail sketch of new approach control airspace and sectorization for Lima.

Returning to Atlanta, I resumed my duties, albeit different duties, writing waivers for a number of off-the-wall operations such as high-altitude balloons and rockets—boring but different from anything I'd ever done, so from time to time, it was interesting too.

In January 2014, I met my wife, Kay. She was five foot two with chestnut-brown hair, and I fell for her on the first date. She's very well educated and works as a program manager from our house. She loves to travel as much I do, and we've traveled extensively since our marriage. For our honeymoon, we went to Sydney and stayed with some old friends of mine who live there; Graham and Jackie. Fom there, we were headed for a couple of days in Auckland, New Zealand, then onto Tahiti for a 7 day sailboat cruise to Bora Bora and back. I had invited Graham and Jackie to to join us, but they had previous reservations with a group of friends. Having breakfast in their house the last morning in Sydney, Graham stated, "You know mate, I can only take you in small doses. So, I'm going to work today but, we've decided to join you on the cruise. I think I can handle you for a week."

My immediate supervisor, who was a nice guy and a real air traffic controller, had been the manager at a choice facility in southern Florida. Atlanta was good duty, but he had come to us from a garden spot. Curious, I asked for the reasoning. Apparently, a militant NATCA representative had come to his facility and made life rough for him. NATCA reps can indeed make life rough for a facility manager—sometimes rightfully so, but often because the NATCA rep has an ax to grind and has an ax to wield. My supervisor saw it as the latter and told his wife that if there were ever three days in a row in which he didn't want to go to work, he would transfer or retire. He transferred.

As previously stated, I was never the controller expected to sail through any training program. I struggled mightily at Whiting, Cubi, Oxnard, and Tucson TRACON. But due to my outstanding instructors and my dad's philosophy of preparing and performing at 100 percent, I managed to certify in five towers and one TRACON. In those years, the thought of an ATC manager who had never been certified to sequence and separate airplanes was as laughable as the idea of going to an MD who hadn't finished medical school yet had been certified to practice medicine. But it's happening in the FAA, now.

ATLANTA

I took this personally, which flies in the face of a controller's mentality. Logic and deductive reasoning, not emotions, are the order of the day for controllers. It was foolish. Kay saw my frustration, and we talked about it one weekend in August 2014. I was eligible to retire but didn't want to go. Speaking objectively, which she is best at, she helped me realize it was time to go. My career field, which I loved, had morphed to a point that I couldn't accept. I couldn't accept it because I had worked too hard to achieve in it, despite my personal limitations. People in management now had never certified to sequence and separate airplanes, yet, were being promoted into those positions. Management must abide by the NATCA contract, but, when it comes to management positions, management can do whatever they want.

The following Monday, I walked into my supervisor's office, closed the door, and stated, "It's day four."

"Does that mean what I think it means?"

"Yep, I'm retiring."

"When?"

"Effective immediately."

I turned, went to my office, put my personal belongings in a box, and walked out.

Having stated all that, the FAA was very good to me, and I am very fortunate to have been hired. This new policy is about the only thing I would change. The FAA air traffic control system is the most effective and efficient in the world. No other country moves airplanes like the FAA ATC system. Chest thumping? A case could be made for that, I suppose. I've worked with foreign countries who do a great job, but the U.S. ATC system sets the standard.

The FAA allowed me to have a career that I truly enjoyed, good health care, a great salary, adequate vacation time, and a sound retirement. I was surrounded by upstanding, moral controllers and supervisors who took the job seriously and put forth their best effort every time they plugged in and bellied up to a radar or tower position.

14

"GROUND, SIMON 22 IS WITH YOU, CLEAR OF THE ACTIVE RUNWAY, AND TAXIING TO THE GATE"

I sit here, hammering at the keys on my screened-in lanai (a South Pacific term for a porch that I picked up in Guam) in Peachtree City, fifteen miles south of the Atlanta airport and the *real* home to Delta, with an Astros baseball cap casually perched on my noggin. The size 7 1/4 hat doesn't fit right since I became a writer and decided to look the part by growing a goatee and ignoring my hair, which has a distinctly 1970s look that I have come to appreciate. Kay takes it all in stride.

Tonight, it's the Brewers against my 'Stros, and I make a mental note to call Eldred and flick him some shit regardless of who wins the game. At our age, a baseball game is an excuse to call and say, without the actual words, "I miss you, and I'm thinking about you." It's like a guy hug—two pats on the back and back off. If you feel queasy at all about having another guy's ding-ding that close to yours, a nervous laugh is in order. I find myself making these calls with more frequency and wish there were one or two I could still make. Life is life, and sadly, I look around my personal radar room and notice a few unmanned sectors and empty chairs. It's tough realizing that some calls will no longer be answered. I miss those the most.

LIFE WITH A VIEW

My humble "office" is filled with pictures of Tomcats, Hornets, and old friends smiling, while in the background, Gordon Lightfoot serenades me with "The Wreck of the Edmond Fitzgerald," making me believe that my life is a ship at sea, taking me where the winds decide. I am a controller who is not really in control.

Life catches up with all of us. The rain hitting our lanai reminds me of the monsoons in the Philippines—great times, great people. Now I'm retired, and my great times and great people are narrowed to a small handful of close friends and my irreplaceable wife, Kay. Her big boobies and morning laugh are but two of her assets. She awoke this morning, smiled at me, raised her tank top to expose her breasts, and said, "Hey, mister, throw me some beads!" She's priceless and a perfect fit for me.

Memories are not just important; they're a critical part of all of us. I remember a week spent in the boundary waters of International Falls, Minnesota, fishing with Scotty and a former brother-in-law, Billy. It was always good to see Billy and stay at his cabin on Stop Island on Rainy Lake. Remembering the sun coming through his east window, the chickadees singing, and Chippy the chipmunk on the front steps noisily announcing feeding time, I realize I don't get up there often enough. Memories, which are directly connected to "mental health" days for me, are extremely important not only for controllers but also for writers. I've decided that it is possible to think too much, but it's a problem many of my friends will surely insist I've never had.

One of the most memorable moments from one of those trips came when Scotty and I had an old friend–to–old friend talk. He was casual but insistent in the delivery, as only an old friend could be. "Why have you moved around so much? Everyone I know loses money when they move that much."

It was then that I realized one of the people who had unknowingly initiated my insatiable desire to sail, travel, and search the globe for whatever treasures it would give up did not share my need. He had enjoyed the Philippines but wanted nothing more than to return home to Florida. It is now clear that I am the exception to the rule, having been born with my grandfather Edwin Excel Smith's genes and a predisposition to wandering. If it had not been for a heart attack that forced his recuperation at my aunt's house, he would have suffered the

> "GROUND, SIMON 22 IS WITH YOU, CLEAR OF THE ACTIVE RUNWAY, AND TAXIING TO THE GATE"

second and fatal heart attack on the road instead of in her kitchen. I've always had a stirring in my soul, but I didn't realize or appreciate the full extent of it. What Scotty didn't realize, and I just recently have, is that I am a very rich person, even if my bank account doesn't reflect it. All the people, places, and experiences—great, good, and even less-than-good—have been deposits and amortizations in my very, very rich life, a life composed of many acquaintances, friends, best friends, girlfriends, ex-girlfriends, and yes, three ex-wives. I wouldn't change a thing. I can honestly say, if I crossed paths with any of them again, I would embrace all of them warmly. Well, there is one exception, but that will remain personal. On rare occasions, time does not heal all wounds.

In the original *Gumball Rally*, Raul Julia, when leaving New York City, rips the rearview mirror from his two-seat sports car, throws it over his shoulder, and states, "What is behind me is not important." Same for me. Most people, my dad included, view my roaming affliction as a hindrance to normalcy. I never questioned it but did wonder where it was taking me. Personally, I simply embraced it and threw the rearview mirror over my shoulder, replacing it with photos and the memories that came with them.

I discussed the affliction with my uncle, the helo pilot, for he too is afflicted and could relate to my situation. He voluntarily re-upped in the army during the mid-1960s, accepted a commission as a lieutenant, and attended helicopter flight school, all the while knowing he was destined for a tour in Vietnam.

"What in God's name were you thinking?" I asked.

"I was an insurance adjuster in west Texas! An old farmer threw me off his roof when I told him I wouldn't cover the hail damage. Life sucked, and I was bored!"

I realized that he had a good point and further realized that I probably would have done the same thing. Maybe lunacy runs in the family too.

Things change, and we change with them. From time to time, I talk to my controller buddies who have yet to retire and contemplate what I am missing. It was an exciting moment every time I walked into a radar room or tower, but they insist that it's not the same now and that I am better off where I am.

Some of my life's paths were chosen for me and some chosen by me. But those I chose were dictated by two creeds or mottos I learned a very long time ago.

The first one is my dad's "ask forgiveness, not permission" attitude. He is a cocky, I-can-do-anything-I-want sort of person, and on occasion, he paid the price for it. However, more often than not, it got him what he wanted. The second, thanks to David Dodd, became a part of me the day I keyed a mike and uttered my first air traffic control words. I have lived by his advice: "if you're going to break a rule, just know which rule you're breaking, and be prepared for the consequences." Fair enough.

It would be easy to make the case that I have broken a few rules in this book—and I've broken a few bones along the way also. My neck, which has a plate in it, both of my shoulders, and my right elbow have been rebuilt; my left elbow was broken when I was a kid; and just recently, at the grand old age of fifty-eight, I shattered my fibula in a few places and the tibia (the big bone) in two places—while walking the dog. Seriously. It was a hot July morning, and as usual, I let Zelda take a swim in the Flat Creek, which runs along a golf course, to cool off. She pulled a little too much on the leash, and I slipped into the water, wedging my foot between two rocks and falling sideways. I'm convinced the people in the tee box five hundred yards away heard the screams. A nine-inch plate and fourteen screws later, I proceeded to heal and push Kay's easygoing demeanor to the limit. The straw that nearly broke the camel's back came one Sunday as I was finishing this book and decided I wanted a coffee with Kahlúa. Thinking I had pushed Kay's patience far enough, I decided to get the Kahlúa off the top pantry shelf by myself—which is when my knee slipped off my knee scooter and I fell, wedging my now uncasted, unprotected leg under the scooter and twisting it into a very compromising and very painful position. As I screamed, she came to the rescue. Once things had calmed down and we realized that nothing was broken, or rebroken, she stated with finality, "There will be *no more* of that in this house!"

"I just didn't want to ask for help anymore!"

"Yeah, and look what it got you!"

Except for my ATC instructors, I had never been dependent on anyone to achieve a goal, until now. Kay was pissed. But I didn't break the Kahlúa bottle! Or any more bones.

Many people ask me why I wrote this story. It was a story that needed to be told. I got tired of hearing the media state that "the control tower was talking to the aircraft at thirty-five thousand feet." My favorite, though, was when a woman reported on a midair between two F-18s in the Arabian sea. "The cause of the collision was two aircraft trying to assume the same airspace at the same time," she reported. I almost peed my pants. That phrase is an old smart-ass controller-ism. Both pilots ejected safely and survived without injuries. She'd been had. But, it *was* funny.

For some reason, we feel a need to classify everything, and when I decided to write this story, people asked me what sort of book it would be. A memoir? A biography? A narrative? An exposé? A tell-all? Yes, all of the above. And no, none of them. It's a real-life novel—a nonfiction novel. The simple answer is that it's our story—my generation of controllers, the poststrike controllers, those who wanted nothing more than to be air traffic controllers in the FAA and work where our talents would take us.

A few friends who read parts, if not all, of this book as it was being written commented that I beat up pretty badly on the air force, different administrations, NATCA, and contractors. I don't think so. The stories are either irrefutable or clearly designated as "the world according to Robin."

Let me be clear about something very important to me: I voluntarily served my country on active duty for eight years and two months along with many others, partly because of the examples set by my dad, mom, uncles, and cousins who served before me and partly because of the beliefs instilled throughout my early years. We, as Americans, fight like cats and dogs among ourselves because of our deeply embedded competitive nature. We enthusiastically debate and defend our hometown baseball, football, hockey, and basketball teams down to the individual players. We have a very strong desire to constantly strive to be better than we were yesterday and better than anyone else, on any day. Air traffic controllers are no different. We debate the way the world should be run with great enthusiasm yet form a cohesive unit when the headset is plugged in and *it* hits the fan.

Understanding the positive effect the US military has on the world, I cannot emphasize strongly enough my admiration and respect for all the uniformed services and their dedicated members. I am proud to have served and feel fortunate that I did not have to experience the reality of my service more than I did. Although I was not in the navy during combat, while I served, pilots and aircrew were injured, and some died defending the Constitution of the United States. It all happened while the armed services were maintaining peace and keeping citizens of not only the United States but also countless other countries free and safe.

As members of the US armed services, we revel in interservice rivalries yet form an impenetrable wall when threatened. The agitative nature of portions of this book were written good-naturedly, and I expect them to be taken with a grain of salt and hope that the Michael Jackson "blue suiters," jarheads, and grunts will refrain from coldcocking me on the street. Please. Kay would appreciate it. But if you do, make sure to break something. My orthopedists (yes, that's plural) need to make a boat payment and are depending on you.

Controllers are nothing if not dependable. Dependability is the essence of life. With it, we can step out of our routine anytime we like, take a walk on the other side of the road, and return when we've had our fill or things get a little too hairy. Air traffic control was the same way. Consider two aircraft moving in opposite directions three miles apart, at the same speed; when they are directly abeam each other, they turn one at the other and roll out three miles in-trail, every single time—or until an anomaly in the equation occurs, and then all bets are off. Two and a half miles in-trail, some smart ass (realizing you've just had a deal and would not be working the midwatch) shouts across the radar room, "Can I have your midwatch?"

This book is dedicated to the dependable air traffic controllers with whom I grew up and have grown old. They were there, day and night, assuming the enormous duties and responsibilities that came with managing the nation's most effective and efficient form of commerce. The fact that people do *not* read newspaper articles about "errors leading to mishaps" is their claim to fame. In their case, "out of sight, out of mind" is the ultimate compliment. Jimmy Buffet sang, "If the phone doesn't ring, it's me," and that should be the motto of all air traffic controllers worldwide. If the NTSB phone isn't ringing, controllers are doing their job, and it is a job that very few people understand and, unfortunately, even fewer appreciate. Hopefully, this book will change all that.

So the next time you are sitting on a commercial flight or look skyward from a backyard barbecue to see an airplane flying overhead, think of the dedicated people whose days off are Wednesdays and Thursdays. Or those who sit in a tower or in front of a radar scope watching the clock strike midnight on New Year's Eve and wonder who is kissing their spouse. Or those who are anxious to get home from a midwatch so the kids can open Christmas presents. Or those who look forward to the Fourth of July pictures, once again missing the oohs and aahs of the fireworks. Or those who, all too often, fight back panic attacks when things fall apart. Or, just as important, those who didn't certify despite their best efforts. God bless them—they tried. They are typically labeled "training failures," but nothing could be further from the truth.

Well, that's it. The book is written, and I have told the story as best I could. I have always enjoyed writing and wanted to write this book for a long time. I hope you've enjoyed reading it as much as I enjoyed writing it. It was a cathartic opportunity to relive my life one chapter at a time and a journey that I highly recommend to anyone willing to make an effort. My controller buddies and I are in our fifties, and it's a strange feeling to look back and see more life behind us than in front of us. But we do have memories.

Despite the best efforts of two editors, Robin Bourjailly and Heather Hutchins, I'm confident grammatical mistakes will be found in this manuscript—dangling prepositions, among others. But my life will probably end with a preposition, or another broken bone—hopefully, the former.

Many asked how long it took to write this book. A lifetime is the correct answer, but twenty years is the answer they're looking for (sorry again—"for which they are looking"). I am told my writing style improved as chapters were written, and as the early chapters were edited, I realized it was true. Consequently, I wasn't happy with the early stuff and debated rewriting some of it. I finally got to a point where I just wanted to finish the book, and rewrites are time-consuming and a lot of work, so I mulled the issue with myself and decided, "It's my book." Whew! Dodged a bullet. But just when I thought my "hit the high points and keep going" lifestyle was intact, I reconsidered. "Don't you want it to be your best work?" I asked myself. Yeah, yeah, yeah, I can live with it.

But I hadn't shamed myself enough, and my conscience got the better of me. "The book is as much about controllers in general as it is about you—don't you want them to be well represented?" Damn! So I did a bunch of rewrites, timely rewrites. Talking to yourself is one thing, but arguing with yourself is another. Losing an argument with yourself is a sign you've probably pulled too many midwatches.

As scientific as air traffic control may be, controllers are some of the most artsy-fartsy folks I've ever met. They don't conform to rules. I see them as "artfully limited" by the governing laws—coloring inside the lines when being watched and freely expressing themselves at other times. I think that's what made my career so much damned fun. The art of science.

Simon 22 is shut down and tied down and now resides in the Davis-Monthan boneyard.

Printed in Great Britain
by Amazon